'Be Careful, Don't Rush'

Celebrating 150 years of train travel between Holyhead and Bangor

Robin Masefield

Published 2015 by Bayburn Historical Society

First Edition
First Impression

A catalogue record for this book is available from the British Library.

Published with assistance from Colourpoint Creative Limited, Newtownards
Designed by April Sky Design, Newtownards
Tel: 028 9182 7195
Web: www.aprilsky.co.uk

Printed by W&G Baird Ltd, Antrim

ISBN 978-0-9570869-1-3

Front cover image by Norman Whitla, courtesy of the artist

Contents

Introduction

This book has been written specially to commemorate the 150th or 'sesquicentennial' anniversary of the opening of the railway line from Holywood to Bangor on 18 May 1865. It is hoped that it will have a wide appeal to residents along the route.

The book is an unusual combination of social, railway and personal history. It starts with a look at the make-up of the two towns prior to the advent of the railway, and the impact of its arrival. Historical archives have been probed to reveal in the next chapters the dubious dealings of two competing companies both facing initial financial challenge. The triumphs and the tragedies are laid out, as well as descriptions for the lay reader of locomotives and rolling stock. The book then chronicles the story of the individual stations along the line, and concludes with some delightful personal stories.

The illustrations are also an unusual mixture of those which may be familiar to readers with railway expertise and a range of other personal or historic photographs.

Railways made a vast difference to the lives of many people. Prior to their arrival, less than 1% of the population ever journeyed more than ten miles from their home. Most lived within walking distance of their place of work. Through railways, people could travel and meet a far wider range of other people, thus leading to major changes in working and marriage patterns, for example.

Railway mania affected Ireland in the 1830s and 1840s, just as strongly as it did Britain. The first line to be built on the island of Ireland was the Dublin and Kingstown route which opened in 1834, and the first in Ulster was between Belfast and Lisburn in 1839. Plans for a service between Belfast and Holywood had been hatched as early as 1836, though it was not to be in place until August 1848. There were many schemes put forward, some in direct competition with each other, and others over-ambitious. (HC Casserley estimated that across the sweep of Irish railway history no fewer than 200 schemes were formulated of which only a minority came to fruition.)

So it is not surprising that the story of the line between Belfast, Holywood and Bangor has both twists and turns. The route from Belfast Queen's Quay to Holywood was built first by one company, the extension to Bangor nearly 20 years later by a second, and less than a further 20 years after that opened, the first company had swallowed up the second.

This book tries to blend the historical facts and figures with insights into the people and the personalities that either led the railways' charge or struggled to come to terms with the implications.

Much like our own times, not everyone was in favour of modern technology. It also has to be remembered that rail travel in that era was neither particularly safe nor certain. For example, Charles Dickens was involved in a major accident at Staplehurst viaduct in Kent on 9 June 1865 – less than a month after the Bangor line opened – about which he wrote to a friend:

'Suddenly we were off the rail and beating the ground as the car of a half emptied balloon might. We were then all tilted down together in a corner of the carriage … and stopped… I got out through the window… with great caution and stood upon the step… No imagination can conceive the ruin of the carriages.'

Dickens had been travelling on the boat train from Folkestone which was given insufficient warning of repair work being done on the bridge. Ten passengers died and 40 were injured, as most of the carriages ended in the river bed. Dickens was said to have lost his voice for two weeks as a result; understandably he thereafter avoided travelling by train, when possible.

The wider world was full of shocks too – in April 1865, the American President, Abraham Lincoln, was assassinated, and the following year a number of British banks became bankrupt (no Government bail-outs then), imperilling a range of railway projects.

The author of this book has sought to use original material wherever possible, quoting the actual words from railway prospectuses, legal documents, company minute books and contemporary newspapers. But he has also been hugely helped by both previous and current experts in this field. Northern Ireland is fortunate that it has produced generations of railway recorders and aficionados, as well as attracting the interest of parties from elsewhere.

The author is indebted to all those who have proffered advice, shared texts and reminiscences, and provided photographs and other memorabilia. There have been many and they have been unfailingly helpful and patient.

Although there is a full list of acknowledgements towards the end of this book, there are some individuals and organisations who must be thanked here. The author has drawn heavily on a number of writers with great expertise in railway matters, some sadly no longer with us. Among these, Desmond Coakham is pre-eminent, but RM Arnold, Grenfell Morton and DB McNeill also deserve mention.

Charles Friel has most generously shared his splendid photographic collection, while Andrew Crockart has very courteously given the author access to the treasured albums of Desmond Coakham.

Denis Grimshaw and Ian Sinclair have offered valuable guidance and help, as have Richard Whitford and Bob Pue. The expertise of local historians Tony Merrick, Con Auld and Sandra Millsopp has been much appreciated, along with the help of Lola Armstrong at the Clandeboye Archive. The Holywood U3A Local History Group have also been supportive in a number of ways. Material in the Holywood Library Archives has proved a valuable source, while Tom Kerr has generously allowed his works to be reproduced. Colin James' photographic skills have been vastly appreciated.

Clare Ablett at North Down Museum has nobly transcribed many articles about the railway in the *County Down Spectator*, on which the author has been grateful to draw. The exhibition at North Down Museum and the topical interest shown by a range of other local organisations are very welcome.

The McCutcheon Collection, at the Hill Street offices of the Northern Ireland Environment Agency, has proved a fecund source of fascinating correspondence and legal documents from the 19th century, as has the Public Record Office of Northern Ireland.

In addition, the author is most grateful to all who have kindly read through draft sections. While some pitfalls have been avoided, responsibility for errors and omissions remains the author's alone.

Special thanks are due to Norman Whitla for permission to feature on the cover his charming painting of BCDR 4-4-2 locomotive No. 12 heading a passenger train up the embankment from Holywood, bound for Bangor.

The author is again grateful to Brian McCourt for his input to the design. He is indebted to April Sky Design for their expertise.

Profits from this publication will be given to two local charities – Age North Down and Ards (AGEnda) and Holywood Shared Town. It is correspondingly hoped that if the author has unwittingly failed to attribute the source of any material correctly, this will be overlooked.

Finally the author would like to add that had the 150th anniversary on 18 May 2015 not been an immovable date, further researches and in particular additional interviews with those formerly connected with the line in a range of capacities, would have proved beneficial. It is to be hoped that this book will prompt recording of additional material.

Timeline of Relevant Railway History

27 September 1825
Stockton and Darlington Railway opens

October 1829
Rainhill Locomotive Trials won by Stephenson's *Rocket*

15 September 1830
Liverpool and Manchester Railway opens (and William Huskisson MP is killed)

17 December 1834
Dublin and Kingstown Railway opens

26 December 1836
Belfast and Holywood Railway Circular

12 August 1839
Line opens between Belfast and Lisburn

25 February 1845
Inaugural meeting in Belfast of businessmen and landowners to discuss the establishment of what became the Belfast and County Down Railway (BCDR)
Also that year, promotion of a rival scheme for an 'Atmospheric' Railway between Belfast and Holywood

26 June 1846
An Act of Parliament provides for the BCDR to construct a line from Belfast to Downpatrick with branches to Holywood, Donaghadee (and indeed Bangor)

2 August 1848
Opening of the line from Queen's Quay, Belfast to Holywood

October 1858
Meeting held to promote plans for a line between Holywood and Bangor

25 May 1860
An Act of Parliament provides for the Belfast, Holywood and Bangor Railway (BHBR) to build a line from Holywood to Bangor (joining the BCDR line at Holywood)

19 November 1860
Initial BHBR contract with Alexander Thomas Gordon to construct the Bangor line

3 June 1861
Opening of the BCDR line to Donaghadee

December 1861
Gordon defaults on the Bangor line construction contract

26 March 1862
New contract with John Edward Campbell Koch to construct the Bangor railway

24 June 1862
Formal sod-cutting ceremony at Cultra

13 July 1863
Second Act of Parliament extends the time for completion of the Bangor line

25 September 1863
Laying of the foundation stone for the Crawfordsburn Viaduct

Early 1865
Belfast and County Down Railway (Holywood Branch Transfer) Act

18 May 1865
Opening of the BHBR line to Bangor

29 June 1865
Purchase by the BHBR of the Belfast to Holywood line from the BCDR

1868
BHBR placed in receivership for the first time

13 May 1871
Accident at Ballymacarrett in which two passengers were killed and 55 were injured

1872
BHBR placed in receivership for the second time

Spring 1873
The BHBR Arbitration Bill is drafted, and negotiations proceed between the two Companies

August 1873
The BHBR line is leased to the BCDR (within limitations)

October 1875
Reconstitution of the BCDR Board of Directors

1876
Repeal Act reduces the rental paid by the BHBR to the BCDR

1877
Belfast, Holywood and Bangor Extension Railway Bill considered

28 December 1879
Tay Bridge Rail Disaster

1880
The Belfast Strandtown and High Holywood Railway is proposed as an alternative route from Belfast to Holywood

1881
Belfast, Holywood and Bangor Railway Act provides for the Company to run steamship services

14 July 1884
The end of the Belfast, Holywood and Bangor Railway as a separate company when it was purchased by the Belfast and County Down Railway

May 1893
The BCDR begins its Bangor – Belfast steamer service, with the *Slieve Donard*

1896
Original Cultra station destroyed by fire

1897-1902
The line between Holywood and Bangor is doubled

1903
King Edward VII travels to Bangor by train

May 1905
The Holywood to Belfast Railmotor service introduced

1 January 1917 (up to 15 August 1921)
The Government takes control of all Irish railways

1920
The four 4-6-4 'Baltic' tank engines were built by Beyer Peacock, and introduced on the Bangor line

1924
Morrow's Enterprise Bus Company provides competing services from Bangor to Belfast

1926
First automated signals introduced on the Bangor line

October 1928
Belfast to Holywood motor bus service introduced by the BCDR

1932
Signalling on the line from Tillysburn to Bangor fully automated using Sykes Banner signals

1935
Road and Railway Transport (Northern Ireland) Act nationalises the BCDR road transport

1 August 1944
Management of the BCDR transferred to the Great Northern Railway (Ireland)

10 January 1945
Major accident at Ballymacarrett Junction leading to 23 fatalities and 71 injured

1 October 1948
The BCDR is sold to the new Ulster Transport Authority (UTA)

24 April 1950
The line to Comber and Donaghadee is closed (the BCDR lines to Downpatrick, Newcastle, Ballynahinch and Ardglass also closed that year)

1952
Introduction of the original three coach multi-engine diesel railcars (MEDs) on to the Bangor line

1953
Withdrawal of goods services on the Bangor line

26 November 1953
First day of completely diesel operation on the Bangor line

July 1963
Benson report on Northern Ireland Railways produced

November 1964
Withdrawal of first-class tickets

1965
Serious fire at Holywood station
Crawfordsburn Halt opened
Closure of the 'Shaky Bridge' over the River Lagan joining the BCDR with the Great Northern and Northern Counties (LMS) Railways

1966
Seahill station opened

1967/68
The Ulster Transport Authority disbanded, with rail services taken over by Northern Ireland Railways (NIR)

1969
Closure of the nearly all the remaining ticket offices at intermediate stations on the Bangor line

1971
Realignment of the Holywood to Marino section of the line, providing more room for the dual carriageway bypass through Holywood town

10 April 1976
Closure of Queen's Quay station in Belfast

12 April 1976
Opening of the Belfast Central Railway with the new Central Station

2002
Bangor station rebuilt

2004
Upgrading of the Bangor Line completed

Chapter 1

Holywood in the 19th Century

Before the Coming of the Railway:

This section traces the development of Holywood, from before the arrival of the railway in 1848.

Local historians Anthony Merrick and Con Auld have written extensively about the town, and this chapter draws heavily on their work.

One of our earliest sources is the account of Rev WA Holmes, vicar of Holywood from 1810, who wrote an account of the town in the 1819 *Parochial Survey of Ireland*. He noted that:

'The language in use here is… strangely tinctured with the Scottish idiom and accent. Indeed there is little difference between it and that used by inhabitants of the opposite coast. The Irish is unknown except to a few individuals, and these not natives of the parish… In their manners a stranger would suppose them to be rough and intractable, but amongst themselves they manifest as much courtesy as is to be met elsewhere.'

Agriculture and seafood were important sources of livelihood. Holmes recorded there were three cart and plough makers in Holywood, among the population of 600.

One of the important contemporary sources of information about Holywood in the first half of the 19th century is the *Memoirs* of the Army Engineers who carried out the first Ordnance Survey of this part of County Down in the 1830s. At that time, what might be described as 'greater' Holywood consisted of 845 families, though this took in a generous geographical area which included the areas of Strandtown and Ballyhackamore. By contrast Bangor did not have more than 550 houses.

The *Memoirs* describe Holywood as a *'pleasurable summer residence, especially for those who are daily obliged to be in Belfast'*. There were 13 three-storey houses, all of which had slate roofs, although there were still 95 single-storey dwellings, less than a third of which were slated. It was also commented that *'the whole shore of Belfast Lough in this parish is studded with gentlemen's seats'*. The commentary added:

'The drive from Belfast to Holywood is agreeable. On Sundays, vast numbers drive from one town to the other several times on the same day for the pleasure of the drive!'

G Scott had observed in the 1834 *Memoirs* that *'as a bathing place it is much in its infancy'*. However more pertinently he observed:

'It appears much land might be reclaimed along the Holywood shore – or a railroad made from Belfast without causing any other level than that which at present exists to be made.'

Above: Holywood as painted about 1843; courtesy of Holywood Library

In terms of transport, the town had gained its first coach service as early as 1810; one run by John Rowley of Holywood plied between Ann Street, Belfast and his own house at 2 High Street. Improved transport, together with healthier living conditions, were factors in making Holywood one of Northern Ireland's first commuter towns, as well as a seasonal watering place. By 1834, the *Memoirs* noted '*a great number of cars running in the road between Belfast and Holywood at different hours*'.

Although from nearly one hundred years later, we are fortunate to be able to get a feel for what such travel entailed from a late 19th century photograph of horses and carriages outside the Wallace Posting Establishment at 31 Downshire Road, Holywood. According to Betty McLaughlin, the two ladies in the photograph are probably Misses Charlotte and Sarah Wallace; the latter went on to marry the coachman William Hugh Matchett. The sisters also ran a grocery shop from the same premises. The horses and carriages were certainly used to convey passengers and luggage to and from Holywood station, and further afield. The splendid chestnut tree in the photograph survived for nearly another century before being cut down in the 1980s to make way for town houses on the site.

The first post office in Holywood opened in 1818, with Hugh Stewart (who built the house next to the current police station) being appointed postmaster four years later. In addition, Stewart opened the resort's first public baths on the Strand in 1824. We know that at this time a number of the residents supported themselves by letting their houses to visitors during the summer. Fishing for cod was already by then a dying industry, although the mussel banks off Kinnegar continued to provide an important food source.

In 1840, Marine Parade began to be developed, though Holywood's euphemistically named '*House of Industry*' (or poor house) had been situated there since 1813. This was instituted following a survey by the Rev. WA Holmes who had found 70 destitute families in the parish from Grey Point to Connswater. In the *Memoirs*, it was noted in respect of the House of Industry that the '*Holywood poor house is very small*'. It then contained about 15 inmates (commonly 'very old people'), and those who could work were employed spinning. It also referred to a '*Cholera Hospital*' though this may have been a separate building on Ean Hill. (Some in Holywood had died in the 1832 cholera epidemic.)

In addition to a number of lodging houses, Marine Parade also had the large Marine Hotel. The local Surgeon Thomas Kelly described it in his 1850 '*History of Holywood*' as:

'*An extensive establishment, where unfailing attention and civility always attract a large concourse of the highest reputability of strangers and visitors. Here there has been established an American Bowling Alley which simple amusement is abundantly practised. The village now contains many players of no mean proficiency.*'

It is nice to think that the Holywood characteristics of welcoming visitors and sporting prowess were already exemplified 150 years ago.

By 1841, the town's population had risen to 1,500 living in 263 dwellings; it was to more than double over the following 25 years. Holywood was considered to have an excellent climate and was in the latter part of the 19th century a favourite residence of '*Belfast merchants, professional gentlemen, clerks and respectable artisans*' on the account of its '*rare healthiness, moderate house rents and comparative low taxation*'.

In 1841 the Presbyterians built a Gothic-style church on the Bangor

Above: Wallace Posting Establishment, 31 Downshire Road, late 19th century, courtesy of Betty McLaughlin

Road, designed by their own Minister, the Reverend William Blackwood. Three years later the Church of Ireland left the old Priory church for the new building on Church Road, designed by Charles Lanyon. In 1849 the Non-subscribing Presbyterians moved to the classical-style premises in High Street, also designed by Lanyon. (It is interesting to note that a building which had previously been used as a Presbyterian church – No. 40 Shore Street – had by 1860 been turned into a gymnasium.

There was in addition a flourishing temperance movement. The *Northern Whig* in May 1843 carried a notice placed by:

'Joseph Campbell [who] begs to inform the public that he has opened a Teetotal Hotel and Coffee Rooms in the main street of Holywood... NB The choicest slimcake always made to order for parties and generally on hand.'

It is also interesting to note that coffee shops are nothing new in Holywood's High Street. (And the low calorie confection known as slimcake then available might indeed be a good choice for today's weight-focused society!)

In 1846 Henderson's *Belfast Directory* recorded that a 'Manor Court' was held alternate third weeks at Holywood for *'the recovery of debts not exceeding £20... Andrew Cowan Esq., Seneschal'*. These terms have a splendidly mediaeval ring to them. (Bangor still had a similar court at that time.)

In the same year, the *Parliamentary Gazette* stated that *'a small pier at the town requires repair and extension'*. The pier was then used for bringing goods from Belfast and exporting sand. The *Gazette* also noted *'a badly attended fair is held every three months in Holywood'*. There were then still four mills in the town – three using water power from the Ballykeel river, and one wind-driven.

In an article in the *East Belfast Post* in 1983, John Patton records another dimension to this period of growth for Holywood. In 1847 chemists from Glasgow discovered a seam of magnesium-limestone to the north-west of the town. For a while it was shipped to Scotland for use in making sulphate of magnesia. The medical experts also agreed that the air round Holywood was good for the health – there were reports of Belfast residents suffering from consumption being cured in Holywood. The waters from local springs were seen as healthy, being impregnated with 'metal-oxide', and were in much demand. Alas Holywood missed its chance to become a famous Spa, bemoaned Patton, pinning the blame on the coming of the railway in 1848.

From the 1850s on

In 1852, the Holywood Baths Company opened salt water baths at the bottom of what was then called Shore Street (now Road). This was an important commercial concern providing hot and cold, and salt and fresh water baths as the advertisement shows. From the beginning visitors could purchase discounted train and bath tickets, and four years later the Baths came under the railway company's direct control.

Later the premises were used as a cinema, with forms laid in the sloped swimming pool which ensured good lines of sight for the audience, remembers John Graham. The projectionist had to climb up a ladder to reach his eyrie, which projected out over Shore Road. (Sadly this historic location was destroyed in a fire in 1940, though had it survived, it would no doubt have been a casualty of the Bypass, as was the Star and Garter

Above top: 1854 advertisement for Holywood Baths. *Above bottom:* The Cyclist Arms Hotel, Shore Street, Holywood, Holywood Library

public house which was one of Holywood's earliest licensed premises, trading under a variety of names. It appears to have been the Cyclist Arms toward the end of the 19th century.)

In January 1852, the Town Commissioners were set up, recognising Holywood's status as a town rather than a village. (This remained the form of local government until 1899, when the Holywood Urban District Council was created.) As we shall see, a similar development in local government did not happen in Bangor until the coming of the railway in 1865. The Town Commissioners were principally responsible for practical public amenities such as the supply of water and sewage disposal. (That said, a spring-fed fountain for public use for drinking water was erected, outside where the Methodist Church is now, by Viscount Dungannon in 1854.)

The Town Commissioners also had some role in relation to the railway. Although it dates from some time later – 1870 – it is interesting to read the relevant bylaws laid down by the Commissioners. With a surprising amount of detail, these prescribed the 'car' fares to be paid for a journey, for example,

'From railway station, Post Office, Maypole, or any other intermediate point, to Marino, Farm Hill, the Palace or any other intermediate place within the boundaries – 1/2 persons, luggage not exceeding 56 pounds, one shilling…. The foregoing fares include driving to the doors of the various residences although this may be some distance from the public road.'
[This was the Bishop's Palace – see below.]

The same bylaws also set down the fares for luggage porters carrying 'boxes, trunks, portmanteaux'. In addition they – somewhat fiercely – laid down that

'Any male person, excepting children under 10 years, bathing in the sea, within the boundaries of the town of Holywood, except in proper bathing places approved by the Commissioners, shall be liable to a penalty not exceeding 40 shillings.'

In the early 1850s, another development associated with the railway came into being. The Railway Tavern had been established in Hibernia Street, and more grandly took on the title of the Railway Hotel in 1854. Its proprietor, James Withers, died aged 90 in 1870, when his wife took over the business – one presumes she was a bit younger!

In 1854, there came the first valuation of the town of Holywood. An advertisement dating from the same year refers to *'the rising town of Holywood'*. It goes on to say that it is:

'Particularly valuable to capitalists and building speculators from its contiguity to the Port of Belfast and Railway communication thereto. Holywood is a pleasing and healthy resort, the favourite and most fashionable bathing place on Belfast Lough and the resort of the Residents of Belfast.'

Messrs Fairbrother and Clark of London
Donegall Arms, Belfast. Tuesday, 25ᵗʰ October 1854.

Under Order of the High Court of Chancery made in the case of
Higgins v Earl of Shaftesbury and Others

The whole of the rising town of Holywood.
Numerous private residences, shops, hotels, parcels of land and
building ground.

The Holywood Demense, most of Knocknagoney, Priory Park,
The Kinnegar and Woodlands.

Gentlemen's residences – Ashfield (the Bishop's Palace),
Westbrook, Clifton House, Maryfield, Richmond House,
Knocknagoney House, in all about 1,500 acres producing a
gross rental of £1,600.

(It seems curious to find reference to 'building speculators' over 150 years ago!)

In 1855 a wooden jetty some 50 yards long was built at the cost of £250. Captain Henry Harrison paid the largest 'subscription', but the Holywood Railway also subscribed £20. Con Auld noted that Holywood resident John McGee, a master tailor, who made the long, loose, heavy overcoat, known as the 'Ulster', a world-wide term, organised the subscription list. (McGee who lived on Marine Parade, had an outfitters in High Street, Belfast and died in 1883 while returning from New York on the steel-hulled Cunard ship *Servia*, which is often considered as the first modern ocean liner.)

The Holywood Gaslight Company was incorporated in 1856 – a year after Bangor had its first gas supply, but over 30 years behind Belfast. Unlike the position across the Lough in Carrickfergus, Holywood residents took up

Above right: *1854 Holywood Property sale notice.* ***Bottom right:*** *Some of the last surviving evidence of the Holywood Gas Company, courtesy of the Flame Museum.*

KERR

The Lamplighter, by Tom Kerr, courtesy of the artist

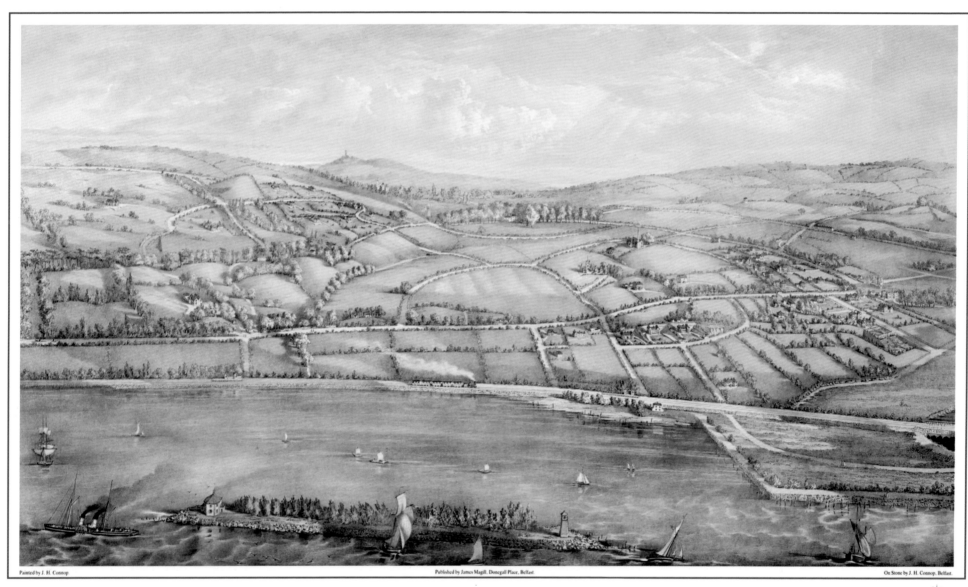

Painted by J. H. Connop.   Published by James Magill, Donegall Place, Belfast.   On Stone by J. H. Connop, Belfast.

VIEW OF SYDENHAM, BELMONT AND GLEN~MACHAN.

WITH THE VILLAS ERECTED AND IN PROGRESS, PART OF WHICH IS LAID OUT FOR BUILDING AS PER MAP ACCOMPANYING THE VIEW, SITUATE WITHIN TWO MILES OF BELFAST,
AND COMMANDING EXTENSIVE PROSPECTS OF THE LOUGH, AND COUNTY ANTRIM MOUNTAINS.

the four hundred shares rapidly, but installation still took three more years. The gasometers, retorts and works buildings were erected in Kinnegar, adjacent to the Holywood railway station. Curiously – and to criticism from travellers – the station itself continued to use old-fashioned oil lamps for a number of years.

The *News Letter* in November 1871 reported an explosion at the Holywood Gasworks, which completely demolished a brick shed:

'The town was in its usual state of tranquillity, at about nine o'clock, when the sound of an explosion, which shook the surrounding houses, alarmed the inhabitants…the man who was in charge of the place shortly before the occurrence had gone into this shed, and by mistake turned one of the valves the wrong way, and allowed the gas to escape. There was a gas jet kept burning in the shed which ignited the gas and caused the explosion…the manager was absent at the time of the occurrence, but he was on the spot in a few minutes after, and acted with such promptitude that no inconvenience was caused to consumers in the town by the accident'.

When gas was piped from east Belfast to Holywood in the 1950s, it ceased to be made in the local gas works, although the gasometer remained a local feature for many years thereafter. (A few relics from the Holywood works are preserved in the Carrickfergus Gas Museum.)

The means of bringing in the necessary supply of coal by boat was an issue that would reverberate for several decades. The then chairman of the Gasworks Company, Captain Harrison, himself paid for the upgrade of the 1855 Marine Parade jetty, but it remained unsatisfactory, and many colliers bringing deliveries were simply run onto the shore and unloaded when the tide was right. In 1862, 13,000 tons of coal were landed by that means.

In 1863 a public meeting, again chaired by Captain Harrison, was called to discuss the provision of a pier and coal quay. The proposal was to build it at the foot of Shore Street far enough out to land passengers at low as well as high tide. An Act of Parliament duly permitted a pier and a promenade. The Holywood Pier Company was formed to take on the task – McGee and Hugh Stewart were both among the Directors.

In 1869 the pier was completed with a fine promenade, extending for 1,360 yards with a shorter coal quay alongside. It cost some £20,000. Rates for loading or unloading goods at the pier included 6d per ton of carrots, and one shilling each for a live animal. Promenaders were charged one penny for the privilege, but a further sixpence if conveyed in a bath or sedan chair! (Clearly there were no concessions for the elderly or invalid in those days.)

The pier always struggled. In January 1882 a gale blew part of the pier down, and in July a vessel slipped its anchor and made another breach.

But the denouement came on 25 August 1883, the day of the Holywood regatta. The pier was used by the Yacht Club for a fireworks display. Some of the dry timber on the west side caught light but was extinguished. Alas it had not been fully put out and at 2am later that night flared up again. The RIC were called and did what they could but the Belfast Fire Brigade took a further three hours to arrive. Another long section of the pier was destroyed. Thereafter a few desultory stumps remained.

In 1857 Dr Archibald Dunlop took up post as the town's medical officer and served for the next 45 years. (Dunlop lived at St Helen's on Holywood

Above left: *Holywood Pier in its heyday, as envisaged by Dan Rainey, courtesy of North Down Museum* **Above right:** *Holywood Pier after the 1883 fire, Lawrence Collection, National Library of Ireland*
Left: *View of Sydenham, Belmont and Glen-machan by JH Connop, courtesy of Alan Rintoul*

High Street.) There were various other local bodies now involved with health and poverty, including the Dispensary Committee and the Destitute Sick Society, founded in 1841. Indeed in the 18th century there had been the splendidly named Holywood Society for the Suppression of Mendicity which had as its aims 'encouraging honesty, industry and frugality and for relieving distress; for promoting a reverent observance of the Sabbath and generally bettering the conditions and improving the morals of the poor'. Its work was clearly only partially successful! Moreover the Holywood Bequest Fund had been a charitable body founded around 1771, to distribute blankets and warm clothing to the destitute. (Rev. Holmes had observed in 1819 that 'mendicity is practised by a very few individuals but strolling beggars are frequently to be met with'.)

The Dispensary:
'Was founded for the purposes of alleviating the ills of humanity by affording gratuitously, advice, medication and attendance to such as require its aid within the town and adjacent country'.

In 1850 it was recorded – during the potato famine which admittedly did not affect this part of North Down as badly as much of the rest of Ireland – that

'A relief society is established which affords wholesome and nutritious food to many needy families and for the most part, during the severity of winter coals are distributed among the poor.'

Con Auld notes that Holywood had a good record in local philanthropy, long before the creation of the welfare state.

During the mid-19th century, a number of big houses were built both in east Belfast and Holywood. The attractive painting by JH Connop, entitled 'View of Sydenham, Belmont and Glenmachan' dates from 1864 and is reproduced by kind permission of Alan Rintoul. The line of the railway along the shore from Belfast to Holywood can be clearly seen, as can the steamer Erin. The big houses are individually identified. (Connop, an Englishman, was rumoured – probably untruthfully – to have painted such views while riding in a hot air balloon!)

The growth of Holywood came quite largely from the influx of Belfast merchants who were benefiting from boom years in the growing city. They included individuals whose wealth came from whiskey, banking, linen, tobacco, tea, newspapers, and Bernard 'Barney' Hughes founder of the famous bakery. They were joined by academics from the recently established Queen's College (later University) in Belfast and others from the middle classes, all of whom in turn created a demand for additional trades, shops, suppliers, hostelries, medical provision and a local supply of gas, in the town.

As the Provincial Directory described Holywood in the mid-1860s:

'It is now to be regarded as one of the most agreeable and accessible suburbs of Belfast. Large sums of money have been expended in speculation, chiefly by the Belfast merchants, in the erection of numerous elegant mansions in the town and neighbourhood; while gradually the old, uncomfortable cottages and houses have been removed, and replaced by dwellings of a superior class... Holywood is a particularly healthy locality... The opinion of the late eminent Doctor Forsythe was that no place in the neighbourhood of Belfast was so favourable as a residence for invalids; and numbers of his patients, acting under his urgent advice, took up their abode in Holywood.

There are no mills or factories in the town, but there is a constant demand for labour, and the sewing trade gives regular employment to great numbers of the families of the working classes. The railway has proved of great advantage to the place, as many Belfast merchants, clerks and respectable artisans, through its convenience, have been enabled to become permanent residents. The schools are, in general, admirably conducted. A very fine National School has lately been erected by Professor Sullivan.... Public Bathing Basins, also, are to be constructed by the Holywood and Bangor Railway Company.'

Robert Sullivan was a key figure in the history of Holywood at this time. His father had been press-ganged into the Royal Navy when Robert was a very young boy, and had subsequently fought at the Battle of Trafalgar in 1805, though he lived until 1853 when he died aged 89.

In 1832, the National System of Education was introduced in Ireland. In that year Robert Sullivan was appointed Inspector of Schools for the North of Ireland; in 1838 he became Professor at the Training College in Dublin. There he laid down principles for trainees to learn to be effective teachers and also wrote what became the definitive textbooks. This made him a not insubstantial fortune. Dr Robert Sullivan himself died in 1868.

Holywood's Sullivan National Schools were opened on 28 April 1862, also designed by Charles Lanyon's firm (at a time when that gentleman was very preoccupied with getting the Bangor line off the ground – or perhaps more to the point, onto it!). The boys' school was downstairs, the girls' upstairs – Sullivan declared some years previously that *'girls' education was of equal and indeed greater importance than boys'.'* Sullivan School thrives in Holywood to this day.

However a progressive but sadly far shorter-lived educational establishment was the County Down Agricultural College, at the corner of Victoria and Croft Roads, at that time quite a way out of the town. This stemmed from the 1837 Irish National Commissioners' Report which called for agricultural schools to produce *'an intelligent class of farm labourers and servants'.* The island of Ireland was divided into 25 districts, each to receive a Government grant to establish such a school. The Holywood medical officer of the day, Dr McKittrick, was instrumental in the County Down College for one hundred students coming to the town, together with a model farm. It opened in 1849. The master, William McMeekin, acquired two cows, nine piglets and 23 hens, but alas when the Head Inspector visited in October 1851, he found just seven boys in attendance – heavily outnumbered by the livestock. The following year the Commissioners closed the College.

Bassett's *Guide to County Down* published in 1886 is a good source of information. Holywood was then said to be *'one of the most highly favoured of the County Down towns. The compensations for residents in Holywood are numerous'.* They included first-rate public and private schools. Bassett goes on to note that *'before the bathing attractions of Bangor were so easily taken advantage of, Holywood was more popular as a summer resort for families making a stay of a month or longer'.*

Bassett was right to note, as we shall see later on, the extension of the railway to Bangor in 1865 led almost inexorably not to the demise of

Town Hall and Sullivan School, Holywood (Co. Down) Valentines Series

Holywood, but to a reduction in the pace of its growth and – it might be argued – a changed role for the town. As the *BCDR Guide* said a number of years later *'Holywood … is, to all intents, a suburb of Belfast'.*

The splendid Town Hall was designed by William Batt and built by local contractor William Nimmick in 1876, in a style that complemented the Sullivan Schools. It had a concert room for an audience of 500. Arthur Hamblett remembers being taken at Christmas time to the Town Hall to see Santa Claus who would give young children a brand new penny – incidentally the price of admission to the Picture House. (Sadly the building was burnt down just before Christmas in 1940. According to the account in the *Belfast Telegraph* for 24 December, the alarm was first raised by a resident on his way past it to the train station.)

According to the *Directory*, Holywood at this time boasted a saddler, a pawnbroker, two hotelkeepers, a coal merchant, and a boot manufacturer. Sergeant G Beattie was in charge of the Royal Irish Constabulary barracks.

However the origins of the local police force go back considerably before that. The County Down Constabulary was established in 1825. By 1830 both Bangor and Holywood were listed as stations, under the command of Sub-Inspector Spotswood who was based in Newtownards. Each had one Constable and two Sub-Constables. The first known names are Constables

Above: Old Town Hall and Sullivan School, Holywood

R Carson at Holywood and W Scott in Bangor in 1846; by 1865 their replacements were Constables James McGuinness and Austen Watters. The Holywood house that had originally been lived in by Sir Samuel Bristow in 1800 later became the Royal Irish Constabulary Barracks. The Barracks were subsequently on the site where the former cinema stood. Bertha Geddes giving a talk on old Holywood in 1977 recalled that:

'The police officers used to rest themselves on an iron seat outside the door whilst keeping a sharp eye on events taking place on the main street at the same time.'

The Constabulary were not alas keeping a watch on Victoria Road on 30 December 1872 when two sisters, Charlotte and Mary Rawe, murdered Miss Isabella Kerr and her maid Jane Toner in Glenbank, there. The milkman found the bodies the following morning. A contemporary street ballad laid part of the blame on the railway!

'O, Charlotte Rawe do you not think shame
To come to Holywood in the train
And kill Miss Kerr and her servant Jane
With a great big salamander.'

Above: Ballymenock Dairy Milk Delivery, Holywood Library

(A salamander was a heavy iron plate, with a long handle, heated and held over food to brown it.)

We know a good deal about the lives of those who lived in the big houses, but what was it like for those in the lower strata of society in the 19th century? The Holywood Library Archives contain some fascinating material recorded by those who had lived in Hill Street which was demolished in the 1960s. People lived in little terraced houses with half doors – taps and toilets were confined to the back yard; originally candles were the only form of light, with a pump for water in the middle of the street. One elderly resident remembered about the neighbourhood in the 19th century:

'The people were very kind. Everyone had little or nothing and we all shared with one another. Many of the women had their babies in their own homes and the neighbours came in to help…. There was an old chimney sweep called Arthur Diamond… He would sit on his window sill and when any children came near, he would charge at them with his black hands'.

Many people in the street kept animals. Another octogenarian resident recalled:

'There was an old woman at the top of the street who kept chickens and she spent her whole day running to the front of the house to make sure that none of the children had stolen any of them. My own mother kept pigs and a man called Greer would come up from the Kinnegar to kill them. We would hang them up and drain the blood out and then sit up all night to watch that the cats did not get them. All the women were very close. In the summer they would sit outside in the evenings with their big white aprons on and smoking their clay pipes…'

In his volume of poems *The Quiet Shore*, Tom Kerr wrote about the neighbouring Spencer Street where he was born:

'The terrace houses straggled
down the street where I was born,
red brick, grey stuccoed family homes,
the chimney sweep's, the sweetie shop,

the milkman's yard,
And on the sunny side,
Door steps and window sills,
Where we would sit, our homeworks done,
And watch the cows come home
To Granda Thompson's byre.
Or 'hang behind' the binman's cart,
And yell 'Old Rags'
In chorus with the beggar man.'

One resident worthy of note was a character called 'Billy Liver' in Holywood. He was so called because he came from Liverpool, and slept among the coal at the old railway station, according to an article in the *Holywood Advertiser* of November 1984. It appears the railway had many uses!

It is also worth noting that by 1890 the former Bishop's Palace had been acquired by the War Office as the site for the new Holywood Palace Barracks. The first regiments were stationed there from 1897/98 on. The Barracks, along with the growing facilities at Kinnegar camp, must have increased the business for the railway line. The story of the Barracks and their relationship with the neighbouring garrison town is another fascinating one which deserves to be recorded by local historians.

Above left: *Spencer Street, Holywood, by Tom Kerr, courtesy of the artist*
Above right: *Postcard of Palace Barracks, posted in 1903*

Chapter 2

Bangor in the 19th Century

Before the mid-19th Century

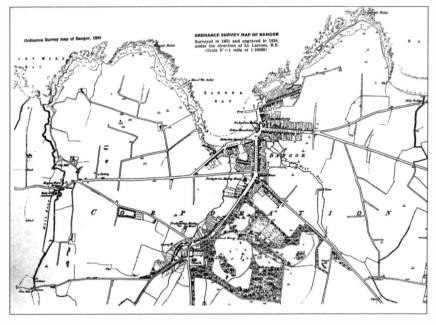

There are a number of different sources on what life was like in Bangor in the 19th century. Two are 'Victorian Bangor', by members of the Bangor Local History Study Group, edited by Grenfell Morton and published in 1972, and William C Seyers' 'Reminiscences of Old Bangor' (first published in 1932). Seyers was born in 1854, so he would have known Bangor in the pre-rail era.

In terms of transport, before the railway, the sea was a vital link for the town. The recorded development of Bangor Harbour began as early as 1757, when a pier some 300 feet long was constructed near the bottom of what is now Victoria Road, with a grant from the Irish Parliament. The Harbour thus formed was however reported in the *Parliamentary Gazetteer* of 1844 to be 'very turbulent' in North East gales, and was also dry at low water. Coal was then the main import at the harbour, beside which stood the historic Custom House which had been completed in 1637.

During the first half of the 19th century, there was a thriving cotton industry in Bangor, with two mills (Old and New, powered by steam engines) at the foot of High Street and at the site of the present McKee Clock. Alas, a series of fires in the 1850s brought Bangor's cotton industry to an abrupt end. The *Ordnance Survey Memoirs* of 1836 had remarked on the mills' smoky chimneys which provided a '*manufacturing, crowded and dirty appearance*'. They employed over two hundred men and women. The mills represented one of the main forces of change in the first half of the 19th century, as against the Abbey and the Castle.

From early times, Bangor, like Holywood, was known for its summer sea-bathing. An advertisement in the Northern Star in May 1792 announced:

'To be let for the bathing season. A large and commodious house in the town of Bangor, adjoining the quay.'

Then in 1816 the Bangor Corporation ordered a place to be prepared for bathing in the harbour.

The *Memoirs* also noted that the Harbour was 'an extremely bad one', so it was perhaps not surprising that Bangor does not seem to have ever seriously been considered as an alternative to Donaghadee for the mail service to Portpatrick. It was not until 1863 that a provisional order of the Board of Trade set in motion the granting of powers to Robert Ward to widen the pier and build an extension to it. (The Harbour remained in the possession of the Ward family until it was transferred to the Bangor Urban Council in 1920, for a price of £22,500.) Seyers recorded that the new part of the pier was added after the railway was finished, the same contractor making it, bringing his plant and equipment from the one to the other.

Above: Ordnance Survey Map of Bangor, engraved 1834

The authors of the *Memoirs* were comparatively impressed with Bangor's housing, even at the poorer end of the spectrum – while the older cabins had mud walls, '*glass windows are in all cases employed, and a tolerable degree of cleanliness and neatness may be seen to prevail in some instances*'. That said, there were 146 cases of two or more families sharing one cabin. The town itself was described as '*narrow and straggling*'.

Prior to the creation of the Bangor Town Commissioners, local affairs were run by the Provost and the Bangor Corporation. In practice, an 1834 Inquiry into the state of municipal corporations in Ireland revealed that the entire Corporation was, as it had '*been for many years, composed of members of the Ward family, their friends and dependants.... No Roman Catholic has been a member*'. The chief functions of the Corporation were the letting of land and tenements, and arranging for the repair and cleansing of streets and footpaths. They also paid the salaries of the Town Sergeant, and of the person who wound and oiled the town clock. The 1834 Inquiry did note that the Bangor Corporation's work was '*a rare instance of Irish Borough lands preserved with care, and an income... usefully expended and satisfactorily accounted for*'.

Nevertheless the Corporation was dissolved following the Municipal Corporations (Ireland) Act 1840, and for a period Bangor was under the Newtownards Poor Law Union.

There was a '*place of confinement in the town, called the Black Hole, to which the Provost claims the power of committing disturbers of the peace, and, if detained for the night, of compelling them to pay a fine of one shilling for straw supplied*'. However when asked in 1834, the Provost, then Colonel Ward, could only recall one occasion on which he had felt compelled to use this facility.

Near the Abbey, were the municipal Pound and a Mendicity Institute, from which food and clothing were distributed to the poor.

There was also a Poor House supported by Colonel Ward (considered by Patton to be in the modern Church Street). The First Presbyterian Church, completed in the early 1830s, had an auditorium which could seat 1,000 people. (This denomination was by far the largest in Bangor, outnumbering Church of Ireland members by more than ten to one.) A library had been created by 1837, there was a Friendly Society and a pawnbroker's '*frequented only by the lowest class, dealings confined to the poorest and profligate*'. The Bangor Dispensary which supplied free medical treatment and medicines to the poor who had qualified for medical relief tickets was in Catherine Place (now Dufferin Avenue). The most prevalent complaint there was '*observed to be scrofula, and medical men attribute this to the proximity to and intercourse with, Scotland*', it was noted in the *Memoirs*.

From the 1850s on

The entry for Bangor in Henderson's *Belfast Directory* records that the population in 1851 was 2,850. (This was a drop from the figure of 3,116 ten years before, reflecting in part the effects of the famine and emigration. The population reduced still further to around 2,500 in 1861 and was still at a similar figure in 1871.) The *Directory* noted in 1852 that:

'*Near the beach are many neat furnished houses and villas, built for the accommodation of parties visiting this favourite bathing shore... the sewed Muslin business is carried on to a very great extent, giving employment to thousands of females through the country and town*'.

At the time of the *Directory*, the Post Office was run by Mrs Louden, the post-mistress. Letters from Dublin, Belfast, Scotland and the north of England arrived every morning at 9 o'clock, and were dispatched at 20 minutes to 5. (One might wonder how one corresponded with the South of England, but the *Directory* presumably refers to the origin of the vessel bringing the post!)

Sergeant Murphy was now in charge of the Constabulary station which at this time was in Main Street. The variety of trades recorded is interesting. There were several butchers and grocers, a watchmaker, a haberdasher, a pawnbroker, several car owners, an organist and teacher of the piano, and a bog oak carver. A new two-storey school had been built by 1846, with over a hundred boys and half that number girls on the register, although actual attendance was a good deal lower. A separate school – Bangor Endowed – was built in 1856. Although it was created with funds from the Ward family, this was a fee-paying establishment, for the wealthier boys of the town. (The Ladies' Collegiate and Glenlola came towards the end of the 19th century, although Ireland's first Sunday school had been established a hundred years earlier in Rathgael by J Rose-Cleland.)

Bangor Castle is a mid-19th century construct. In reality a mansion rather than a castle, it was designed by Scottish architect William Burn who also designed Helen's Tower for Lord Dufferin at neighbouring Clandeboye at much the same time. The Castle was completed in 1852

for Robert Edward Ward, brother of the 3rd Viscount Bangor. The estate covered around 6,000 acres and included much of the town of Bangor. As set out in later chapters, RE Ward played an important role in bringing the railway to Bangor.

We know something of local Bangor man William Seyers from his obituary (in 1941). Born in 1852, he was a farmer and a carter (as his father had been before him) who in 1886 took over an important contract with the BCDR for an 'extensive carrying service in and around Bangor'.

In his book, Seyers tells us a good deal of what the town must have felt like in his youth, as well as the actual businesses and characters therein. One of the author's favourites is Sammy Reavey who always wore one and sometimes two tall top hats; once when his hat fell off, Seyers saw the coal, beef, bones and

bread etc. which had been stored under it! When he passed away a poem written about him by MJ Laird contained this verse:

'No longer by the station house,
He waits with watchful patience there,
For gentlemen that often would
Their money with poor Sammy share.'

In Seyers' account of Victorian Bangor, virtually all the road names were different – for example Sandy Row for Queen's Parade, Ballymagee Street for the High Street, and Fisher Hill for Victoria Road. One rhyme of the day ran as follows:

'Ballymagee for drinking tea,
Fisher Hill for brandy,
But Sandy Row can beat them all
For playing cock-a-dandy.'

According to Seyers, James Crosby provided hot salt water baths at the corner of Queen's Parade and Southwell Road. He pumped the water from the sea and charged 5/- for six baths. Main Street then had the principal shops, together with the Georgian Market House. The Police Barracks were at what later became Miloy's barber's shop. According to Seyers, the Gas Works started up on Ballymagee Road on a small scale – just two men did the work initially. (It was begun as a private company, though it was

Above left: Bangor Castle, courtesy of North Down Museum
Above bottom: Sammy Reavey, a Bangor character. Above right: Bangor Harbour, c.1875, North Down Museum

later taken over by the Town Commissioners. A later secretary of the Gas company, Robert Russell, was wealthy enough in the 1880s to build the prominent house Augustaville on Princetown Road, above the Pickie area.)

There were at this time quite a number of hotels, mostly down beside the harbour and the beach – and a rather larger number of public houses. Seyers recorded that at that time, there were about 30 sea captains in Bangor, mostly trading to and from Belfast. They all bought their beef in

Bangor, Co. Down

dear Kate.
This morning after Breakfast, we had a drive on a jaunty car to McCaw's works and rose through it, had dinner and then railed to Bangor a very pretty place as you can see. Off to Dublin tomorrow yours, J. F.

Bangor. Aug 30/01

Ferguson's shop in Ann Street, Belfast, and on Christmas Eve, Ferguson sent a roast of beef to each, by railway, carriage paid.

Before the coming of the railway, Holywood could be reached in thirty minutes with a fast horse. Poor folk in Bangor would have to walk to Belfast. Seyers recorded that the price for carting coal to Newtownards Poor House was 2/6 per ton, a distance of about 5 miles from Bangor Quay. At its busiest, there would have been 20 horses and carts at 6 o'clock in the morning waiting in line for which would be the first to get loaded.

Grenfell Morton quotes McComb's 1861 *Guide to Belfast* which noted the attractions of Bangor in the summer, but added that it was '*not well adapted for a winter residence, owing to the exposed nature of its situation*'.

Under the Towns Improvement (Ireland) Act of 1854, application could be made to the Lord Lieutenant to proceed to an election for Town

Commissioners. The first attempt in 1859 was opposed by the majority of ratepayers.

Morton's book states that a meeting of some 500 Bangor citizens took place in May 1862, although other sources dispute this. There was however an election of Town Commissioners in 1864 who included both RE Ward and Henry McFall. (The Commissioners were in turn replaced by the Bangor Urban District Council in 1899.) One of the more memorable acts of the Commissioners some years later was to prohibit residents from keeping pigs in their backyards, as Morton put it '*a profitable but malodorous sideline*'. (Mains drainage did not begin until 1882.)

The mid-19th century was, even before the coming of the railway, a time of change in Bangor. The almost feudal arrangements exercised by the Ward family were being challenged by the emerging, property-owning, mercantile class, even though specific businesses waxed and waned.

The end of the cotton mills was accompanied by decline in parts of the textile business elsewhere. In April 1863, there was a petition from unemployed muslin weavers of Bangor to the Newtownards Board of Guardians '*praying for assistance in preparing themselves to embrace the privilege of free emigration to Australia or New Zealand*'. Alas their petition was spurned.

In August 1864, a gala of swimming matches took place at Bangor. Mr Henry McFall of the Royal Hotel (which dated originally from around 1840 and the unfortunate closure of which was announced in 2014) had altruistically erected a bathing box for the community on the Pickie Rock, although a contemporary account regretted the absence of a similar facility for lady visitors. (Mr McFall was also the harbour master and agent for the Belfast Lough steamers, secretary to the Gas Company, and himself a keen swimmer.) The Ulster Yacht Club which had for a while earlier in the century had its headquarters in Bangor, was revived in 1866. Four years later it received its Royal Charter. The present magnificent clubhouse, designed by Vincent Craig, was opened in 1899.

Bassett's *Guide to County Down* records that by 1881, the population of Bangor had grown to 3,006, (although another source suggest that the population was nearer 4,000 by that time). The text noted that '*the only industry at Bangor that has survived the changes of time is embroidering*'. It adds that some years previously Mr David McKenzie's

'Designs were so chaste and the needle work done so perfectly that they attracted the attention of the Duchess of Marlborough who brought them to the notice of Queen Victoria. Mr Mackenzie in due course received an order from Her Majesty'.

The items included monograms, crests and even toilet covers! The work provided home employment for a significant number of women and girls into the later part of the 19th century in the parish.

The land of the district was said to be average quality. Oats, potatoes, wheat and flax were the chief crops. Interestingly while the market used to be held in the town weekly on Saturdays, Bassett recorded that it had been discontinued. Cotton and linen manufacturing had disappeared, though lime-burning and brick-making were being carried on extensively.

The *Guide* was not short of what might be called 'purple passages'; in describing the walk to Ballyholme from the Bangor seafront, it noted that *'it would not be easy to find a more delightful retreat from the cares of the world than is afforded here'*.

Referring to the impact of the railway, the Guide stated that:

'After the line of the railway to Belfast had been opened, Bangor's attractions as a watering place brought it into the first rank. It is now also connected with Belfast by steamer … The bathing facilities are favourable for both sexes'.

There was a short lived steamer service between Bangor and Peel on the west coast of the Isle of Man in the summer of 1889, but the following year Belfast superseded Bangor, largely on account of the unsatisfactory pier facilities at the latter.

The impact of the railway on the development of Bangor continued. The provision of 'house free' tickets by the railway company gave considerable stimulus to the town's progress, as is recorded in the later chapters.

One source suggests that the population of the town in 1910 was 9,200, but in the summer, that rose to a dizzying 20,000 or even 30,000. The number of hotels had increased significantly, to meet the demand created by the railway and steamer services. As Morton records, the decade 1891 to 1901 had seen the population of Bangor increase by over 50%. As the

Belfast Directory of 1897 put it, the smoky and dirty appearance of the sea front had given way to:

'A fine promenade for pedestrians faces the bay and a handsome esplanade, comfortably seated, and provided with a band-stand has been constructed, and it is a great boon as a resting place for visitors.'

ESPLANADE, BANGOR, CO. DOWN.

By this time, Bangor was becoming more as we know it today.

The *News Letter* in August 1897 carried an advertisement for Bangor Grammar School of which the Headmaster was one WG Conolly. The terms (ie fees) were described as moderate, but it stressed in particular

Above top: *View from the corner of Main Street and Queen's Parade, Bangor, c. 1900, North Down Museum.* **Above bottom:** *The Esplanade, Bangor*

24

that *'the situation of the School and its grounds, which extend to the margin of the sea, renders it exceedingly suitable for delicate boys.'* One doubts if the modern generation of Grammarians would share that assessment!

BANGOR GRAMMAR SCHOOL,
COUNTY DOWN.
A most successful School for Boys.
———
Work will be Resumed on September 2nd.
Six Entrance 'Scholarships—four value £40, and two value £30—will be awarded among Boys entering next term.

The situation of the School and its grounds, which extend to the margin of the sea, renders it exceedingly suitable for delicate boys.

For Prospectus, all particulars, and terms (which are moderate) apply to
W. G. CONOLLY, M.A., LL.D.,
Head Master.

17681

Above top: *Newspaper advertisement for Bangor Grammar School, Libraries NI*
Above bottom: *Ordnance Survey Map of Bangor, 1903*

Chapter 3

The Birth of the Belfast and County Down Railway (BCDR)

Genesis

The Belfast and County Down Railway has had various 'soubriquets' over the years. The late Dr DB McNeill liked to describe it as '*Every creeping thing*', after the wording in Genesis. He did acknowledge that that was a little unfair, although Robert Lloyd Praeger, writing fifty years later, recalled that in 1848:

'Holywood Railway traffic was worked by two little tank engines about 8 feet long and weighing eight or nine tons. High speeds were not encouraged. On one occasion, the only available engine being out of repair, all 10 hands of the permanent way staff were called out to push the 3 o'clock train to Holywood.'

Another favourite was '*Be Careful, Don't Rush*' which forms the title of this book.

Railway mania affected Ireland, just as it did Britain in the 1830s and 1840s. Many were the plans and schemes to build lines. Sometimes they were supported by noblemen, landowners, clergy and others, sometimes not so. (Alas historical records from that era more rarely tell us the attitude of the majority of the population, who did not fall into these categories.)

The *BCDR Official Tourist Guide* quoted Smiles' biography of George Stephenson to *put* the craze in these terms:

'Railways through hills, across areas of the sea, over or under great rivers, spanning valleys at great heights or boring their way under ground, across barren moors, along precipices, over bogs and through miles of London streets. No scheme was so mad that it did not find an engineer.'

However the *BCDR Guide* added that in this country, '*railway construction proceeded slowly, and perhaps more surely*'.

The basic approach was for a group of promoters, sometimes themselves landowners to work up an outline plan, then get the landowners along the route on board, obtain initial funding through issuing shares, and then get a Parliamentary Act to incorporate the fledgling company and enable it to proceed to construction.

In this age of centralised government (the 'nanny' State), it needs to be remembered that neither central nor local Government played a role in planning an overall railway system.

Railway schemes often competed with or rivalled the proposals of other groups, rarely was there open collaboration. Moreover while the initial plan might be to lay a track to one destination, often enough the final course of the route lay in another direction. Schemes could be over-ambitious and their backers face financial loss or even ruin.

The story of both the Belfast to Holywood and indeed Bangor lines exemplifies all this, and more!

At that time, it took a minimum of 12 to 13 hours to travel by coach between Dublin and Belfast. In April 1835, a project was proposed to establish rail links between the two cities. In October 1836, a Royal Commission was appointed to '*inquire into the manner in which railway communications can be most advantageously promoted in Ireland*'. The engineer responsible was John Macneill who put forward proposals combining horse-drawn carriages and locomotives. (Macneill

Above: Crest of the Belfast and County Down Railway, courtesy of Kay Coulthard

was appointed to the first chair of Engineering at Trinity College Dublin, and later knighted at Amiens Street Station in Dublin.) The Commission recommended a standard gauge of 6 feet 2 inches for all railways in Ireland. The first 7 ½ miles of railway built in Ulster, from Belfast to Lisburn, were constructed on this basis. It ran its first service on 12 August 1839 – just the second line in the whole of Ireland.

Subsequently, by Act of Parliament, in August 1846, 5 feet 3 inches was decided upon as the standard gauge for all Irish railways, including both the Belfast and County Down Railway and the Belfast, Holywood and Bangor Railway (which it remains to this day).

As the new technology came in, so different approaches were promoted. At one point plans were drawn up, for a Holywood Atmospheric Railway. (This would have used the vacuum principle to create momentum, but the basic technology of using leather to seal the vacuum employed in the prototypes at Dalkey and Dawlish proved, among other problems, too attractive to rodent depredation.)

As noted in the Holywood chapter, the authors of the Ordnance Survey *Memoirs* observed that the route from Belfast to Holywood was both level and agreeable, and that on Sundays vast numbers drove between the two locations.

So, as detectives might say, there existed both the means and the motive. Developments began shortly after that first Ordnance Survey exercise.

We are indebted to the archive collection built up by William McCutcheon for much of the early material and records.

As early as – curiously – Boxing Day 1836, a circular was produced headed the 'Belfast and Holywood Railway'. It begins:

'I am directed, by the Provisional Committee of this undertaking, to acquaint you that all the plans, surveys etc. have been completed and deposited, as required, in proper time, for applying to Parliament, in the ensuing Session for the necessary Act. Detailed estimates of the expenses and cost of the work have also been received from the Engineers, and an account taken of the present Traffic on the Line, which, alone, without any increase, will afford a large return for the Capital invested. Experience, also, has proved that where railways have been established, traffic has increased from four to seven fold…. As applications have been made for a much larger number

of shares than is required for the undertaking, I am directed to intimate to you, that, if your deposit be not paid within the time specified, you will forfeit your claim to be considered as a Proprietor.'

On the back of the same document, were then set out a number of costings (what we would nowadays call an outline business plan) including two alternative routes – a cheaper one that would carry the railway '*close by the shore*', and the other which would carry it on an embankment on reclaimed land more seaward, at double the cost. It then quoted a daily average of passengers, '*by cars*' during the summer months at some 2,000 each day, rising to 2,500 on summer Sundays! The Committee had also noted that 600 pedestrians walked from Belfast to Holywood each Sunday and estimated that one-third would take the train to save time. At 6d (sixpence) each passenger the line would bring in £9,000 per year. The financial projections seemed to be flawed however, as this was portrayed as a profit of 22% on the capital outlay, with no reference to running costs etc.

Also dated 26 December 1836 is a notice signed by Hugh Wallace, to James Bristow as a landowner on the route of the proposed railway, advising the latter that he was giving notice that it was intended to apply to Parliament for leave to bring in a Bill for making a Railway from Belfast to Holywood. Bristow was invited to inform Wallace at his office in Fountain Street in Belfast, whether '*you assent to, dissent from, or are neuter as to the undertaking, that your reply may be returned to Parliament, as required by the Standing Orders of both Houses*'.

Shortly following that, comes a certificate dated 28 January 1837 recording that James Bristow (who was a senior manager with the Northern Bank) had paid the sum of 5 pounds as a deposit on 20 shares '*in a Company, intended to be formed, for the making of the line of Railway*

Above top: *1836 Notice of intention to create a railway from Belfast to Holywood, from the McCutcheon Archive, courtesy of the Northern Ireland Environment Agency (NIEA)*
Above bottom: *1836 share certificate for the Belfast and Holywood Railway Company, courtesy of the NIEA*

27

from Belfast to Holywood'. Mr Bristow was clearly neither dissenting from nor being neuter to the undertaking!

The Promoters Try Again

The formal origins of the Belfast and County Down Railway, as such, go back to a meeting in the Donegall Arms Hotel in Belfast held on 25 February 1845 *'of parties favourable to the promotion of the railway to Holywood, Comber and Newtownards'*.

The succession of minute books of the Belfast and County Down Railway from 1845 onwards is held in the Public Record Office in Titanic Quarter, where the aficionado could while away many a happy hour! Alas space limits the scope for quoting other than selectively.

The first book opens with what is ostensibly a contemporary account of that 25 February meeting. The author very much doubts whether the promoters had the prescience to bring to that occasion a brand new folio-sized minute book. Nevertheless, we learn much from it, not least the identity of the key backers most of whom had direct connections with properties along the intended routes. Reflecting the importance of Holywood as a destination, John Harrison, then almost the laird of Holywood, living in Mertoun Hall, was invited to take the chair. Guy Stone, later chairman of the BCDR, John Andrews from Comber, Samuel Delacherois Crommelin (living at Carrowdore Castle), the engineer John Godwin and Thomas Ward (who acted as secretary from the beginning) were there. Three propositions were put to the meeting, as follows:

'It is the opinion of this meeting that the construction of a Railway from Belfast to Holywood and to Comber, and Newtownards would be highly advantageous to these towns and the surrounding country,

that a committee be now appointed for the purpose of procuring the necessary information and taking the proper steps preliminary to the formation of a Company carrying out these undertakings, and

that the following gentlemen be appointed to a committee to carry the foregoing resolution into effect.'

Those appointed included Harrison, RF Gordon of Holywood, John Andrews, William Coates of Glentoran, Thomas Gregg of Ballymenoch, J Henry Kennedy of Cultra, SD Crommelin, and John Howe of Ballyleidy. The minutes were signed as accurate at the following meeting by Guy Stone.

There was a rival scheme, also registered that year, entitled the Grand County Down, Belfast, Newry and Warrenpoint Railway. There was much toing and froing between backers of the various different schemes. As noted above, one was for an Atmospheric railway between Belfast and Holywood. However, its promoters, which included the Marquis of Donegall and the entrepreneurial Montgomery brothers of Belfast, were bought off, and gave up their application for an Act of Parliament. There was also a rival plan for a Belfast, High Holywood and Bangor Railway.

The second meeting of promoters was held on 28 March of that year, this time chaired by John Andrews of Comber; Hugh Stewart who was to be behind the setting up of the Baths company in Holywood, also attended. On this occasion there was reference to a line to Bangor, as well as to Downpatrick and Donaghadee, *'to meet the views of many of the landed proprietors of the county'*. Meetings both of the subcommittee and the promoters continued regularly.

There was a meeting in May at which a decision was made that no applicant should have more than 50 shares unless he was a member of the Provisional Committee in which case the maximum was 100. The allotment of shares was to be made by a subcommittee including Messrs Wallace, Coates and Bristow. A meeting was held in London in June for the purposes of ratifying the allocation of shares as proposed by them. Those recorded as signatories for the bank, some of whose names resonate over subsequent years, were Messrs Harrison, Bristow (associated with the Northern Bank) and Wallace (a lawyer).

The May meeting had also formally agreed that the necessary Parliamentary deeds be forthwith prepared to apply to Parliament for all the lines including those to Bangor and Donaghadee.

On 23 July 1845, the Provisional Committee considered a proposal from the Grand County Down, Belfast, Newry and Warrenpoint Railway Company that to save costs that company would be willing to enter into an arrangement for the amalgamation of their company and the Belfast and County Down Company and the Newry, Warrenpoint and Rostrevor Railway Company. As any good bureaucratic organisation should, the Provisional Committee duly appointed a sub-committee to liaise with the Grand County Down.

Discussions quickly ensued, with a proposition that a fourth company – the Newry, Banbridge and Belfast Junction Railway – should be added into the grand merger, with a total share capital of £1,350,000 – a large sum of money in those days. Some degree of agreement was reached in principle, including the decision that the name of the amalgamated company should be different from each of the existing four. Did the sub-committees get carried away?

On 18 August 1845, the other three railway companies wrote to record that in their view the proposal of 30 July from the County Down Railway had:

'Exceeded the power vested in them and the persons present under the existing circumstances entirely object to any further steps being taken towards the proposed amalgamation, and accordingly feel compelled to decline proceeding.'

Prudently, a meeting of the BCDR shareholders was held on 30 August, (interestingly with some present from the Newry and Banbridge Junction Railway) at which it was decided that:

'Further delay in the allocation of the shares of this company [would] be highly injurious.'

A motion was put commending the committees of those two companies in suspending negotiation with the Grand County Down. A contrary amendment to ratify amalgamation was rejected by a large majority, with the original motion then being carried with just one dissentient. Reading between the lines, one gets the feeling that in this era of railway mania, those who wished to hold shares in the BCDR and anticipated getting rich as a result did not want to have the prospect of early gains jeopardised through delay in negotiations and uncertainty through going into a grander scheme with other companies further removed from Belfast.

In November 1845, the *Down Recorder* included a notice that application was:

'Intended to be made to Parliament, for making and sustaining the railway and branch railways following…a main line of railway commencing at a point at or near the South side of the Queen's Bridge in Ballymacarrett in the Borough of Belfast, and passing thence …and terminating in the Borough of Downpatrick. Also a Branch railway, commencing at a point on the main line in the Townland of Ballymacarrett, about five furlongs distant from Queen's Bridge… passing thence, from, in, through, or into the Parishes, Towns, Townships, Townlands, extra-Parochial and other places following or some of them… Knocknagoney and Holywood,… the strand slob or soil of Belfast Lough… and terminating at or near the Shore Street, in the town of Holywood aforesaid.' (NB Extra-parochial land was that not included in the parish such as land reclaimed from the sea.)

The same notice listed extensively the route of the proposed branch line to Donaghadee, but in addition, from that line, at or near 'Six Cross-roads' a further branch would go via Ballygrainey, Gransha, Balloo and Ballymagee terminating at or near the Quay in Bangor. The scale and impact of the lines was announced in that the Act would also permit the Company to *'cross, divert, alter or stop up all such Turnpike, County, Parish or other Roads, or Highways, Rivers, Streams, Canals, Navigations… for the purposes of the said proposed Railways.'*

It would appear that – reflecting the views of the many landed proprietors – the embryonic BCDR's strategists wished to have as wide a range of options as possible. They and their supporters duly had their way, and their Act obtained Royal Assent on 26 June 1846.

The way was now clear to raise funds for construction, and the authorised capital was – the not insignificant sum of – £500,000, with powers to borrow up to one third of that sum. The gathering of capital was however slow, and the Directors were cautious *'in view of the bad effects which the late mania for railway speculation has had on the money market, involving the crushing of many sound and legitimate undertakings'*. Indeed a number of shareholders defaulted, including the Marquis of Londonderry. Accordingly the Directors decided to restrict construction initially to the Belfast to Holywood, and the Belfast to Newtownards portions.

Construction and Opening of the Holywood Line

Contracts were let in February 1847 to Ireland's leading railway engineer and architect William Dargan, who was born in 1799 and died in 1867. Dargan was the son of a Carlow farmer who sent his son to England for education and to serve an apprenticeship in surveying. In 1831, when he was just over thirty – about the age for 19th century engineers to be making their mark – Dargan won the contract for Ireland's first railway line between Dublin and Kingstown which was completed in 1834.

Dargan rapidly became the country's leading railway engineer (so much so that by 1853, he had built more than 60% of all railways in Ireland, including by his death three other railway lines radiating from Belfast). In 1839, the Belfast Harbour Authority commissioned him to cut the first stretch of the Victoria Channel, the spoil from which was deposited to form the 17 acre island in the Lagan initially named after him. (After Queen Victoria's visit 10 years later, it became Queen's Island.)

Dargan's tender of £33,000 for the Holywood line was the lowest of the three submitted.

From the beginning, Charles Lanyon was the Company's official architect. John Godwin who had come from Swansea as engineer to the Ulster Railway Company was then appointed as chief engineer by the BCDR. Godwin, as we have seen, attended the first public meeting of February 1845. His challenges included tackling subsidence problems on the line between Belfast and Holywood and the selection of engineering personnel. (Godwin was an interesting man. He first studied at the age of 14 with Sir James McAdam who introduced the system of road-making known as tar macadam. We are fortunate he turned his attention from road to rail, as so many later were to go in

the reverse direction. Godwin was subsequently the first to be appointed, in 1849, to the chair of Civil Engineering at Queen's College, Belfast. Most of his time clearly continued to be devoted to railways as in the eight years of his tenure at Queen's, no students graduated in civil engineering!)

These issues having been overcome, the level route to Holywood, beside Belfast Lough, was finished first, inspected by the Railway Commissioners in late July and opened to traffic on 2 August 1848. The track was single, although it was built to take a double line of rails in due course. The Holywood terminus was built on Marine Parade.

The *Belfast News Letter* reported:

'Holywood Railway – This branch of the Belfast and County Down Railway was first opened to public traffic on Wednesday. The line runs parallel with the Belfast Bay, on the County Down side, and being a perfect level, the movement is very easy. The carriages are fitted up very elegantly and with every regard for comfort. The arrangements for the transfer of traffic are carried out with the utmost satisfaction and punctuality.'

One might expect the BCDR minute book to be full of this happy event. Curiously, there is only a comparatively short reference in the meeting held in the Board Room on 3 August 1848, a meeting attended by the engineer and the secretary. It was noted that Captain Laffan RE had inspected the line on the part of the Government on 28 July and approved of it; and that *'the Branch line to Holywood had been yesterday opened for traffic'*.

Interestingly, within 24 hours of the line opening, the Directors were considering the first representation from their service users! The Board noted an application from a number of inhabitants of this town (i.e. Belfast) and Holywood for a *'later train in the evenings than that fixed upon'*. This encouraging development was readily agreed to by the Directors who decided that the last train from Belfast should leave at 7:30pm, while that from Holywood would leave at 8:30pm from Monday 7 August. A postcard, though of much later date from the turn of the century, provides a vivid illustration of the last train and its customers!

Engineer Godwin reported on a number of discussions he had had with the County Surveyor and the Railway Commissioners on the bridges over

Above top: Portrait of William Dargan, from the book by William McCutcheon, courtesy of the NIEA
Above bottom: Portrait of John Godwin, courtesy of Queen's University Belfast

THE LAST TRAIN
for Holywood

(which were partly subsidised by the company) were run that day. Over 5,000 passengers were carried with the total takings of what seems a paltry sum by today's standards of £86. Guard Smyth was assaulted by a 'party' for which successful prosecution ensued, but they may not have been entirely in the wrong, as Smyth was subsequently sacked in 1850.

The weekly Board meetings continued in 1849, recording the income and expenditure on a weekly basis. This showed the significant variation; for example in May of that year the weekly takings varied between £36 and £59, with wages of £15, although in the previous month, over Easter, the income had been as high as £163.

A number of crossings were facilitated in the Kinnegar area to allow landowners to exercise their right to gather seaweed on the shore!

William McCutcheon, in his book *The Industrial Archaeology of Northern Ireland*, records that in the first six months, the operating costs were £1,100, while the takings amounted to over £1,800. Traffic was – as expected from the prospectus – seasonal, with monthly takings in the summer four times those of the winter.

Holywood surgeon Thomas Kelly writing in 1850, recorded that:

'The distance to and from Belfast is performed by this locomotory mode of travelling, in from 8 to 10 minutes. In the summer months a train leaves each terminus hourly from seven o'clock am till half-past nine pm.'

It seems however that the doctor still chose to travel himself by road – rather more sedately – when he needed to go into town!

Newtownards was reached by the BCDR in May 1850, and steady traffic began to build up on the two lines. Shareholders were rewarded in 1851 with a modest initial dividend of 2%.

As noted in the chapter on Holywood, from 1852 the company offered a combined rail and bathing ticket. Interestingly, the BCDR was one of the first companies to offer an ostensibly integrated transport system. From 1854, the company advertised a horse-drawn omnibus leaving Bangor at 9.45am that would connect with the train to Belfast leaving Holywood at 11am, though there was apparently no guarantee of the arrival or departure of trains or indeed omnibuses at the scheduled time. (A through fare from Bangor to Belfast cost one shilling.)

the Turnpike roads, and that he could get no satisfactory guarantees on deviating from the provisions of the Parliamentary Act. He was instructed to erect the bridges accordingly. (Was this early evidence of the BCDR seeking to cut corners and costs?)

The minutes also record that the great William Dargan was kept waiting that day. He had attended the Board with a request for a further payment on account of works; it was ordered by the Directors that a 'check' (ie a cheque) for £500 be drawn in favour of Mr Dargan and handed to him.

The Railway was run on a somewhat rudimentary basis. The company secretary, Thomas Ward, combined his duties with being stationmaster at Queen's Quay, for no additional stipend. The chief ticket clerk was responsible for traffic matters, according to Desmond Coakham, though he was soon replaced by the original parcels clerk! One driver was dismissed in the first year for allowing an unauthorised person to travel on his engine. (That seems a bit harsh given the generations of boys who have subsequently been permitted to ride on the footplate!)

Nine trains were run in each direction daily, including Sundays. The first class annual subscription ticket would be just £8. From the first year, there were season tickets and concessions for families, young people etc. On Christmas Day 1848 the service faced a real test as the Holywood Races

Above: Postcard cartoon depicting the last train to Holywood

The original Parliamentary permission having lapsed, the Directors had to obtain a new Extension Act in May 1855. This provided for expansion of the embryonic system in several directions, and also for the realignment of various parts of the track. However, in this as in the original scheme, Bangor was to have been reached by a branch leaving the Donaghadee line near Conlig, coming into the town from the south, with a terminus at the quay.

In October 1855 a meeting was held with Lord Dufferin to seek his support for the Donaghadee line. According to Coakham, he expressed his willingness 'on public grounds alone' to help it obtain financial assistance for these routes.

Over the years, the Directors began to appreciate that Bangor had growth potential, and saw that there might be advantage in reaching it via the more direct 12 mile route from Belfast through Holywood, than from the Donaghadee line. Accordingly, in 1861, the BCDR formally abandoned its plans for a branch off the Donaghadee line into Bangor.

Prior to that, at an extraordinary meeting of shareholders in November 1857, Captain Henry Sharman Crawford, whose family estate at Crawfordsburn would be traversed by the line, had proposed that authority be given to 'promote or concur in the promotion' of a direct line to Bangor. Captain Harrison of Holywood was a dissentient landowner, while Thomas Greg (or Gregg), a former BCDR director based at Ballymenoch near Holywood objected most strongly. The Bangor extension was presented by Sir John Macneill the following year with alternative stations either at Catherine Place (close to where it is to this day), or at the west end of Queen's Parade. Both alternatives had the support of Robert Edward Ward and Viscount Bangor. The Directors were authorised to negotiate with any other parties who might wish to make the Holywood to Bangor line; that story is taken forward in the next chapter.

The significance of Donaghadee of course lay in its proximity to the harbour of Portpatrick in Scotland – a distance of only 20 miles. That sea crossing had been used for a long time historically, but grew more prominent with the introduction of the penny post and the requirement of the Post Office for dependable conveyance of the growing volume of mail. Accordingly a mail steam packet service had built up between the two ports, which provided for significant passenger traffic as well.

As long ago as March 1793 the (short-lived) *Northern Star* reported that:

'On the 16th inst. the Palmer packet boat, with the mail and passengers on board, sailed from Donaghadee to Portpatrick, where she arrived having a passage of only 2 hours and 5 minutes, the shortest ever known on this ferry.'

While this was clearly exceptional, it is curious to think that over two hundred years later the 'superfast' service from Belfast to Cairnryan takes ten minutes longer!

There were plans too on the Scottish side for a railway system linking Portpatrick into the Dumfries line and thence onto the rest of Britain, thus providing an arterial route between London and Belfast via Donaghadee. However there were a number of challenges, and with hindsight it does seem surprising to say the least that so much effort was put into servicing the cramped harbours of Portpatrick and Donaghadee.

EM Patterson records that from 1859, the finances of the BCDR were weak, although by 1864 the frequency of trains to Holywood had increased to 16 a day, except on Sundays. As we shall see, in 1865 the company sold its Belfast to Holywood branch to the nascent Belfast, Holywood and Bangor Railway, for £50,000 which gave the BHBR access to the city of Belfast. In addition the BHBR paid the BCDR an annual rent of £5,000, though even so the newcomer had to build a separate station at Queen's Quay with its own access and booking office. In the agreement between the two companies, the Bangor Company was not permitted to extend its railway to Donaghadee nor to compete with the BCDR's traffic to that town.

The BCDR Expands

Additional funds enabled the BCDR to construct the line on from Newtownards to Donaghadee. The track curved north just short of the village of Conlig where for some years a station principally served the dower house of the Dufferin family. Near the road junction of Six Road Ends, a station was also built, grandly named Groomsport and Bangor (later Ballygrainey), despite being in practice near to neither.

On 14 January 1860, his cousin WS Blackwood then at Ballinderry wrote to Lord Dufferin (in a letter in the PRONI collection):

'My principal reason for writing at present is to tell you … that I fear the prospects of the short sea passage are very materially damaged by the bad management and dilatory conduct of the County Down Railway Company. In fact I can hardly believe they are serious in their desire to make the line from Newtownards to Donaghadee … The scheme for establishing communication between Belfast and Lough Ryan (Stranraer) is supported by the most influential parties in this County and if it succeeds, I fear it will be a death blow to the Portpatrick line … I wish to put you on your guard. I always thought they would throw you over if they could.'

However WR Anketell, the BCDR chairman (a former land agent), wrote to Lord Dufferin on 17 July that year, in relation to the County Down Railway:

'The line from Stranraer to Portpatrick is in progress and apparently with great spirit and will there is no doubt be opened in the autumn of 1861. Our line to Donaghadee will likely be completed by March to April next … The only remaining issue is the Donaghadee harbour'.

The construction of the harbour at Donaghadee had not been finalised by the time the railway opened on 3 June 1861. Sir John Macneill and William Dargan were again heavily involved in this line's construction. The brothers John and Robert Edwards of Dublin successfully tendered to build the track (as they also had to construct the line to Downpatrick). The full harbour works at Donaghadee were subsequently completed in 1863.

The *News Letter* commented in June 1861 that with the opening of the rail communication:

'As a bathing station and a place for summer residence, Donaghadee will soon be a formidable rival to Holywood and Bangor.'

The Portpatrick Railway was authorised on 10 August 1857. By 12 March 1861, the line connected Stranraer to Castle Douglas, where it joined the newly constructed Castle Douglas and Dumfries railway. The branch to Portpatrick opened the following year, on 28 August 1862, while the Stranraer Harbour branch opened on 1 October 1862 – the same day as the railway from Carrickfergus to Larne commenced. No fewer than 600 passengers most of whom had travelled from Belfast to Donaghadee by train were carried on a special sailing from Donaghadee to Portpatrick that day. The line was affectionately to be known as the Port Road.

However – and it was a major caveat – Portpatrick's importance as a port declined almost before the Portpatrick branch was completed. The Donaghadee line continued to lose money. Portpatrick Harbour railway station both opened and closed permanently in 1868! It opened on 11 September and closed in November.

Several factors served to undermine the Donaghadee and Portpatrick route. First, Portpatrick Harbour was much more exposed to the elements than the safer anchorage of Stranraer at the head of Loch Ryan. A series of bad storms did little to encourage the confidence of passengers in the Portpatrick route. Second, there was competition in Northern Ireland from the Belfast and Northern Counties Railway which was linked with the Carrickfergus and Larne Railway. They naturally wished to promote the rival route between Larne and Stranraer, which they did with increasing success.

Thirdly, the increasing size of the steamships plying the seas between Northern Ireland and that part of Scotland inevitably demanded larger harbours with deep water.

Finally, it is even rumoured that foul play was involved at one stage with the Donaghadee train being unlawfully delayed, to the advantage of the competition on the County Antrim side.

The concerns of WS Blackwood in 1860 were indeed prophetic.
The *News Letter* gives us a feel for what has been termed railway mania, with the daily prices of shares in the individual railway companies (including those in Northern England unhappily associated with George Hudson) being given great prominence in the paper. (The later 1860s were a time when the value of many railway company stocks dwindled alarmingly.) On the other hand, an article in the newspaper on 1 September 1863 bemoaned the fact that at the half-yearly shareholders meeting held by the BCDR at the Queen's Quay, only 15 turned up and it was not quorate, despite proceedings being delayed for an hour in case they had dined too well.

Chairing on this occasion, William Wallace, was not able to do more than – most conveniently – declare the dividend. There was then a period with no dividend paid, although a minimal 1% was declared in the years 1869-71.

Nevertheless, despite these setbacks, the BCDR survived and even thrived, with a line to Newcastle opening in 1869 which the BCDR first worked and then acquired outright. (The Railway subsequently opened the splendid Slieve Donard Hotel in 1898.)

Up to the late 19th century, most large towns kept their own local time. Until the spread of railways this caused little inconvenience, with the vastly slower speed of mail coaches. Up to 1862 the BCDR kept Belfast time, which was one minute and nineteen seconds in front of Dublin time. Curiously from then until 1916, when Greenwich time was adopted not just in Great Britain but right across the British Isles, its trains ran on Dublin time – 25 minutes behind Greenwich Mean Time. The change probably caused many to miss their trains at first, as previously they benefitted from the 79 second advantage conferred by Dublin time.

Another sign of the BCDR's later financial strength was the purchase of steamships by the company. (This is dealt with in the chapter headed Steamer Competition.)

However this was not the case in the late 1860s and early 1870s. William McCutcheon says that the:

'Entire system was badly managed… The railway stock was continually… breaking down… and the Directors were short of money and well into arrears with the preference interest.'

There was a serious accident at Ballymacarrett on 13 May 1871, while the work on the Junction there had not quite been finalised. Two passengers were killed and five others seriously injured. As luck would have it, the BCDR chairman WR Anketell, as well as a large number of 'excursionists' who had been to Portpatrick, was travelling on the train from Donaghadee via Comber that ran into an engine that had been derailed out of Queen's Quay. A contemporary newspaper provided a lurid account:

'In an instant the engines met; there was a terrible crash; the two engines, a carriage and the guard's van were hurled down the embankment; two lives were lost; many persons injured… the spectacle presented by the shattered carriages, as well as by the running to and fro of the excited passengers, was a very painful one.'

Anketell *'escaped with but a slight abrasion of the leg'.* The two dead were a Queen's University student and a thirteen year old girl. The driver and fireman were accused of being intoxicated, and the latter was tried for manslaughter, receiving a sentence of 12 months hard labour, though he does not appear to have been allowed to give evidence at his own trial. The incident was a further setback for the BCDR shareholders, as the company had to pay more than £12,000 compensation to the injured. (The guard in the wrecked brake van was praised for staying at his post. He was subsequently made station master at Knock where in 1888 an irate passenger threatened him with a knife, and then climbed a tree reportedly in a state of nudity!)

In October 1875 the Board of Directors of the BCDR was reconstituted, largely as a consequence of the company's poor financial state. Shares worth £50 were now worth only a fifth of their value. The existing Board resigned, following an investigation into the company by a committee of shareholders. The fateful meeting was held in the Board Room on 25 August 1875. Anketell was in the chair, Crommelin was still a Director but several of his colleagues had only come on board comparatively recently. The minutes record candidly:

'The question of the resignation of the Directors of the Belfast and County Down Railway having been considered, four of the Directors and Mr Wallace retired for consultation and on returning there being seven Directors present, it was proposed by Mr Crommelin and resolved unanimously to tender their resignations at an extraordinary meeting of shareholders to be called for that purpose.'

A later newspaper account reported Anketell as saying *'All hopes of a compromise were ended'.* The author observes that in some ways Anketell had done well to last as long in the role, as he had. Living initially at Ardtullagh in Holywood (a big house within the estate of the Dunville family's Redburn House), he was renting by 1875 the historic Quintin

Castle, outside Portaferry. (Captain John Harrison subsequently moved into Ardtullagh.) He had changed his name to an earlier spelling of Ancketill, and was writing Irish Novels.

William Pirrie, who had become the year before a partner in the great shipyard of Harland and Wolff, joined as a Director at this time. (Another member of William Pirrie's family, Dr John M Pirrie, a son of the older William Pirrie of Conlig, had earlier been one of the Directors of the company, even chairing a meeting during the stormy times on 7 May 1873, before his death later that month.) Also appointed then was Thomas Andrews of Comber who was married to Eliza Pirrie, William's sister. (These were the parents of Thomas Andrews who was later to design the Olympic and Titanic steamships.) The tradition of family service on the Board was to continue well into the 20th century.

The new Board was chaired from November of that year by Richard Wood Kelly, who had an address in Dublin, and the company's fortunes were transformed within 10 years. By 1877 a 2½% dividend was declared, rising to no less than 6% in 1884, while in the following year the shares were worth ten times what they had been at their nadir.

The BCDR minute book continues to provide a rich source of fascination during this period. We learn such intimate details as the indisposition in October 1882 of Mr Miller of the Locomotive Department who 'was taken with a sort of cholera on Wednesday night last, but he suffers now from weakened stomach…'

At the same meeting, the Directors also considered an appeal against dismissal from engine driver Muldoon. They decided to dismiss his appeal, but did give him an extra £5 for long service. (Presumably he forfeited any pension rights. Speaking of which, Harry Welshman tells a lovely story of meeting a retired Indian Railways official on a train in Rajasthan. The man explained that he was going to Headquarters to prove that he was still alive and therefore still entitled to his hard-earned pension. Two years prior to that, he had forgotten to make the trip. When he next showed up, the Personnel Department refused to pay the arrears until he provided proof that he had been alive throughout the intervening period!)

At the strategic level, events took a different turn in 1883-84, as a subsequent chapter records. But first we need to return to the creation of the Bangor line.

The *Rules of the Belfast Engine Drivers and Firemen's Protection Society*, were printed by the Evening Telegraph at 12 Arthur Street, Belfast, as early as 1872. This impressive pamphlet states that the object of the Society was to:

'*Protect its members against all injustice, oppression or tyranny no matter from whence coming…*'

Entrance to the Society cost three shillings, followed by subscription of three pence per week. It was open to those who agreed to work "*not more than 10 hours per day and six days per week*". In addition, members were not permitted to accept less than the stipulated wages –

'*Drivers, five shillings per day for the first six months, rising progressively to seven shillings per day after two years' service.*'

A footnote in the pamphlet states that:

'*These Rules are virtually the conditions agreed to by the Locomotive Superintendents of the various Railways having a terminus in Belfast, and which have been acted on (so far as possible) since 1 January 1872.*'

Each Branch Committee was required to elect an equal number of drivers and firemen. Should the General Committee decide on a strike, the secretary was to enclose voting papers for each man. The question was to be debated at a special meeting and a vote taken, with the decision of the majority being binding. If members of one or more Branches were to go out on strike, the other members were to guarantee them not less than half their own wages while out.

The *General Classification of Goods (including a list of the Railway stations and junctions in Ireland)* was published on 1 December 1888 by the Irish Railway Clearing House. Every conceivable item of goods was identified into one of six classes for the purposes of pricing, starting with acetic acid and ending with zinc and zoedone (which had been launched as an ambrosial nectar in 1880). The classification included some other splendid items such as anvils, beeswax, bath chairs (if not packed at owner's risk only), clay pipes for smoking, ornaments for military clothing, theatrical scenery, and whalebone!

Chapter 4

The Belfast, Holywood and Bangor Railway

(from its origins in 1858 to its demise in 1884)

The Genesis of the Bangor Line:

Compared to the Belfast and County Down Railway (BCDR), there are, regrettably, fewer original Belfast, Holywood and Bangor Railway (BHBR) Company papers that have survived. One reason, of course, is that the BHBR was operational for less than twenty years – from 1865 to 1884 – compared to the one hundred years of the BCDR. Alas too, many documents were lost in the Blitz during the Second World War. So any account of the BHBR is more dependent on (second hand) newspaper accounts, rather than original documents. The era of the BHBR predated the *County Down Spectator* which only began in 1903, so the two main sources are the *Belfast News Letter* and the *Downpatrick Recorder*. Fortunately, in addition, William McCutcheon who was working for the Northern Ireland Government many years ago, as amongst other roles an industrial archaeologist, put together a collection of papers relating to both railway companies on which this chapter can also draw. They include a serendipitous small assortment of letters, contracts and legal documents which shed unique insight into the challenges that faced both the originators of the Bangor line and their successors who ran it.

In any scheme for a new railway, one important factor to take into consideration was the attitude of the major landowners along the course of the proposed line. In terms of the route from Holywood to Bangor, the

evidence suggests that on balance, more were in favour than against. Those who objected most strenuously were the Kennedy family in Cultra.

The *Downpatrick Recorder* printed a most helpful article on 30 October 1858 which sheds light on the position:

'*Railway from Holywood to Bangor:*

A private meeting was held on Wednesday of a number of gentlemen anxious to promote an extension of the line of railway from Holywood to Bangor. The project was not only exceedingly well received, but an amount of support was secured that places the success of the undertaking beyond question. The principal landowners along the line gave in their adherence to the project. Mr Greg, who was at first rather hostile, is now a convert, and Mr Mulholland, who was also supposed to be hostile, will not, we believe, oppose what is for his own good, as well as for that of the public. Mr Sharman Crawford took £4,000 in the new Company, and other landed proprietors gave an equally warm support. The County Down Directors gave the best evidence of their opinion of the extension by offering a subscription of £30,000 towards carrying it into effect. The line has already been surveyed and favourably reported upon by Charles Lanyon Esq., C.E., and it is estimated that the total cost of its completion will not exceed £100,000.'

(Thomas Greg – a banker – and his family were living in Ballymenoch House, Holywood. William Sharman Crawford was then nearing the end of his political career, at Crawfordsburn House. As an individual, he was well-known for looking after the interests of tenants and he seems likely to have believed in the benefits of the new technology for all classes of society.)

A full article appeared on 20 November 1858, also in the *Downpatrick Recorder*. This began by listing the members of the Provisional Committee which was chaired by Robert E Ward of Bangor Castle. The other members were Viscount Bangor of Castleward, William Sharman Crawford, David Ker of Montalto, Captain Hamilton of Craigdarragh, Robert Gordon of Holymount (who was also the secretary), Henry Higginson of Carnalea House, John Preston, John McGee, Thomas McCammon, James Coleman,

Above: The Seal of 14th Century Bangor Abbot, John Kennedy, North Down Museum

James Corry and John Finlay – all of Belfast, David Connor and William Cowan both of Bangor, Robert Nicholson of Ballow (presumably Balloo) and Captain Despard of Killough (see below). Charles Lanyon, who was better known as a great architect, was the engineer. Lanyon, who is clearly a very busy man, was also Mayor of Belfast in 1862 and knighted in 1868. (It is interesting to note certain names not present, including Lord Dufferin and the Kennedys of Cultra.)

Under the heading 'Belfast and Bangor Junction Railway (provisionally registered)', the article then proceeded to provide an amended prospectus, describing the proposed line as a 'continuation of the Belfast and Holywood Branch of the County Down Railway Company'. It is interesting to note that the stated intention was to make only a single line in the first instance, but to 'purchase land for a double line'. (The term 'junction' in this era meant 'connecting'.)

Then followed two key issues – the justification for the line, and the attitude of the landowners:

'The town of Bangor has, for several years, been a favourite summer residence of the inhabitants of Belfast, and there can be no doubt that, upon the formation of this Line, its importance and population will rapidly increase. The railway will run in the immediate neighbourhood of a district admirably suited for the erection of Villa Residences.

The landed proprietors along the proposed Line have, with a few exceptions, evinced the warmest interest in the undertaking and several of them have already proposed to become large Shareholders.'

The proposed capital for the company was £92,000, with the Belfast and County Down Railway Company contributing £30,000. In return for their financial input, the BCDR were to have representation on the new Railway's Board.

Charles Lanyon had already been busy – since the original prospectus was issued, he had 'examined the country between Holywood and Bangor, with the view of ascertaining whether it would be practicable to adopt a more desirable line than any of the inland lines hitherto suggested.' There were now in effect two alternative routes – one along the coast, and one more inland, on which the gradients would be more severe. Sir John Macneill pointed out that with steeper gradients, more powerful engines would be required.

The Provisional Committee agreed on the improved route, known as the Shore Line, effecting a saving in the capital required from the original £110,000. The article stated that as a result of the reduction in the anticipated expenditure through following the Shore Line, the Committee thought it 'unnecessary to do more than to lay Mr Lanyon's report before the public, feeling… every confidence in the merits of this project'.

However their confidence was a little premature, as there were still objectors to the proposed line running along the shore.

It appears also that Lord Dufferin of Clandeboye whose views were not recorded in the October article, may have continued to harbour somewhat mixed feelings. On 21 March 1860 WS Blackwood had written from Glenghana at Conlig to Lord Dufferin:

'I think ultimately you will not find the line from Holywood to Bangor so great a nuisance as you first anticipated, and that if it should ever be made the convenience it would afford for communication with Belfast, will more than compensate for any injury as regards your drive to Greypoint. I say "if it ever be made", because many wise people here seem to doubt the possibility of the money being forthcoming. I hope this may not prove true, as the line will certainly be a desirable one for the public.'

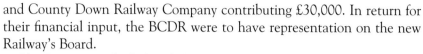

Above left: *Portrait of Charles Lanyon, courtesy of Queen's University.* **Above right:** *Portrait of Lord Dufferin, later Marquess of Dufferin and Ava.*

37

'Make and maintain a railway commencing by a junction with the Holywood Branch of the BCDR, at or near or at a short distance from the South West corner of the passenger station in the town of Holywood and terminating in the town of Bangor at or near the point where Catherine's Place forms a junction with Church Street.'

It is clear that Gordon did actually start building the line; Charles Lanyon as the Engineer of the BHBR Company certified various initial stages of work, such as the purchase of rails. The company ledger has an entry on 23 July 1861 recording payment to the contractor of £5,000 for rails etc. delivered at Bangor. Gordon is also reimbursed £1,000 for sums expended by him in discharge of Parliamentary Agents' fees.

In fact the very first payment recorded in the ledger is to Charles Lanyon on 10 April of that year. Later in proceedings, he receives £800 for engineering and surveying services.

Moreover Gordon received some initial payment in ordinary shares in the railway company. However things began to go wrong the following year, and by 12 December 1861, Gordon had been accused of unacceptable delay and he agreed to default on the contract.

It is very interesting that the most frequent entries on the company ledger for the year 1861 are in connection with printing and stationery. The Belfast firm, Marcus Ward, whose printing services were also used by Vere Foster, received regular payments of up to £15. This seems a little premature if they were already at that stage preparing tickets for the line.

January 1862 sees the first call made on proprietary shares at £2 per share. (Later on the ledger records on two occasions the names and amounts due from individuals who declined to respond to further calls; they included Lanyon and Koch themselves!)

In February 1862, the hotel proprietor Henry McFall was paid the significant sum of £34 for the rent of his yard at Bangor.

The Directors Try Again

We then find a new Article of Contract dated 26 March 1862 between the company and Mr John Edward Campbell Koch (also spelled Kock), of the London Financial Association, in which Mr Koch now undertakes to make

and complete the said line of railway. The contract contains a detailed specification of works, with specific provision relating to items such as sea embankments, temporary defences and dwarf walls. The width of the railway was required to be 13 feet, with 9 inches depth of ballast.

Interestingly the BHBR ledger reveals that Koch was paid £10,000 by the company as early as 25 February 1862, well before the contract was finalised. He also then was paid a regular, quarterly, fee for management of the contract.

We know that Koch subcontracted the building of the line to Messrs J and R Edwards (who had already built the Donaghadee line) to whom payments on account were made, again on the basis of certifications by Lanyon. Even here things do not appear to have run smoothly, as there were delays due to the death of one of the Edwards.

We know the first sod was cut on 24 June 1862. According to the *News Letter*:

'*Belfast, Holywood and Bangor Railway*

Today, at two o'clock, the ceremony of turning the first sod for this railway will be performed by Robert E Ward, chairman of the Directors, in the Cultra demesne, and a dinner to which a limited number of invitations have been issued will subsequently take place at the Royal Hotel, Bangor. The contractors of the line, Messrs J and R Edwards, will present Mr Ward with a very handsome mahogany wheelbarrow and a spade to be used in the ceremony. Both the articles bear appropriate inscriptions.'

(It seems curious that the first official sod was cut at Cultra, part way along the line, rather than at either end which would appear more logical. This may perhaps have been a sop to the Kennedys at Cultra?)

One of those directly responsible for building the line was John Carroll, described as the Superintendent for the extension to Bangor. He was born

in 1827 and died in 1898 – there is an obelisk memorial to him in Bangor Abbey graveyard.

The estimated costs of the various items involved in building the line included a sum of £69,000 for contract claims from Mr Edwards, rails and sleepers at £10,000, and £8,000 for the cost of building stations.

William Seyers, who wrote his recollections of Bangor in the 19th century, fortunately has left us a good deal of information about the building of the line and these personalities:

'The two brothers Edwards were the contractors for the Belfast and Holywood and Bangor Railway. It took three years to make. Owing to the death of one of the Edwards, work was stopped for six months. The navvies were in starvation; wages were 12/- per week and each man had to buy his own shovel at a cost of 2/6. Their wives were glad to get fieldwork at 9d per day. The engineer was called Stoney. He lived at Little Clandeboye. The late John Carroll was Superintendent. He was over all gaffers and foremen, looking after the building of bridges and also the station houses. I well remember getting the loan of a wheelbarrow to take some road scrapings off the street. He came along, saw the brand, put his foot against it and tumbled it over. The horses and carts were carting stones from rock cutting to the station, so he got it put on [a] cart and left me thinking what I should do to him. Many a time I told him about it in after years. When he finished with the railway he got the licence to sell spirits in the 'Hole in the Wall'. His name is above the door at the present time; he kept the house going until the late Company wanted the licence changed up to the platform, when he took the licence to Ava Hotel and the Company had to apply for a new one for the platform. He remained there until his death. He was a man well respected in Bangor, and was at one time elected a member of the old Town Commissioners. He was a Roman Catholic and a Unionist. This same house [the Ava] was called 'The Railway Hotel' over 60 years ago and was owned by Mrs Austin, mother of the late harbour master… The licence lapsed and it was a private house until John Carroll's time…

I knew a man, named George Boyd, who took my father's two horses down at 12 o'clock on Sunday night so as to be first on Monday. Five shillings was the price paid for horse and man at making the railway and they had to be at Craigavad at 7 o'clock sharp. If 10 minutes late, they lost a quarter of a day. Men's wages were 11/- or 12/- for the best.'

Seyers gives other fascinating insights into aspects of the construction of the railway line. Where Bangor station was built, there had been a market garden owned by one Hamilton Halliday. Bricks made at the brick field at the top of May Avenue were taken to Craigavad and Cultra to build the station houses there. Mickey Loughrey was a rag and bone man who also took in metal for which he exchanged his wife's confectionery. Seyers recorded that *'the railway was in making at that time, so boys began to take bolts, spikes etc. to him [Loughrey], but were stopped'*.

The *Downpatrick Recorder* of 6 September 1862 provides an interesting update on the progress and the challenges encountered. Notwithstanding the earlier reduction in the amount of capital that the Provisional Committee thought would be required, the total sum had then risen to no less than £150,000. By now a formal Board of Directors had been appointed – Robert Ward as the chairman, Captain Despard, John McGee, Robert Henderson and Robert Gordon. William Mackay of Castle Chambers, Belfast, had taken over as secretary.

The article, which again contained an updated prospectus, stated that the contract for the construction had been entered into with Messrs Edwards who were described as *'eminent Irish Railway Contractors'*. The prospectus then again cited the factors that were bound to *'produce a very profitable return to the Shareholders – a large dividend may safely be calculated upon… The shares therefore may be looked on as GUARANTEED'* (original capitals). The various firms of stockbrokers who were handling applications for shares were based in Dublin, Belfast, Cork and London. The actual application form was itself printed at the end of the article – the Directors were making every effort to ensure they got their money! (Not for the first time, such a prospectus proved hyperbolic – it was to be many years before

Above: *Carroll Family Obelisk Memorial, Bangor Abbey*

the weary shareholders began to see a return on their investment.)

As an indication of the competition between rival railway companies in Ulster at that time, right alongside the prospectus was an article placed by the Northern Counties and Larne Railways advertising the merits of the short sea passage via Larne and Stranraer, of just two hours, which would be served by *express trains and fast steamers*.

In September 1862, John Rynd of County Westmeath, who had been appointed by the Commissioners of Public Works in Ireland as the Arbitrator under The Railways Acts (Ireland) 1851 and 1860, advised those whom it may concern that he had made his draft awards setting forth the price for compensation to be paid by the BHBR *in respect of the several interests in portions of the lands required to be taken for the purposes of the Railway authorised by the BHBR Act 1860, or injuriously affected by the execution of the works of the said company*.

Mr Rynd's notice set out the route of the line from Belfast to Bangor which is worth quoting in full:

'The Slob and Strand of Belfast Lough, and Bed and Shore of the Sea, the Townlands and Townparks of Holywood, Townlands and Townparks of Ballykeel, Townlands of Ballymena, Ballycultra, Craigavad, Ballygrainey, Ballyrobert, all in the Parish of Holywood, and in the Poor Law Union of Belfast and County Down; and the Townlands of Ballygrot, Ballymullan, Ballykillare, Carnalea, Ballyvarnet, Townland or Townparks of Corporation of Bangor, all in the Parish of Bangor, and in the Poor Law Union of Newtownards and County of Down, aforesaid.'

A public meeting was then held on 15 October 1862 in the Ulster Hall in Belfast to hear any objections against the draft award.

We know that the building of the line was not accident-free. The *News Letter* reported in November 1862:

'Yesterday, an accident occurred at the works on the Holywood and Bangor Railway line, by which a man employed on the line lost his life. It appears that at the bridge which is being erected near Ballymenoch, a windlass had been in use, raising stones to their place, and the unfortunate deceased was attending this windlass when some portion of that upon which it stood gave way, perhaps owing to the effects of the frost, and he was thrown down with the whole, and killed on the spot.'

The article records that the unfortunate man was a widower from Armagh – his mobility for employment is interesting to note.

A second Act of Parliament was obtained by the BHBR on 13 July 1863; this extended the time for completion by 18 months and granted powers to raise additional capital (in £35,000 of shares and £11,000 of borrowings) as well as to build facilities at Bangor such as a hotel and promenade. Coakham is of the view that it was Koch who entertained ambitious notions about making money out of such ancillary ventures.

The Symbolism of the Crawfordsburn Viaduct

The *Downpatrick Recorder* on 3 October 1863 reported on the ceremony of the laying of the foundation stone of the Crawfordsburn viaduct which had taken place on 25 September in the presence of a large assemblage among whom were Lord Dufferin, and JD Cooper (here described as *'director of the line'*). It is also interesting to note that by this point Captain Despard was named as the Deputy Chairman reflecting the lead interest of those at Bangor Castle.

The article explained that the construction of the Crawfordsburn viaduct was by then in an advanced state, although what was conventionally termed the 'foundation stone' had only recently been laid. The viaduct was to consist of five arches, each of 50 feet span, and would be about 80 feet above the river.

Major John Sharman Crawford, by now the owner of Crawfordsburn House, following his father's death, then:

Above: *Shares in the Belfast, Holywood and Bangor Railway Company are reportedly guaranteed, Libraries NI*

'Deposited in a cavity in the stone a hermetically sealed bottle containing copies of the Belfast newspapers and several coins of the present year. The opening in the stone was then covered with a brass plate, bearing an inscription listing [the names of all involved] … The stone was then adjusted in its place; Major Crawford put some water about it, and thereupon declared it duly laid – an announcement which was received with great cheering. After the termination of the ceremony, Major Crawford invited the spectators to his magnificent residence, situated a short distance from the scene of the operation which he had just performed and there he entertained them at a special déjeuner.'

The toast called by Major Crawford was 'prosperity to the Holywood and Bangor Railway'. He said that the undertaking had been prosecuted with considerable vigour, though it had now 'arrived at a stage in which it would necessarily encounter a good deal of difficulty'. The Major also proposed the health of Mr Lanyon 'in the most eulogistic terms'.

In response, Mr Lanyon said that the public were deeply indebted to the landlords for the interest taken on the line which occasioned applause. 'The inhabitants must feel grateful for the interest taken by Major Crawford and his late worthy father in this railway and kindred undertakings'. Toasts were then drunk to the health of Mr Edwards, Mr Koch and Lord Dufferin about whom Mr Ward said that 'the interest he had taken in the line was all the more appreciated, because it had not been dictated by any motive of self-interest. The line was to him not very desirable, nevertheless he not only gave no opposition to it, but he favoured it in many respects.'

Responding, Lord Dufferin admitted that the support supplied by some of the other landowners along the line had been 'more thorough and more enthusiastic' than his own. He was very sure that whatever his private aesthetical feelings on the subject might be, 20 or 50 years hence those who stood in his shoes would be very much obliged to him for not having given any opposition to the carrying out of the project.

The article ended by assuring readers that 'the men employed at the works were not forgotten, as they too had festivities provided for them'.

The viaduct was the most impressive construction along the line. William Seyers recalled being taken, as a child:

'To see the viaduct at Crawfordsburn, just before the railway was finished. The scaffolding was taken down, planks were projecting out over the edge and loaded with stones. Tradesmen were lowered down to paint and clean the joints. These planks extended out about eight feet. My brother went out on them and danced, turned and extended his arms. I was dumbfounded and could not look. He would be about 12 years old at that time.'

The last keystone of the viaduct was laid on 13 February 1864, carrying the inscription 'this stone was set by WHS Crawford Esq, February 1864'.

As a postscript to this section, it should be noted that the foundation stone was removed in 1990 by the Country Park authorities, the year after the centenary of Lanyon's death. The contents of the hermetically sealed bottle were found well preserved.

Above: Newspaper report of the laying of the Crawfordsburn Viaduct Foundation Stone, 1863, Libraries NI

The Line Nears Completion, but the Company faces further Obstacles to Success

An article in the *Downpatrick Recorder*, in 1864, records an account of the progress being made in constructing the line given at the company's half-yearly meeting for shareholders. The secretary read a report which started with the expenditure up to that point:

'£58,900 on the permanent way and works; £25,347 on land and compensation including expenses of arbitration; and £12,300 on parliamentary and law costs, engineering and general expenses; a total expenditure of £96,548 to 1 December last. Your Directors have much pleasure in announcing the near approach of your line towards completion, and opening for public traffic.'

The engineer's report stated that the progress which had been made in the works on the line had not been so great as in the preceding six months, *'consequent upon the usual difficulty of carrying on work in heavy clay cuttings during the winter season.'* (Clay is a challenge with which gardeners along the line are very familiar to this day!) It added that more vigour was expected in the spring, in expectation of being able to complete the line by the middle of the summer.

Interestingly the secretary's report advised that the BCDR was being somewhat 'duplicitous'. He pointed out that it might be inferred from the BCDR's report a little earlier that the BHBR was itself planning a separate line between Holywood and Belfast. This was not so, although the BHBR Directors

'Would have been glad to have acquired the entire line from Belfast to Bangor by the purchase from the Belfast and County Down Railway of their line between Belfast and Holywood on reasonable terms; but, from the conferences which have taken place on this subject, there does not appear to be a probability of any such arrangement being effected.'

That said, the BCDR management clearly had a fairly swift change of heart in relation to their willingness to discuss selling the Belfast to Holywood stretch of line to the newcomer.

A further article in the *Recorder* later in 1864 advised readers in respect of the railway from Holywood to Bangor that:

'This important line of railway is now almost completed, and will be one of the most substantial and best constructed lines of railway in Ireland, while it is believed it will be one of the best paying – being the Kingstown line of the North, as the railway from Belfast to Holywood will soon be in the possession of the same company. Although the railway will be shortly completed to Bangor, we understand that, at the suggestion of the Directors, it will not be opened till the forthcoming spring, in order that the opening of the line may take place when the greatest amount of traffic is to be expected.'

Perhaps one of the difficulties which the speakers at the déjeuner had in mind, concerned the company's funding. Finance had remained tricky, particularly in relation to unforeseen costs that had fallen to Koch in purchasing the land needed for the line. In a letter of 15 October 1864 from John Douglas Cooper (written on behalf of Koch) to the BHBR Directors, he noted that Koch had bought all the requisite land for a total of just on £39,000, for which he had actually paid net cash of £36,694. However it had originally been suggested on behalf of the Directors that the land would only cost at most £22,000. Cooper continued in his letter that had Koch known that this would be exceeded by nearly £15,000,

'He would have declined the contract altogether… I need not point out to you Mr Koch's mortification and surprise to find how far he had been deceived (by no means wilfully because the extravagant awards of the land took all parties by surprise) … The bulk of the payments to him are in ordinary shares of no marketable value.'

He ended the letter by saying that as Koch had to pay for the land in cash, he had a claim on the company for (at least) £15,000. Under the full contract with Koch, he was to receive £153,000, of which less than one third was to be in cash, with the rest in ordinary shares of the company. (An example of the sort of deals that Koch had to make with landowners along the line can be seen in the chapter dealing with Marino station.)

As we noted in the chapter on Holywood, many gentry and business people were keen to escape the pollution and unhealthy atmosphere of Belfast in the 1850s and the improved communications meant that the price of what had formerly been agricultural land in this part of North Down increased markedly in that and the following decade.

After a gap of some months in the paper trail, (during which we know the Directors asked Koch to prepare a full profit and loss statement) we next have a fascinating memorandum from the BHBR Directors dated 16 May 1865 – just two days before the line opened – to their legal counsel in Dublin, seeking advice on Koch's claim. To be fair the Directors were clearly not unsympathetic to the claim:

'The delay in the opening of the line beyond the period fixed for its completion, the extra cost of the land and the state of the money market have no doubt rendered the contract an unprofitable speculation on the part of Mr Koch.'

The memorandum pointed out that prior to obtaining the Act, the land that needed to be purchased had been valued by 'the most eminent land valuers in Ireland' who had calculated the cost at £16,000. In discussion between the Company's solicitors and Mr Koch in London, the former had – perhaps rashly – advised the latter that the extreme figure would be £22,000.

The Directors summed up their dilemma thus:

'The Directors feel that every consideration should be bestowed on his application for the excess, but some of them have serious doubts as to their right to comply without the express concurrence of every shareholder and creditor of the Company.'

It was proposed to call a Special Meeting of the shareholders and submit the matter to them. Counsel was asked to advise whether they could issue Koch with a further 20,000 shares, recognising that that would depreciate the value of the shares already assumed, and if so could a minority of shareholders give trouble to the Directors, and was it in any case lawful under the 1863 Act?

Counsel responded to the effect that whatever the unfortunate solicitor had said would not be a foundation for legal action by Koch. There nevertheless remained the question of how the application should be dealt with 'to the Company's sense of justice or generosity'. He went on to address the issue as to whether a minority shareholder could 'impeach the transaction'. Counsel rightly pointed out that, under the terms of the original contract, Koch was in any case by far the largest holder of ordinary shares and therefore stood to suffer the most financial loss if a further tranche of shares was issued. He drew on 'the language of the Court' in its judgment in a case between the York and North Midland Railway against the so-called Railway King Hudson. The Directors were also reassured that it was most unlikely that a successful attempt could be made to fix personal financial liability on them. In summary, if it were to be found subsequently that they had acted illegally, the remedy open to the court would probably be confined to a re-transfer of the shares irregularly allotted.

From payments to Koch recorded in the BHBR ledger in May and June 1865, it does appear that he was given a further £20,000.

On 19 August 1865, the ledger has a less than crystal-clear reference to 2,465 shares (under the Unissued Shares Act of 1863) which feature alongside the sum of £50,000 paid to the BCDR for the purchase of the Holywood branch after the resolution of shareholders as at an Extraordinary General Meeting on 18 August. These 2,465 shares – and their status – feature prominently in vitriolic correspondence between London and Belfast some eight years later.

Before the Bangor line could open, the BHBR had to reach agreement with the BCDR on access to the latter's Queen's Quay terminus on the County Down side of the river Lagan. A contract between the two companies dated 13 September 1864 allowed – or perhaps rather required – the Bangor Company to provide a separate access and booking office. In the event of dispute it would be resolved by an arbitrator, John Horatio Lloyd, a barrister.

Notwithstanding the rather negative criticism by the BHBR secretary about the BCDR's readiness to reach an agreement with the BHBR, further Articles of Contract dated 26 February 1865 between the BHBR and John Douglas Cooper of Killymoon in County Tyrone, following authorisation under the Belfast and County Down Railway (Holywood Branch Transfer) Act 1865, provided for the BHBR to purchase from the BCDR the Holywood branch (as delineated on a map with the signatures of Charles Lanyon and Charles Domville) for the sum of £50,000 and an annual rental of £5,000. In addition, the BHBR was required to take on the contract entered into by the BCDR with the Railway Carriage Company of Oldbury near Birmingham for the purchase of engines and rolling stock on the Holywood line. Furthermore, as part of the arrangements, Cooper as 'contractor for public works' was to double the line between Belfast and Holywood.

Again, however, this was not entirely plain sailing (or should it be steaming?). An article in the *Downpatrick Recorder* dated Saturday, 13 May 1865, less than a week before the Bangor line was due to open to the public, reported on a special meeting of the proprietors of the BCDR held in the Boardroom at Queen's Quay for the purpose of giving their approval to the bill for the sale of the Holywood line. Mr Anketell was in the chair and

'Read the several clauses of the bill. He did not see there was any necessity to say any more to them at present… and he would therefore take the liberty of moving that the act… be approved.'

However Mr John Jamison of Donaghadee said that he wished to say a word or two – in fact it was to prove considerably more than that! Since the previous meeting in February, he had been in correspondence with indignant shareholders who took a very different view of the matter from the BCDR Directors. Taking issue with the financial arrangements, Jamison said

'You have sold the best portion of your line – the portion that might, and in all probability would have, redeemed your finances in a few years. Railway companies were often in difficulties and redeemed themselves in a short time. You have sold your line to a railway, I may say, next door to you; and to align which, from the apparent spirit of its management, the number of trains, and the cheapness of its fares, will keep you in hot water all your days. They will now compete with you for the Donaghadee traffic, seeing their fares are but half your prices, which will render two of your stations perfectly useless – Groomsport and Conlig.'

In support of his argument, Jamison drew on the significant fall in the value of the BCDR shares in the previous months, such that a £50 share was now only worth £40. Moreover, he even cast doubt on the good faith of the landowners associated with the Bangor line and their reassurance that they would not seek to extend their railway from Holywood through Bangor to Donaghadee. In response, Anketell initially tried to call Jamison's intervention out of order; that approach having failed, he said that the financial arrangements had been referred to a committee consisting of Mr Gray, Dr Pirrie and himself. Mr RM Wilson was so bold as to suggest that some of the (ordinary) shareholders could be brought together with the Directors to consider the bill of costs, not least as these included the payment of a considerable sum to one of the other Directors, Mr Wallace. (This Wallace, a lawyer, had been both the company's solicitor and for a period in the 1860s its chairman, and was now demanding no less than £19,000 for hitherto unclaimed legal expenses!)

Notwithstanding these objections, 'the resolution was then put, and declared carried'.

Mr Jamison was not done yet. Changing the subject, he asked if the chairman had done anything to prepare for the anticipated opening of Portpatrick Harbour in August that year, e.g. providing boats to be put on the crossing. Anketell, (whose approach seemed to rely on keeping his cards close to his chest and saying as little as possible), replied that as he would be meeting the Caledonian directors shortly, he did not consider it prudent to make any statement on the subject.

(As an aside, the author was very struck by the immediately following item in the *Downpatrick Recorder*. That was an article recording the address that had been forwarded through the American Minister at the Court of St James in London on behalf of the Grand Lodge of Freemasons of Ireland conveying the unanimous feeling of execration and horror with which they had learned of the assassination of the late President Lincoln.)

Above: Advertisement for the Railway Carriage Company, Oldbury, from Bradshaw's Railway Almanack, 1885

Operationally there were issues also. Two bridges were found not to allow sufficient headroom for the chimneys of some of the BCDR locomotives, while Desmond Coakham records that the formal inspection on behalf of the Board of Trade of the BHBR on 30 March 1865 refused to sanction opening until a proper junction signal had been erected at Holywood and the line doubled there for 200 yards. Re-inspection took place on 13 May.

Open at Last,
but still with Financial Problems

The Bangor railway opened on Thursday 18 May 1865, according to the Belfast *News Letter*, with:

'The first train leaving Belfast at eight o'clock. All the trains were despatched with the utmost punctuality and the numerous travellers seemed greatly pleased with the excellent arrangements of the company…Mr TC Haines, Manager of the County Down Railway, Mr Domville, Engineer, Mr Kirkwood and others, passed over the line during the day. We congratulate the inhabitants of Bangor on the opening of the new line of railway which will very much increase the popularity of that pretty and convenient watering-place.'

Under the terms of the agreement between the BHBR and the BCDR,

the latter was to supply rolling stock for working the Bangor line – indeed the BCDR continued to work the BHBR's engines until the end of 1870. Two locomotives provided the traction, while eight composite carriages and two guard's vans were the main rolling stock.

To start with there were eight trains a day in each direction, reduced to six on Sundays. Monthly tickets were issued at 25 shillings First Class, and 18 shillings Second Class.

The three original intermediate stations were Cultra, Craigavad (the only passing place beyond Holywood) and Clandeboye (later renamed as Helen's Bay).

The line had its first accident on Sunday, 4 June 1865 when the last two carriages of the late evening train leaving Bangor were derailed, as a result of the ill-judged placement of the points. The crowds were reportedly so dense on the platform at that time that it was difficult to distinguish between those who were going by train from the lookers on. (As so often in accidents over the subsequent years, action had been requested of the engineer to move the points the previous month, but the work was not done until the day after the accident).

At one level, the early years seem generally to have gone well. William McCutcheon records that during the period 1867 to 1869, the Bangor line carried over half a million passengers annually, and the annual receipts worked out at over £1,200 per mile, a better rate of return than other railways in Northern Ireland.

However Coakham records that the BHBR rapidly slid into debt, paying to the BCDR the monthly instalments of the £5,000 annual rent for the Holywood branch, often well in arrears. One early challenge was the failure of Overend and Gurney's Bank in 1866 – one of the key bankers for the new company. It is clear from the very limited early records that London Directors, including Koch, were playing a significant role. (In that year Koch is paid £56 as attendance fees in his capacity as a Director.)

As early as 1866, a new contract is entered into with JD Cooper for works executed as per their engineer's certificates.

William Seyers recorded that John Dodds was the General Manager of the BHBR. His name first crops up early in 1866. (Dodds was apparently well-known for holding an annual football match on Easter Monday near the Pickie Pool!)

Above: 2-4-0 Tank Engine, Number 1, built by Fowlers of Leeds, photographed in 1867 at Donaghadee, courtesy of the Belfast and County Down Railway Museum Trust

The BHBR had Dodds appointed as the receiver in 1868, and again was adjudged bankrupt in summer 1872 when the secretary was William Mackay. At the half yearly meeting of the BHBR shareholders in August 1868, the Directors pointed the finger of blame at the BCDR and made as good a fist of the overall position as they could:

'The increase in receipts continues. The management of the line, it is believed, is in harmony with the requirements of the district, and has secured the approval of the various classes frequenting the railway.... notwithstanding the almost insurmountable difficulties arising from the want of the second line between Belfast and Holywood... with greater motive power, much improvement in train arrangements can be effected... The Directors however regret that the rolling stock as far as the carriages are concerned is not in a satisfactory condition'.

In the same year Charles Lanyon, by now Sir Charles, and a Member of Parliament for Belfast was appointed to the Board. By 1870, the Bangor company owed £13,000 to the BCDR.

Moreover the early plaudits from the *News Letter* did not last. The paper was more critical in an article dated 3 April 1872:

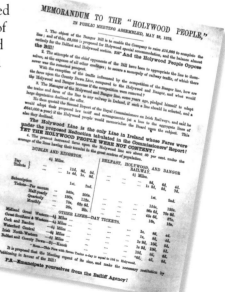

'No railway managed as this Bangor railway is – by a Board of Directors residing in London – can be conducted with profit to the concern, or satisfaction to the public. We are not Home Rulers, I believe, in the political sense, but from an economical point of view this Bangor railway ought to be managed by a home Board.'

There were also complaints in the same newspaper about the timetable, in that the last train left Belfast for Bangor at 9.45pm except on Friday evenings when it ran at 11.15pm. Indeed, a leading article criticised the company for not *'consulting the public convenience'*. It continued:

'No wonder there is opposition by steamer to Holywood; but the long walk on the pier to and from the boat would render any opposition of this kind inoperative if proper railway accommodation were given.'

Feelings ran high, with the *News Letter* reporting on 24 May 1872 on:

'A public meeting of the inhabitants of Holywood held in the Assembly Rooms for the purpose of protesting against the management of the Belfast, Holywood and Bangor Railway and against the Bill then before Parliament. There was a large attendance.'

Two of the Holywood Presbyterian clergy were prominent – Rev Henry Henderson took the chair and reportedly spoke as follows:

'As one who had resided in the town for the last 28 years, the railway management had been disastrous to the interests of the town and most obnoxious to the people travelling on the railway (Loud applause).'

Henderson graciously said that he was not personally criticising the Company's Manager Mr Dodds, whom he held in high esteem. But he pooh-poohed the suggestion that the petition critical of the management of the BHBR, entitled *Memorandum to the "Holywood People"* had been got up by the rival company's chairman.

Rev Charles McAlester moved the first resolution critical of the absentee Board of Directors in London. He said that there had been dissatisfaction previously with the management of the BCDR, and the Bangor Company had been seen as a change for the better, but Holywood residents had since learned *'they were quite mistaken'*. He hoped that better steamboat communications with Belfast would keep the railway management in check.

Above left: *Belfast, Holywood and Bangor Railway - Division of Shares, NIEA.*
Above right: *1872 Memorandum to the Holywood People, courtesy of the Deputy Keeper of Records, Public Record Office NI*

Summing up, Henderson described the abolition of the late trains as *a great and unspeakable grievance*. (He added that it was no longer possible for Holywood residents to attend evening lectures or performances in Belfast and stay until the end before they were obliged to leave to catch the last train home. Henderson, by the way, wrote a column in the *Belfast Weekly News* under the pseudonym 'Ulster Scot'.)

In a newspaper item on the deliberations on the Belfast, Holywood and Bangor Railway Bill in early June 1872, it was reported *the company being in a state of hopeless insolvency*.

There were other unsettling issues at play as well. In the late 1860s, the Government had received the second report of the 'Royal Commission on Irish Railways' which had been appointed to enquire into the propriety of the State purchasing Irish railways. In Opposition at this time, the Liberal leader WE Gladstone had opined in favour of nationalisation, stating *'I know of no boon that could be conferred upon Ireland so comprehensive in application'*. The Royal Commission had looked carefully at the example of the Belgian State Railways, which effectively subsidised fares at a level some 40% cheaper comparatively.

In 1873, Third Class was added which must have gone some way towards reducing the cost of the fares.

Another of the intriguing records from that era (sadly not dated, though it cannot be before 1868) is a list, literally written on the back of an envelope – or rather the front of it – of the division of shares in the BHBR. The total quantity was 105,120 ordinary shares, and 68,560 preference shares, making an increased total of 173,680. There were six named shareholders – Messrs Bristow, Wallace and Valentine each of whom owned 7/36ths, Mulholland and Robinson who had one sixth each, and finally Sir Charles Lanyon had one 12th of the total stock. Lanyon had been elected to the Board in 1868 and later became chairman. He was clearly not the easiest of customers to deal with, as the following section brings out.

The Crisis of 1873 and intrinsic wheeler-dealing

After eight years of operating the single line to Bangor, the BHBR found itself heavily in debt and under-capitalised. Indeed, in 1873 the company was in receivership; William Mackay the secretary was paid approximately £1,000 per month for this role – a huge sum given that annual receipts were only £18,000 that year. The company is also working out the financial consequences of the 1866 bankruptcy of the British bank Overend and Gurney; on 30 April 1873, it had to pay £5,000 under the scheme to the liquidators.

At the beginning of that year, a Belfast, Holywood and Bangor Railway Arbitration Bill had been put to a special meeting of the company's shareholders to discuss the arrangement by arbitration of the affairs of the company.

The BHBR Directors seem to have concluded at this time that further independent operation would be profitless, so they now sought to enter into a lease of the whole line to Bangor to the BCDR. This was concluded in a formal statute, in August 1873. Arrangements were to be made to pay off the Bangor Company's debts, particularly those relating to the leasing of rolling stock.

However this arrangement was not easily agreed, the suspicion between the two companies clearly continued and Coakham suggests that in practice much of the deal was never actually put into effect. There was much toing and froing in April to June 1873. The McCutcheon archive contains a good many items of correspondence – some of it positively vituperative – from the three months of the negotiations.

There is a fascinating letter from William Valentine to James Bristow written in London on 4 April 1873. Valentine is clearly highly frustrated by the delay of the City Bank – one of the railway's two principal backers at that time. He writes:

'This is my fourth [his underlining] visit here today – nothing yet settled – City Bank can't make up their minds – truth is they don't like to face the loss in their ledger – so I have hit on the idea to loan them £10,000 of ordinary stock abating the money £250 on 5/- per share and whether this will work I can't say'.

Nearly 150 years on, it is unclear whether this was financial chicanery or legitimate business practice, but one suspects that it reveals both a certain

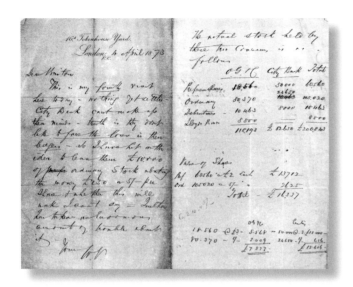

lack of transparency and a degree of ingenuity (sometimes known as creative accounting) that would not have been out of place in some recent financial scandals! (And if the ordinary shares that had been purchased for £10 each were now worth just five shillings, this was hardly an indication of financial soundness.)

It is clear that the handling of the 2,465 shares referred to earlier in this chapter was a key issue. For example, Coates wrote to Wallace on 7 June headed BHBR:

'I wish you would not touch those shares either individually or jointly; unless you acquire them on behalf of the Bangor Board and cancel them... now supposing an evil day to come and the Bangor Company to be wound up, and supposing it to be shown that a man well worth the expense of affecting with liability has held the shares and has exercised rights founded upon the holding of the shares, I cannot doubt that he would be involved in very disagreeable litigation and with very doubtful result. Weigh these things I pray you.'

Three days later the scheming Wallace wrote to Bristow:

'I have had a long interview with Harrison… and put my views before him and I have written to Anketell and sent the letter to the Belfast office so that you may see it.… I think there is nothing for it but to get control of the rents but of course I'd like to do this in the mode that could be least injurious and less hurtful to Anketell. The letter lays the foundation for this and probably may induce him to resign which would be the best course.' (Author's underlining)

Interestingly Anketell writes courteously to Wallace on the very same day, blithely unaware of the latter's intentions, beginning 'My dear Wallace'.

Wallace was not the only one laying down the law. Koch's man McArthur wrote to Bristow:

'There can be no director appointed for the Bangor Railway without my consent… The party making a show of opposition has not a leg to stand upon.'

McArthur clearly had Wallace's measure though; he complained to Bristow that Wallace had an unhelpful *'knack of carving out work for a fellow'.* Wallace usually writes on headed paper from the Reform Club, Pall Mall. This could be why he submitted an expenses claim for £19,000 many years later. He was still writing to Valentine from the Reform Club, in July 1886 complaining of his treatment by the BCDR – beginning one letter *'what is the meaning of having such a letter… sent to me?'*

The correspondence refers briefly to two Holywood landowners who seem to be playing walk-on parts in this drama – Harrison and Kennedy. The correspondence provides fertile grounds for conspiracy theories not least in shadowy references that are made to the *Syndicate* (whose members are not fully named). Finally to complete the list of dramatis personae, reference should be made to the unfortunate Thomas McClure, the manager of the Midland Wagon Company to which a small fortune was owed by the Bangor Company. He writes protesting to Bristow at being obliged by the BCDR Board to become a Director of the BHBR, and wishes to make entirely clear that he will not be liable for any part of the debts of the Company!

As a cutting edge technology, telegraphs make their first appearance in the correspondence; there is one of 21 April of that year from Koch and

Above: 1873 Letter from Valentine to Bristow, McCutcheon Archive, courtesy of the NIEA

William McArthur saying *'my letter of 17th confirmed by all parties here Bill will be withdrawn and arrangements made as wished'*. (Note the saving made by omitting any punctuation!)

However on 25 April, there was then a BCDR meeting of the Parliamentary Committee at which Mr Coates advised the group chaired by WR Anketell that what the Bangor Company (the BHBR) were proposing was *'unsatisfactory if not illegal'* and he could not recommend it. The dispute appears to have been about the size of the abatement of the annual rental of £5,000 under the Transfer Act of 1865.

Further we have a letter dated 26 April 1873 written by William Wallace to James Bristow, in which he makes clear his concerns about the attitude of Charles Lanyon (who it appears was by now chairman of the BHBR) and his fellow Director HL Mulholland of the BHBR:

'We were getting on very nicely until a telegram from Lanyon suggesting a postponement of arrangement with County Down until we settle with Holywood and Bangor; then a proposition that the County Down should not be paid any 'arrears'… V[alentine] and I both agreed that we must adhere to our bargains carrying out all in good faith – as to waiting for him [Lanyon] that is nonsense. We shall have a good deal of difficulty to get through Lord Redesdale's scrutiny but when he understands I think we may be able…

If Mulholland and Lanyon raise any difficulty we can do without them; scheme we have now is County Down to receive £4,000 for four years, £4,500 for 5th year; then £5,000 per annum and no <u>repayment</u> of the £4,500 abated in the five years.'

Lord Redesdale was at this time the redoubtable Chairman of Committees, a role which ensured that he chaired consideration of the vast number of Private Bills coming forward on behalf of railway companies. He was exercised to ensure that the companies promoting Bills had sufficient financial backing, which earned him disfavour with some of the more 'ambitious' schemes. He was clearly not a push-over!

Wallace clearly has an issue with Lanyon; in a further letter to Bristow, he writes: *'I should not be at all surprised at Lanyon being obstinate enough even to his own injury to try and succeed at the [Wharncliffe] meeting'*. In another letter from Wallace to Valentine, he repeats *'I have your letter today and taking all into consideration it is just as well to leave Lanyon alone,'* and in another to Bristow, he wrote *'Coates says that the greatest amount of caution should be used in negotiation with Lanyon'*.

In the midst of all this, there are various purchases of shares (which look suspiciously like potential insider trading all these years later); William Valentine bought stock in the BHBR worth £983 on 29 April, while a telegram the following day from him to his banker James Bristow transferred 50 ordinary shares in the same company from Valentine to James Alexander of Holywood who had become a BHBR Director.

The author's favourite item in all this correspondence is a scrap of paper no bigger than a modern post-it note with some scribbled pencil writing to the banker James Bristow on it, with neither a date nor a signature. It reads as follows:

'Mr Wallace has returned from London and we have had a long communication with him as to Kock's opposition – he seems to think that if City Bank will free Kock from all further liability to them on the foot of the Belfast, Holywood and Bangor shares he will agree at once to withdraw his opposition. Do you think you can give me a <u>private</u> assurance that this will be done? If as I believe, the whole matter can be settled at once, you may rely on my discretion in not making any use of such an assurance, but it will <u>enable me</u> to assure those who are with us on the purchase of the shares that the matter will be all right.' (Author's underlining)

Who said *'side deals'* were a modern creation of politicians?

Even after most of the bigger issues had been ironed out, in July 1873, there was a further dispute about the value of the rolling stock, with the BHBR Directors briefing Counsel anticipating legal action. McArthur again cited Lanyon as the one being difficult. In the light of all this, it is remarkable any sort of deal was secured the following month, even if it was not properly implemented thereafter. (One might almost suggest that the evident lack of trust between the two main parties has modern echoes!)

Ambition Exceeds Capital

Notwithstanding all these apparent financial difficulties, the BHBR did for a period get its head above water.

Coakham credits Lanyon with improving the finances during the 1870s. The line itself was thriving, notwithstanding the growing steamer competition. It had now become the second busiest in Ireland, after the original Dublin and Kingstown railway line.

The expenditure is all detailed in the one remaining company ledger. For example it records that the cost of running the Bangor railway for the six months ending 31 December 1873 was £68,639, an increase of nearly £10,000 on the first six months of that year. The same book records payments down to the last penny for items including locomotive oil and tallow; coal and coke running at about £150 each month; and water for which the company was charged around £20 monthly. (It is interesting to think that there were separate water charges nearly 150 years ago!) Another regular payment came under the heading of 'horses, harness, provender etc.'

A Repeal Act of 1876 gave the BHBR greater independence, retrospectively reducing the Holywood line annual rental, so maybe eventually Lanyon got his way on this issue too. His son John became the company's engineer.

Thus the BHBR continued to run the line, and to introduce additional attractions. The *News Letter* on 21 July 1876 reported that:

> 'The Belfast, Holywood and Bangor Railway Company have, thanks to their enterprising manager, opened bathing places at Cultra for ladies and have made the railway fares to that place so moderate as to enable the poor as well as the upper class to take advantage of the bathing season. Bathing boxes, towels etc. will be provided at low rates.'

The article added, to reassure gentlemen, that the company also intended to open a bathing station at Cultra for men as well. (It is interesting to note that in terms of the construction of these facilities the ladies received priority.)

At this time Belfast had high volumes of passenger traffic. Perhaps for this reason, the BHBR harboured hopes of expansion and connection with the rest of the railway network in Belfast.

The company sought legislation to provide it with the requisite powers. The minutes of evidence given in relation to the Belfast, Holywood and Bangor Extension Railway Bill during the Parliamentary Session of 1877 are interesting. This was a Bill to 'incorporate a company for making railways to connect the BHBR and the town of Belfast, and for other purposes'. The Bill's main purpose was to provide for a connection (still a single line only) between the Bangor line and the railway system on the other side of the river Lagan, with a new terminus at Victoria Street. The configuration of modern Belfast might have been very different had this proposal succeeded.

Extensive evidence was taken in Westminster over a considerable period; sadly from the point of view of the railway, the conclusion of the chairman was that:

> 'I have to announce that the Preamble of this Bill has not been proved to the satisfaction of the Committee'.

One of those giving evidence was Edward Harland, in his capacity as chairman of the Belfast Harbour Commissioners. While we may have our views on the linguistic formality of our Victorian forebears, the official record has the Parliamentary Committee chairman interrupting, when Harland was expatiating in considerable detail on the level of steamer traffic on the County Antrim side of the river, with a terse 'stop a minute'. Mr James P Corry and Mr JS Crawford MP also gave evidence – the latter in favour of the extension, as did his namesake CH Crawford, at that time an assistant to Charles Lanyon. In addition CH Crawford helpfully made a model which he presented in his evidence. The questioning did get into some very practical issues, including concerns about a recent level crossing accident on the line, and whether there was sufficient height to enable one railway line to cross over another, given the gradient that would be required. The BCDR was not well-disposed to the project, while the Belfast Central Railway objected vociferously.

The record gives a feel for the vested interests of the wealthy businesspeople and landowners in the North of Ireland then, and also for the surprising amount of time that Victorian legislators were required to devote, at the height of the Empire, to individual railway Bills in Parliament – especially those that proved to be still-born.

The BHBR was not yet done with proceeding to Parliament, notwithstanding the expenditure inherent in doing so. In 1881 a further Act enabled it – among other things – to operate steamer services to Holywood and Bangor. The full ambit of that legislation authorised the company to alter the gauge of their railway, to raise additional capital to use steam vessels between Belfast, Holywood and Bangor, and for the reduction of the rent payable to the BCDR, and for other purposes. On such steam vessels, 'passengers, animals, minerals, goods, merchandises and things of every description' might be conveyed between any of the three ports.

Fascinating insight into the previous challenges faced by the BHBR is included in the narrative content of the Bill (which no doubt includes some of the 'other purposes'):

'whereas the Belfast and County Down Railway (Holywood Branch Transfer) Act 1865 authorised the BCDR to sell and transfer to the Bangor Company for £50,000 cash and rent or sum of £5,000 per annum, and

whereas the Bangor Company having been unable to meet its engagements and the income derived from its undertaking being insufficient to pay the said annual rent of £5,000 on 8 February 1867,... a receiver was appointed by the High Court of Chancery in Ireland over the entire undertaking of the Bangor Company;

whereas by the Belfast, Holywood and Bangor Railway (Lease) Act 1873 the Bangor company should grant (to the County Down Railway) a lease of the whole undertaking on terms therein in agreement between the Companies bearing the date 21 July 1873 (a copy appearing in the schedule of the Act), and

whereas difficulties having arisen in carrying into effect the provisions of the Lease Act,

and whereas the Bangor Company and before the passing of the Belfast, Holywood and Bangor Railway Act 1876 spent £25,000 putting all their line into repair and working order in completing a second line of rails from Belfast to Holywood,

the Belfast, Holywood and Bangor Railway Act 1876 repealed the 1873 Act and the agreement in the schedule be cancelled and the Bangor Company should issue debenture stock not exceeding £159,500.'

The debenture stock was to pay interest of 4% per annum. The legislation then laid down the specified items on which the capital might be expended, which included paying the Midland Wagon Company the total of £21,000, with interest at 5% per annum since 1 June 1872.

The last entry in the BHBR ledger held at the Public Record Office is dated 31 December 1882. In that year, there are some most intriguing payments including £20 to John Arnott & Co for curtains, £10 to John Riddel for wax cloth, £6 to Robert Watson for flock, and the rather larger sum of £60 to the Belfast firm of McIlwaine and Lewis for foundry work.

Given all these progressive plans on the one hand, and the company having made arrangements to try to pay its way out of its problems, it is perhaps a little curious that in spring 1883, the BHBR Directors concluded, as they did, that amalgamation with the BCDR should be explored. What happened next is described in the next chapter.

As a postscript, it is interesting to record the entries in the ledger that related to the company's response to recommendations of the external auditors. Fascinatingly the auditors picked up on the handling of a payment to the Bangor Gardens Committee of no less than £119 which had initially been put to a suspense account by order of the Board minute of April 1882, and which was then transferred at the request of the auditors in August. Alas posterity has not recorded what the town's green fingered burghers had done to deserve such treatment.

Chapter 5

Takeover by the Belfast and County Down Railway in 1884, and the Company's Heyday

The 1884 Takeover

In 1884 the Belfast and County Down Railway bought up the Belfast, Holywood and Bangor Railway which then ceased to exist as a separate company. With this additional 12 miles, the total track subsequently run by the BCDR at its zenith amounted to 80 miles. Even by Northern Ireland standards, that did not make it a big railway. Nevertheless, the BCDR was always a significant player in the railway history of this part of the island.

While that is summary headline, the story is both complex and intriguing. The BCDR minute book provides a fascinating insight into the incidents and practical challenges that beset anyone then running a railway. It reveals that the Directors were required to have a keen focus on operational matters, a close eye on financial issues, and a weather eye for strategic challenges and opportunities.

On operational matters, in the years 1882 to 1884:

- a bullock is killed on the line near Saintfield;
- an engineer's man falls out of a shunted wagon on the ballast train in the Belfast yard and is killed when the wheels of a third class carriage pass over him; the Manager notes in his report that if screw couplings were provided for the ballast train it would almost put an end to the process that led to the fatality and at a total cost of about

£14 would be 'money well spent' – alas a number of years were to pass before safer ballast wagons were acquired;
- a letter from Messrs J Andrews of Comber asks if the 7.30am morning train can specially stop to pick up their manager at Bloomfield – the Directors do not appear to have been sympathetic;
- the very next entry records the unfortunate John Quinliven, the station master, being run over and killed at Bloomfield station; (there was then considerable correspondence and debate about the compensation payable to his widow – the Board ratified the payment of £75 to her 'provided it is accepted in full settlement of any claim on the company', being added as a subsequent amendment to the minutes, one suspects by a cautious financial manager);
- the Board agrees to adopt the rates proposed by the Central Railway for the carriage of manure;
- the Manager reports on his inspection of the whole line, noting that signals were well maintained as were the engines, though locomotives Nos. 3 and 11 required repairs;
- the signal at Ballynahinch Junction had been blown down in a storm and was found as a result to be altogether in the wrong position.

The BCDR had also established a number of Committees, reporting to the main Board, which dealt with specific issues, including Committees covering Clothing, Salaries, and Traffic.

As noted above, in 1883, the Directors of the BHBR decided to explore amalgamation with the BCDR. Preliminary discussions were entered into between the two – hitherto often sparring – companies.

There is good evidence in the BCDR minutes. Once they reach the start of 1884, much of the Directors' attention is clearly devoted to the implications of the Bangor Railway Bill. On 22 January, the BCDR Directors received a letter from the BHBR recording a resolution that had been passed at its Board the previous day in reference to the draft Agreement with the County Down Railway. Both Railways formed Sub-Committees of Directors to negotiate the differences between them that then remained. Those differences were resolved except for the question of the debt due to the County Down Railway of £7,000 for arrears of rent under the Act of 1876 which the BHBR were bound to pay.

Just three days later, on 25 January – they clearly didn't hang around in those days – Messrs Richardson and Pirrie on behalf of the BCDR met Mr Valentine of the BHBR and agreed the final arrangements in respect of the debt; the cost of the complete purchase by the BCDR was £138,000. Engrossment was sealed on 19 February of that year. The Parliamentary Bill was approved by the respective shareholders on 19 March 1884.

Responsibility for the running of the Holywood to Bangor extension then transferred to the Directors of the County Down Railway. The six

engines with which the BHBR had worked its line were transferred to the BCDR's stock and given new numbers. The two stations that had been built adjacent to each other at Queen's Quay were merged – by the practical method of creating an archway through the dividing wall. (A complete merger of the two stations was made in 1911.)

On behalf of the BCDR, the engineer Berkeley Deane Wise inspected the acquisition, and found all the stations needing repair and all the signals in bad order. BCDR Manager Joseph Tatlow reported in June 1885 that Holywood was a 'curious and confused sort of station', while the facilities at Marino were 'wretchedly small and inconvenient'. On the other hand, in his opinion, Cultra station was very fair.

The new management were not however prepared to continue the servicing of the 10 bathing boxes at Cultra.

Coakham suggests that the Bangor Company's management had tolerated a free and easy atmosphere amongst their staff. He points to two of the BHBR drivers being disciplined by new management in June 1885 for having passengers on the footplate, while another who had extended hospitality to three men the 'worse for liquor' was sacked.

There were clearly other consequences to be considered. From the same minute book, we find that consideration of an alteration to the curve on the approach to Holywood was postponed after discussion on 18 March 1885. Significant improvements were however carried out the following year. Also in 1885, the Directors concluded that they could significantly reduce the cost of the new goods shed that was required at Bangor by building it in wood rather than brick! One suspects that proved to be but a short-term economy.

In 1885, Bradshaw's Railway Almanack records that Richard Kelly, was the BCDR chairman, with Joseph Richardson of Lisburn the vice-chairman. Aside from Pirrie and Andrews, the other Directors were Henry Mulholland of Ballywalter Park, James Barbour of Ardville, Holywood, and John Campbell and DL Coates, both of Belfast. Thomas Andrews was to become chairman in 1895, and retained the post for 21 years.

Joseph Tatlow, published his memoirs in retirement in spring 1920, covering 50 years of railway life, entitled *Fifty Years of Railway Life, in England, Scotland and Ireland*. He recalls his trepidation at coming to the BCDR as Richard Kelly, the chairman, was regarded as a terror. But he recorded that Kelly's wrath was reserved for 'wrongdoers'. Further insight is in the following extract which particularly praises the support of William Pirrie, at this crucial juncture in the life of the BCDR:

'In 1885 the condition of the permanent way, the rolling stock and the stations was anything but good, and as the traffic showed capacity for development, to stint expenditure would have been but folly. I do not think,

Above left: Belfast, Holywood and Bangor Railway staff at Queen's Quay, in front of a 'Badger' engine, c.1884, Public Record Office NI
Above right: Bradshaw's Railway Manual for 1885

however, the outlay would have been so liberal as it was but for Lord (then Mr) Pirrie who was an active and influential director, though there were also on the Board several other businessmen of energy and position. Indeed, it was a good Board, but the chairman, though a shrewd and far-seeing man had, like John Gilpin's spouse, "a frugal mind" and Lord Pirrie's bold commercial spirit quite eclipsed his cautious ways. One instance will suffice to exemplify this, and also to illustrate the novelty of my new duties, which were delightful in their diversity and activity to one whose life hitherto had been confined to sedentary work.

It was the rolling stock that demanded the most urgent attention – engines, carriages and wagons, and especially carriages. Of carriages there were not enough for the traffic of the line and many were in a very sorry condition, particularly those which had been taken over with the Holywood and Bangor Railway, acquired by the company the previous year. One weekend, soon after I joined the service I had all passenger carriages brought into Belfast, except those employed in running Sunday trains and early on the Sunday morning, with the company's locomotive and mechanical engineer, I examined each carriage thoroughly from top to bottom, inside and out, above and below and, with his practical help and expert knowledge, noted carefully down the defects of each. He worked with a will, delighted that someone as enthusiastic, and even younger than himself, was now in charge. He little suspected, I am sure, how ignorant I was of practical matters as I kept my own counsel which was my habit when prudence so dictated. I knew the names of things and was well versed in the theory and statistics of repairs and renewals but that was all. A fine worker was – and is – R.G. Miller. Well over 70 now, healthy and energetic still, he occupies the position he did then. Age has not withered nor custom staled his juvenility. Daylight failed, and night came on before our task was finished, several carriages remained unexamined. These, and the Sunday running vehicles, we subjected to scrutiny the following week.

At the next meeting of the Board I presented a report of what I had done and urged that a number of new carriages should be contracted for without delay, enlarging upon the return we might confidently expect from a responsive traffic. The Chairman and the Board were a little aghast at what appeared, to a small company that only recently emerged from straitened circumstances, a very large order. But Lord Pirrie came to the rescue, strongly supported my proposal, and commended the thoroughness with which I had tackled the subject. The day was won, the carriages secure and the order for their construction was placed with a firm in Birmingham. This expenditure was the precursor of further large outlays, for it was soon seen that the prospects of the company warranted a bold course.'

By 1885, the traffic on the Bangor line had grown to 14 trains each way on weekdays, plus 12 on the short workings from Queen's Quay to Holywood and back. There were now three morning business expresses from Bangor – at 8am, 8.35 and 9.35 which made the run in 25 minutes with just  one stop. There were even two expresses each way on Sundays, to maximise the attraction for day-trippers from Belfast to the sea.

Tatlow continued to keep a close eye on the finances of the Bangor line. He recorded that the Belfast to Holywood section paid best on weekdays, while it was on Sundays that the Bangor trains brought in the most money. He was though frustrated by the Board's attitude a little later, when he proposed introducing the tablet system on the Bangor line it, stating that:

'It is without doubt the heaviest single line in the United Kingdom.'

Also in 1885 the *Bangor Season* recorded that from Belfast:

'The roadway gives tourists a beautiful drive through the most charming road scenery, and those who can afford the expense would be amply compensated. The rail is fairly cheap, speedy and prosaic. Both road and rail are now available all the year round.'

Travelling by rail was not always prosaic, as the following sad article in the *Down Recorder* of 15 August 1885 relates:

'Strange Discovery in a Railway Carriage:

Above: *What it says on the tin – or in this case the postcard! Written in 1910 the message reads 'It is a pity you weren't here to get a sniff of this air. I have tried it and it is just grand'.*

While one of the porters in the employment of the Belfast and County Down Railway was cleaning carriages on Wednesday evening, he discovered underneath a seat a brown paper parcel, which, in accordance with the usual custom, he handed to the stationmaster, Mr Smyth. The latter… examined it… and found that it contained the body of a newly-born female child. The Ballymacarrett police were immediately informed…. the inquest…jury added a rider to the effect that death resulted from "misconduct, carelessness, or ignorance on the part of the person or persons who were present at the time and on the occasion of said child's birth".'

Competition and Opportunity – the Donaghadee Tunnel

However in the 1880s, competition was never far away, and indeed our island history might have been rather different, had one imaginative submarine proposal been able to proceed.

The *Downpatrick Recorder* carried a brief article on 13 March 1880 about potential competition, under the heading '*Proposed new railway from Belfast to Holywood*'. Directors of the Belfast Central Railway Company, were promoting a bill that would provide for a railway to Strandtown and High Holywood. A public meeting of the ratepayers of Holywood had accordingly been held to engage their support. A narrow gauge scheme, it did secure an Act of Parliament in 1881. It would have competed directly with both the BCDR and the BHBR.

However this plan came to naught. A similar fate was in store for a much more imaginative scheme.

Articles in the *Downpatrick Recorder* on 31 July and 14 August 1886 reported enthusiastically on the potential for a railway tunnel between Donaghadee and Portpatrick. The initial account had clearly been met with some scepticism, as the first article acknowledged when it began as follows:

'An investigation into the telegraphic statement published in the Belfast News Letter on Saturday shows that it is substantially correct. The preliminary proceedings connected with a projected immense work are really on foot,

and the promoters, if they obtain the sanction of Parliament to their great undertaking – the greatest by far, from an engineering point of view, ever yet undertaken within the bounds of the British Empire – are sanguine that it will be a financial success.'

The article noted that those involved in this proposal were some of the principal noblemen and gentlemen, nearly all of whom held high positions in the monetary world, who had promoted the formation of a submarine tunnel between the coasts of England and France which had been defeated in Parliament two years previously. That defeat had not been on account of any engineering difficulties or want of capital, but mainly on the strength of military evidence that it would be a source of continual danger of foreign invasion! No such danger could possibly arise from the construction of a tunnel between the coasts of Downshire and Wigtownshire, the *Recorder* assured its readers. Moreover, Government departments viewed the scheme with favour.

Reportedly arrangements were in progress for sinking a deep shaft near Donaghadee to assess the nature of the strata. The cost of the tunnel had been estimated – by competent authorities – at about £5 million. One major benefit would be that the American traveller and the mailbags from that country could be landed at Lough Foyle, and reach London about 11 hours afterwards, by an uninterrupted rail journey. Indeed, it was anticipated:

'The sight-seeing American would land at Moville and then go to see the Giants Causeway, and would pay his passing tribute to the tradesmen of Belfast instead of to their rivals in Dublin.'

The tunnel would indeed bring considerable advantage to the merchants of Ulster, though the article recognised that for the rest of Ireland the gain to be derived from the proposal was not so evident.

Two weeks later, the newspaper recorded with some excitement that a specimen stone, one foot six inches each way, had been taken from the rocks on the Common not far from the railway station at Donaghadee, and forwarded to London for the purpose of testing its quality. The article continued:

'It is stated, on apparently good authority, that it is intended shortly to commence making a boring 1,000 feet deep one mile inland, and convenient to the present line of railway… it has been announced that Mr Daniel Delacherois has been over in London, and has had an interview with the promoters of the Channel Tunnel project, who are confident of success. The project continues… to be more and more discussed on its merits…. An eminent public engineer, writing on Wednesday on the scheme, says "Personally, I have no doubt as to the ultimate success of the project. Opposition is a thing to be expected and surmounted".'

Immediately following this article, the *Recorder* published a splendid letter written by 'An Irishman' to the *Scotsman* newspaper. The author, who was presumably of a pacifist bent, suggested that were this project to be within the scope of practical engineering,

'It would be the means of introducing what I consider an essential element to the permanent settlement of the Irish question… The Government… would be giving to many starving but honest British workmen the means of earning a living, far more noble and patriotic than throwing away millions of British money and spilling British blood in prosecuting barbarous and useless wars.'

The Development of the Bangor Line

The years before and after the turn of the century were good times for the BCDR, not least for its shareholders. In 1895, an annual dividend of 6 ¼% was declared. Four years earlier the company had successfully raised £240,000 of new capital.

From 1895, the BCDR issued *'house-free'* tickets to all stations, save those in the immediate vicinity of Belfast for *'resident occupiers of new houses built and continuously used as private residences'*. Tickets were transferable on the change of occupant, even if a house was rented for the summer months. On the Bangor line, such tickets were issued for seven years, (although on the main line a period of 10 years was available.) In 1895, a total of 477 such tickets were issued across the BCDR system, though this had more than doubled within the next 10 years.

McCutcheon observes that the company thereby created extra demand;

in addition it benefited from the introduction of what he described as an *'enlightened'* fare structure which included a price of two thirds for those aged 18 to 21, and all ladies. (Wives of annual ticketholders paid half fare.) Moreover workmen's trains ran daily from Holywood to Belfast for just 3d, albeit at a small financial loss, allowing artisans working in the city to live in the country, the Directors felt.

As Grenfell Morton recorded, the BCDR did much to encourage the growth of Bangor as a resort during the 1890s. Subscriptions were also given to the Royal Ulster Yacht Club, the Bangor Swimming races, firework displays, and open-air band performances. To quote an example,

'Many leading citizens subscribed most generously to the fund, and the County Down Railway, through its General Manager, to James Pinion, promised every support, stating that they would convey the bands from Belfast and Bangor and back free of charge.'

Organisations along the line also benefited, with Helen's Bay Golf Club receiving a subscription in the year of its foundation, 1896.

The company also encouraged seasonal tourist traffic by issuing a great variety of concessionary tickets, including day excursions, returns on Sundays for the price of a single fare, and anglers', yachting and golfers' tickets. By 1905, McCutcheon records that these represented around 50% of all passenger tickets on the line. The *BCDR Guide* records that about ten million passengers were now carried annually across the whole BCDR system – *'in every way the Belfast and County Down Railway ranks among the most successful of local financial undertakings'*.

The BCDR Company Secretary's Office record book includes a number of 'sundry contracts' for the year 1896. It records that on 21 January that year, (reflecting the company's better financial position), two new engines were ordered from Beyer Peacock at a price of £5,000. Then, another pair, and after that a final two were ordered on 15 March and 7 July respectively, for slightly lower – and different – sums. These replaced the elderly Vulcan 'Badgers' which had been acquired from the 1860s onward.

Of a different order of costs, telephones were installed on the Bangor line at a cost of £178, dated 14 April last year. Scotch coals – for the locomotives – were purchased from WE Williames at a price of 10/6 per ton.

Similarly, in 1897, according to the *Newtownards Chronicle* of 26 June the BCDR

'Put into service a number of new coaches which were in every way a vast improvement on those currently in use. Six of them were Third Class with a [total] capacity for 480 passengers and the remaining six were of composite design to hold 380 First/Second Class passengers. The First and Second Class was upholstered in luxurious fashion – the material used being velvet moque, while the decoration of the interior was most artistic and pleasing. Lighting was Pope's Patent Gas System in connection with Thompson's Patent Horizontal Flame Burners.'

For the first 12 years after the takeover, the BCDR worked the Holywood to Bangor section as a single line, with a passing loop at Craigavad, and later using the excursion siding at Helen's Bay too. However as the traffic increased, the single line proved inadequate, and the section was doubled in stages between 1897 and 1902.

The first actual steps were made when excavations began on the Carnalea to Bangor section in December 1897, with the first portion of double line being opened six months later. The next stage was the section to Helen's Bay, on which the major challenge was Crawfordsburn viaduct (see the section on Crawfordsburn Station and viaduct for more detail). After that opened in December 1899, work continued on widening the track between Holywood and Craigavad. The new up platforms at Marino and Cultra were given substantial brick buildings (as set out in the sections in this book on their stations). Double line working to Craigavad began in November 1900, but the remaining 2 ½ miles to Helen's Bay proved difficult, owing partly to the

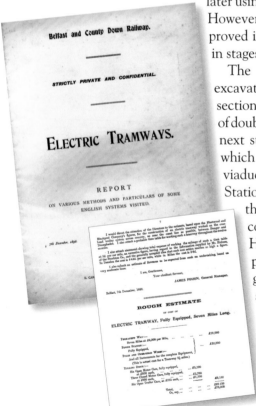

number of bridges several of which provided for private avenues belonging to big houses. The work on the whole line was finally complete and open to double line working on 7 February 1902.

Engineer GP Culverwell reported to the BCDR Board of Directors with some pride that the cost of the delayed doubling had proved less than had the original Holywood to Bangor line been constructed for double line working from the outset. Culverwell's opinion must have been reciprocated by the Board, as he received a bonus of £200 for his work on this project.

In 1898, an English company investigated the scope for a network of narrow gauge tramways in North Down, including one from Bangor to Donaghadee. Naturally the BCDR became intrigued and indeed concerned, so they sent their Manager James Pinion off to check out similar schemes in England (though not curiously to the Giant's Causeway or the nascent Howth system).

Victor Corrie has kindly shared a copy of Pinion's 'strictly private and confidential' report. He considered the alternative merits of extending the railway or constructing a tramway from Bangor station to Donaghadee, through Ballyholme and Groomsport. In favour of the latter were its cost (less than half the capital cost), and the better prospects for attracting both more passengers and house-purchasers along the route due to the additional stops. He favoured using the same gauge to enable goods traffic to be worked over both without transhipment. Accordingly, he recommended the BCDR to construct a tramway, as opposed to letting some rival create unhealthy competition.

Coakham records that while legislative approval was obtained, no actual scheme progressed off the drawing board for want of capital. Subsequent generations of Bangorians may have mixed views on whether they would have wanted their town to be Ulster's answer to Blackpool!

An important event for the Bangor line and the town itself took place in July 1903, when King Edward VII travelled by train from Belfast to Bangor, where he and the Queen then boarded the Royal yacht. They travelled in style in the Royal Saloon which had originally been commissioned by the BCDR in 1897 for a visit by the Duke and Duchess of York. Reportedly the royal party caused consternation by arriving two minutes early. Moreover, according to DB McNeill, it occasioned a scoop for the *County Down Spectator*, as the railway had got most of the reporters in another location.

Above top: 1898 report by the BCDR Manager on the Electric Tramways Scheme, courtesy of donor
Above bottom: The estimated costs of the Tramway

The BCDR Engine for the 1897 Royal Visit, with Locomotive Superintendent Robert Miller in front,
Desmond Coakham Collection, courtesy of Andrew Crockart

Shortly after that, the company moved to cater for the needs of their passengers at the other end of the social spectrum.

In May 1905 the company introduced steam railmotor units on the line between Queen's Quay and Holywood partly to reduce costs, and also to meet the potential (though it did not materialise) threat following the passage through Parliament of the Strandtown and Holywood Electric Tramway Bill. The BCDR looked briefly at electrification of the Bangor

branch, but decided instead to purchase three railmotors from a Leeds company, Kitson.

These trains had only one class – third, with single tickets being issued by the conductor. New halts, such as Kinnegar, were created at the same time. The railmotor service successfully saw off the threat from the Electric Tramway. With this addition, the timetable from Holywood provided for a total of 47 services on weekdays, in place of the 26 that had run previously.

The McCutcheon archive also contains the BCDR Rule Book of 1905. Produced largely in the interests of safety, it begins by specifying that everybody, whether a fireman, ganger or porter is to be supplied with it and must have it on their person when on duty. The first rule seeks to establish that the company is a disciplined service, as it prescribes that

'All persons employed by the Company must devote themselves exclusively to the Company's services… and pay prompt obedience to all persons placed in authority over them.'

However, echoing the terms used on all air travel nowadays, Rule 6 states explicitly that:

'The safety of the public must, under all circumstances, be the chief care of the servants of the Company.'

The Rule Book reinforced the discipline theme: every Servant in uniform must appear clean and neat 'with the number and badge perfect'.

Much of the Book is taken up with the intricacies and idiosyncrasies of the BCDR signalling system. But Rule 157 states that 'Engine drivers must carefully avoid throwing out hot water, fire or cinders in any manner to cause injury to Milesmen'. Finally Rule 448 – for the assiduous reader who makes it that far – relates to 'The Return of Slip Cocks' (one is tempted to comment 'whatever they may be', but readers of a sensitive disposition are advised not to try an internet search for the definition!)

The Queen's Quay terminus was extensively rebuilt in 1911 to provide five platforms, though the original facade was maintained. At Culverwell's insistence, the extended home signal cabin was said to be the largest signal box in Ireland. (The station was superseded by the new Belfast Central Station in 1976, and completely demolished five years later. The site now lies under the cross-harbour motorway.)

At the start of this section we noticed that on the Bangor line house free tickets were only issued for seven years, rather than the ten on the main line. This was a symbiotic relationship between the railway and the burgeoning town, so in the summer of 1913 the Bangor Urban Council took up the cudgels, as the *Spectator* records:

'Mr H.E. Mellor, secretary to the Belfast and County Down Railway Company, wrote stating that the directors of the company would be willing to receive a deputation from the Bangor Urban Council in regard to matters mentioned in their communication.

Above: Railmotor No. 3 at Holywood, undated, courtesy of Charles Friel

The following resolution was passed; as the Council consider that this matter is of very great importance both to the Railway Company and the town of Bangor, it is not only desirable but necessary that a full meeting of the Board of Directors should be present when the deputation presented their views to the directors.

It was resolved; that a deputation from the Council be appointed to wait on the directors of the Belfast and County Down Railway Company to urge upon them the desirability of erecting a hotel in Bangor for the accommodation of the increasing number of visitors and also the extension of the House Free Tickets from seven years to ten years as is granted in other towns adjoining the company's system.'

In October the paper reported success:

'The action of the Railway Company in extending the house free tickets from seven to ten years is bound to be a great stimulus in encouraging building operations in Bangor. This is very much required, as the demand for vacant houses in recent years has been greatly in excess of the supply. A second class ticket is given with new houses of £15 valuation and up to £25, which is the minimum valuation to carry a first class ticket. The kind of house for which there is most demand in Bangor at present, is a house to let at about £30 per annum with free ticket. This is about the extent to which the better class artisans, who are coming to Bangor in ever increasing numbers, are willing to go, and the builder who is prepared to speculate in this class of property will find it a profitable business.

This additional indulgence on the part of the Railway directors is a boon for which the Council have periodically agitated for the past ten or twelve years. Of course the arguments at the earlier date in favour of the extension of the free period were not so convincing, as Bangor then had a reputation, rightly or wrongly, of being over-built. The slump that has during the past year or two been experienced in building has had this benefit at least, it has called forth more encouragement from the Railway directors, and we have no doubt that builders will not be slow to take advantage of the brighter prospects ahead of them. The thanks of the Council to the directors which

were thoroughly sincere have been merited. When Bangor craves a favour it is generally acceded. The directors, through the courteous manager, Mr C.A. Moore, may loudly protest, but we must admit that, if the request is at all reasonable, they generally surrender ultimately to the expression of public opinion.'

Clearly the company's Directors felt sufficiently confident in the forecasts to permit such generosity. This period truly was the heyday of the BCDR, and indeed arguably of the Bangor line too.

It was also a vintage era for the postcard which could be written in the morning and delivered, with time for a reply the same day. Both Bangor and Holywood featured prominently in postcard sales, and many were posted locally to arrange meetings or social calls, or to advise the recipient of train arrival times. The mail was carried by train. Many cards incidentally were printed in Germany – a business that came to an abrupt end in 1914. (Just four years later, Tony Merrick notes, the popularity of postcards reduced at a stroke when the cost of the stamp was doubled from a halfpenny to one whole pence.)

The First World War was to have significant impact on the company also, as a later chapter recounts. Thereafter, the financial fortunes of the BCDR waned as they had so splendidly waxed.

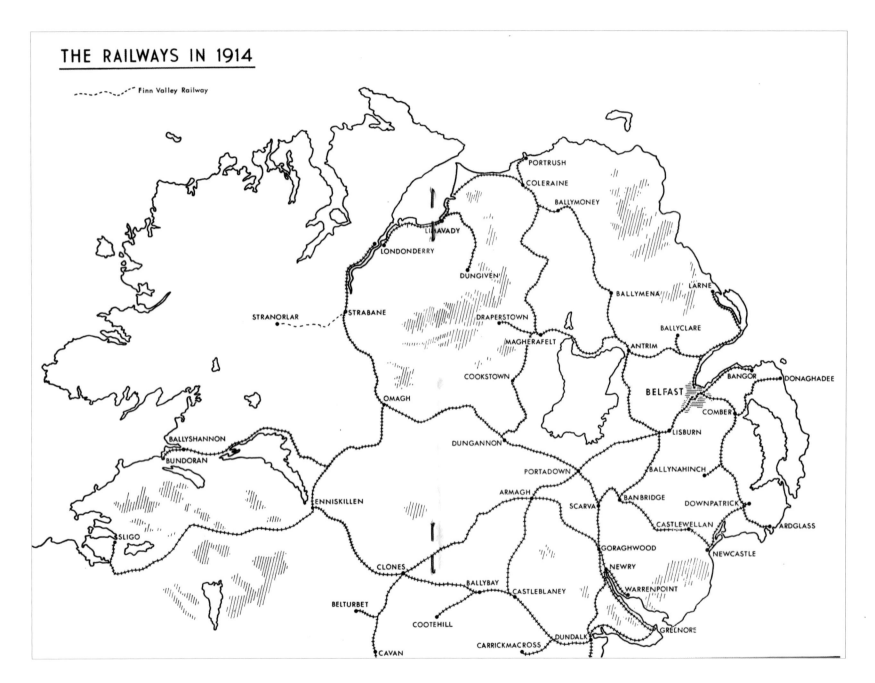

THE RAILWAYS IN 1914

--- Finn Valley Railway

PORTRUSH
COLERAINE
BALLYMONEY
LIMAVADY
LONDONDERRY
DUNGIVEN
LARNE
BALLYMENA
STRANORLAR
STRABANE
DRAPERSTOWN
BALLYCLARE
MAGHERAFELT
ANTRIM
COOKSTOWN
BANGOR
DONAGHADEE
BELFAST
OMAGH
COMBER
BALLYSHANNON
LISBURN
DUNGANNON
BUNDORAN
BALLYNAHINCH
PORTADOWN
ARMAGH
ENNISKILLEN
SCARVA
BANBRIDGE
DOWNPATRICK
CASTLEWELLAN
ARDGLASS
SLIGO
GORAGHWOOD
NEWCASTLE
CLONES
NEWRY
BALLYBAY
CASTLEBLANEY
WARRENPOINT
BELTURBET
COOTEHILL
GREENORE
CARRICKMACROSS
DUNDALK
CAVAN

Above: *Railway Map in 1914, courtesy of Laura Morton*

Chapter 6
Steamer Competition at Bangor and Holywood

Bangor Boats

The introduction of steamships between Belfast and Bangor – and sometimes Holywood – has been well documented by Dr DB McNeill and EM Patterson among others.

The original Bangor boat was an eighty feet long paddle steamship called *Greenock* which on 19 April 1816 became the first steamer to cross to Ireland from Scotland. The *News Letter* published a notice that the *Greenock* would ply daily between Belfast, Carrickfergus and Bangor. The first service only lasted the one summer, but for three years from 1825 the *Bangor Castle* sailed every morning from Bangor and returned from Belfast each evening. (The *Bangor Castle* advertised as '*touching only at Cultra*' for passengers at a comparatively deep water quay there built a few years earlier by Hugh Kennedy.)

Nevertheless, trippers were determined to enjoy the Lough and the delights of Bangor. The *News Letter* of 23 April 1851 reported a trip by the Young Men's Total Abstinence Society which had hired the steam tug *Belfast* and '*the deck of the little steamer was completely filled with well-dressed tradesmen, and their wives and daughters decked in their holiday finery… And well pleased with a day's enjoyment in prospect… Arrived at Bangor, the gay crowd was immediately dispersed, to perambulate the town… A feeling of jealousy was, however, perceptible and the Bangor boys asserted that "their toon was a place whar nae insults wad be taken frae strangers"'*!

It was not until 1853 that Mr Henderson's steamer, *Pilot*, provided a more regular service. She remained on the Lough for a decade, benefitting from the new pier at Bangor which enabled passengers to land at all stages of the tide. William Seyers recorded that she was skippered by a Captain Richardson, and did four trips up and four trips down daily leaving Belfast at 7am, though there was competition from the *Petrel* which left Belfast at the same time and raced to see which would get to Bangor first.

Above: *The Light Beacon constructed by Alexander Mitchell in 1844 off Cultra, courtesy of Holywood Library*

By this time steamers on the route benefitted from the wooden light beacon or pile lighthouse erected by Alexander Mitchell off the shore at Cultra in 1844, at a cost of £1,300.

Mitchell is – for the author – one of Holywood's lesser known heroes. Born in Dublin in 1780, the young Alexander started losing his sight in his schooldays and was completely blind by his early 20s. This did not however stop him becoming a highly innovative marine engineer and inventor. He solved the problem of how to erect a stable lighthouse on a shifting sand bank, through the use of screw piles driven into the seabed by a temporary capstan (on the principle of a corkscrew). The Cultra lighthouse, which was also described as located on the Holywood sand bank, served in addition as a pilot station. According to one account it was damaged in 1889 when a vessel collided with it, and it seems to have been demolished two years later.

Being blind, Mitchell had additional challenges to face. On one occasion he fell into the Lough while visiting the Cultra lighthouse, but apart from losing his hat, suffered no other misfortune. From 1854, he lived in Victoria Terrace, Holywood, though he later moved to Farmhill, dying in 1868.

In 1861 Captain Brown of Bangor (whose capital derived from the muslin business) put the *Heroine* on the Lough and a fare war started; the fare was reduced to three pence. (Subsequently the *Heroine* was sold to the Confederate forces in America as a blockade runner.) Brown's next ship was the *Erin*. Seyers records that the *Erin* had

an oak belt round the iron hull to save damage to pier and ship while berthing. She, together with a sister ship, from 1877, the *Bangor Castle*, both with two funnels, stayed on the Lough until the arrival of the railway steamers in the 1890s. (In 1890, the *Erin* collided with a rival, the *Victoria*, when both were racing, with full passenger loads, from Belfast to Bangor. No great damage was done, but both captains had to appear in the dock – at Belfast Petty Sessions.)

Describing the scene at Bangor, Seyers recounted that:

'Luggage porters, with hand-carts, carted the luggage to and from the steamer. They had a badge strapped on their left arms with name and number on it.'

Charlie Scott still acted as a ship's pilot though he was about 84 years of age. The Bangor steamers were usually laid up in the Long Hole for the winter.

One strange case was recorded in the local press in September 1870. This was an account of attempted suicide by a wife who jumped overboard from the steamer *Erin* because of her husband's dancing on board to the tune of a fiddler!

In 1872 the steamer *Racoon* crossed to Bangor from Scotland on 11 July, bringing in a number of '*Scotch visitors… this being the week of the great Glasgow fair*', according to the *News Letter*.

In 1875 Brown's vessels were bought by Moore Brothers and in turn they morphed into the Belfast, Bangor and Larne Steamboat Company in 1887. In the same year, the *Clandeboye*, built by Workman Clark for the Bangor service, joined them, though she was sold after two years. It was found that three steamers were needed to ensure a daily service of eight round trips to Bangor and two to Larne. Thus the company acquired the *Bonnie Doon*; alas she acquired so bad a reputation for reliability that she became known as the 'Bonnie Breakdown'.

Percipiently the Belfast, Holywood and Bangor Railway Act of 1881 had made provision for that company to operate steam vessels '*for the purpose of establishing an improved and efficient communication between Belfast, Holywood and Bangor*', although the BHBR didn't take up that option before the merger with the BCDR. (It is interesting to note that the Eurotunnel operators have recently been forced to give up their plans

Above top: Painting of Belfast Lough showing the Mitchell Light Beacon and Fog Bell, artist unknown but painted after 1861, courtesy of Belfast Harbour Commission
Above bottom: The Bangor Castle at Bangor Pier taken from near Pickie, date unknown, North Down Museum

to operate a parallel cross-Channel ferry service on the grounds that this would be unfair competition.)

In 1891 the BCDR Directors decided to put their own steamers on the Lough, starting with the 300 ton *Slieve Donard* which operated the service for five years from 1893. In the following year, came the *Slieve Bearnagh*. These were not small boats in terms of their carrying capacity – the *Bearnagh* was certified to carry over 950 passengers between Belfast and Bangor, at a maximum speed of 17 knots with a journey time of 50 minutes. She served for nearly twenty years before being replaced by the paddle-steamer *Erin's Isle* in whose design Thomas Andrews (of Titanic fame) was involved. Her maiden trip was on 12 July 1912. The ships were used by the Navy as mine-sweepers in the Great War, and the *Erin's Isle* was sunk in early 1919. (The earlier *Erin* was purchased by the BCDR in 1894 and scrapped almost immediately – presumably to buy up the competition.)

The records kept by the Company Secretary show that the *Slieve Donard* was insured for £14,000 in 1895, and the *Bearnagh* for £3,000 more; interestingly both were insured to proceed also to Stranraer, Campbeltown and the Isle of Man. The *Erin* was valued at just £1,000. There is also an account of the agreement with one Samuel Roy who took on the contract to supply catering for the 1895 Bangor steamer season. The contract even prescribed the precise makes of spirits to be available, which rather surprisingly given the

Dunville family's eminence in Holywood, included Jamesons, Bushmills and Coleraine or Comber but not Dunville's whiskey. (Coakham records that the provision of liquor caused an indignant protest from the Women's Temperance Society. While this was unsuccessful, the company did make the concession of keeping the bar closed on Sunday sailings.)

H Fayle wrote an account of the Belfast and County Down Railway in the '*Railway Magazine*' in 1906 (which was reprinted in Bob Pue's *25 Years Gone*). Fayle noted that it was unusual for a railway company to have given itself competition from a steamer service, but observed by this means the BCDR had '*protected their own territory and gained a good deal of additional traffic.*' He added that during the sail down Belfast Lough '*a magnificent view of the country on both sides is obtainable*'.

Perhaps tactfully Fayle did not record that Captain McCorquodale of the *Slieve Bearnagh* had been summonsed in 1904 for overloading the vessel.

The *Spectator* recorded during the First World War that there were unintended consequences when the *Erin's Isle* left Bangor Pier for her last trip of the season:

'*By a strange coincidence, the rockets she fired constituted the signal for "enemy's warships entering the Lough". Needless to say the signal caused quite a commotion at Grey Point and Kilroot, the garrisons there standing to the guns to repel the invader.*'

After the end of the First World War, the 'Bangor Boat' service did not resume until 1923, and it only lasted a year. On the other hand Lough cruises did continue. In 1931, the former Lough Foyle paddle steamer *Cynthia* offered 'tea dansant' cruises from Bangor, for an inclusive fare of 2/6.

McNeill states that the 'Bangor Boat' was only ever a summer service, not operating in winter. Passengers purchasing a return ticket on the railway company's boats could alternatively use the train for their return

Above left: View across Bangor Harbour with paddle steamer Slieve Donard or Slieve Bearnagh at the Pier, c. 1894, North Down Museum
Above right: View from Helen's Bay across Belfast Lough, painted by JW Carey, from the illuminated address presented to Rev. Archer, 1909, courtesy of Helen's Bay Presbyterian Church

journey. The fare was not dear – for 50 years up to 1915, nine pence return tickets were available most afternoons. Certainly Bangor and back for a bob was a reality, not just a slogan.

The Challenges of Holywood

While Bangor had a reliable steamer service, the position of Holywood was more complicated, owing in part to the large sandbank just offshore from the town and to constant silting up. This led to at best a chequered service.

In May 1867 Browns of Bangor began to call at Holywood too. As the pier was not complete, passengers had to be rowed to and from the steamer at anchor off the town. On 8 May Brown's paddle steamer *Erin* brought in three Directors of the Pier Company to the cheers of local residents.

In 1869 the pier was completed with a fine promenade, extending for 1,360 yards with a shorter coal quay alongside. It cost some £20,000. The steamer *Lady of the Lake* began on the Holywood run in late August that year. Alas during the winter, presaging what was to prove a repetitive issue, the pier silted up and a dredger had to be employed. An advertisement proclaimed that '*The Lady of the Lake will ply (weather and casualties excepted) between Belfast and Holywood, seven trips daily and on Sunday three.*' The fare for the saloon was four pence, and half that for steerage. Alas by 1870 the *Lady of the Lake* had been withdrawn from service.

The pier always struggled. While Captain Brown sought to establish the Holywood service, he faced competition from smaller vessels, including steam tugs. There was a short-lived Holywood Steam Paddle Company which was expected to place an order with Harland and Wolff for a double-ended boat, but never did. The Company did acquire the *Lily* which ran between Holywood and Belfast for a year, setting a new speed record of just twenty minutes, before the silting became too bad. The *Garloch* achieved notoriety in the early 1870s for the frequency of its accidents. By 1875, all steamer services had had to give up. Thereafter the pier's ownership changed several times, including London firms one of which even drew up draft legislation to allow for the maintenance and regulation of the pier. This required the owners to '*provide at their own expense a site near the pier and build on it a house or other proper accommodation for a lifeboat rocket apparatus*'.

In January 1882 a gale blew part of the pier down, and in July a vessel slipped its anchor and made another breach.

As noted in the chapter on Holywood, the end came on 25 August 1883. Although there were plans to restore it, and Daniel Dixon (Belfast Lord Mayor) purchased it in 1889 to do so and bring back the steamer traffic, they never came to anything.

Above: *Return Ticket for the Belfast to Bangor Steamer, late 1880s, courtesy of Ivor Graham*

Chapter 7

Through Two World Wars and a Recession

The First World War

In the previous chapter, we saw how the BCDR progressed from a near bankrupt organisation to a service business in its heyday. The period from 1914 to 1948 marked the progressive decline of the organisation, punctuated by two world wars, increasing competition from road transport, a financial crash and a disastrous railway crash in January 1945 (which is the subject of a later chapter).

The First World War was to have significant impact on the company. Initially the railway revenue declined, as the 1914 holiday season was cut short. While there was an increase in traffic, there was a reduction in profit. Moreover the Ministry of Munitions did not consider the railway companies' need for replacement equipment a priority for scarce materials, so all the companies largely had to make do with existing stock, as best they could.

It is interesting to look at the minutes of the first meeting of the Directors after the declaration of War on 4 August 1914. Incredibly – at least with hindsight – the first item concerned a report of a horse killed upon the railway line. It is not until the fifth item on the agenda, that:

'It was explained that owing to the European crisis our receipts are seriously falling off and several proposals were submitted for curtailing expenditure… The question of reducing the train service and withdrawing the steamer were referred to the chairman and general manager to deal with.'

In addition, under the heading 'protection of the line during war', the Engineer reported that he had drawn the permanent way inspectors' attention to the need for extra vigilance on their part.

At their meeting on 26 August, the Directors declined to make any donations to War Funds, but decided to pay five shillings per week to the dependants of reservists who had been called up. A little later, it was agreed to extend the same largesse to the dependants of volunteers for 'Lord Kitchener's Army'.

Another challenge to the continuity of the BCDR was the significant number of its staff who volunteered to fight on behalf of Britain. A fine plaque in the modern Central Station records the names of the 130 or so from the BCDR who volunteered, and the 18 men who were killed during the Great War. No doubt at least as many again were unable to resume their work on the railway, when the war ended, as a result of injuries they had sustained when fighting.

However, even at this time of crisis, there were still 'domestic' issues that could take up a good deal of managerial time. One such example concerned Mr Dunlop, a Post Office lineman (as recorded by Tom Wall in the Journal of the Irish Railway Record Society). The BCDR usually granted free rail passes to Post Office staff travelling on official business, though in principle this was for the staff to use when intending to work on the railway line. In 1917, Charles Moore, the BCDR Manager, wrote to the Post Office manager in Dublin complaining that lineman Dunlop had inappropriately travelled using his free pass between Holywood and Belfast on a Sunday, when he was clearly not intending to work. Dunlop's Belfast manager was in turn asked to investigate. His first response was considered inadequate, so further information was sought, including his denial of any wrongdoing, and duly provided to Dublin.

In the meantime, Mr Moore had been getting the story from his railway staff who not surprisingly gave a different version of events. This led to a hearing before officials of both companies (including Mr Minnis, the

Above: *Lamp presented to Sinclair Duncan's Father by the BCDR on his marriage on 29 July 1919, following his return from the First World War*

BCDR Traffic Superintendent), with Dunlop and a number of witnesses. Interestingly, those conducting the hearing were unable to reconcile the conflicting evidence, and it appears that Dunlop escaped without the disciplinary sanction that the BCDR had clearly been seeking.

Another of the issues that regularly occupied the attention of Directors was deliberating over whether to prosecute passengers for 'irregular travel'. In May 1916, the Directors decided to proceed against Messrs Moore and Ryan for such action on the Bangor Branch. Moore appealed to the Directors who subsequently agreed not to prosecute if he made the substantial donation of 5 pounds to the Royal Victoria Hospital and paid their lawyers' fees. Ryan went to court, and got off with the lesser fine of 1 pound and a guinea costs.

The Directors also noted that a 12-year-old had broken his leg when he had pulled over a machine on the Queen's Quay platform provided by the Automatic Sweetmeat Company.

Through an Order in Council on 22 December 1916, the British Government declared its intention to assume control of all the railways across Ireland, and accordingly on 1 January 1917 the BCDR, together with the GNR and the NCC came under the control of the Irish Railway Executive Committee, a position which continued for some time after the end of the war. Coakham says that on 1 January 1920, control was passed to the Dublin-based Irish Ministry of Transport, which continued until Partition.

In the local press, the BCDR advertised, over the name of Charles Moore, the 'train arrangements for demobilised officers and men travelling to and from Belfast on Saturday 9th August'. This was for the major peace day celebrations being held in the city in 1919. They lasted a full day – the train left Bangor at 8.20am and did not leave Belfast on the return journey until 7.15pm. As a consequence, there were no early morning workmen's trains that day, and even the early morning goods trains on the following Monday were cancelled.

John Miller Andrews, later to be Prime Minister of Northern Ireland in the Second World War, took Thomas Andrews' place on the Board; he served until 1921 when he became Minister of Labour in the new Northern Ireland Government.

In 1922, the BCDR leased a portion of land adjoining Holywood railway station to the Holywood Urban District Council. It seems likely that this was the land on which the War Memorial was built.

Bangor and Back for a Bob

Both Culverwell who died that year, and the locomotive superintendent Robert Miller, left the BCDR in 1919. The latter was replaced by John Crosthwait who was to serve until 1945.

As the *Spectator* reported in March 1921, the issue of house tickets was becoming an issue, and would be so for several years. It then advised anxious readers:

'Whether the grant of free house tickets will be continued or not by the Railway Company has not yet been announced. A deputation from the Bangor Urban Council waited on them some time ago and although no decision was come to at the time, it was understood that the tickets would be continued but that the basis of qualification would be altered. Up till the present a valuation of from £15 to £25 entitled the occupier of a new house to a second class ticket for a period of ten years, while a valuation of £25 or over qualified for a first class ticket for the same period. It was suggested that the figure for a second would go up to £20 and that for first to £30, and if new houses had been valued on the old basis that would have been perfectly reasonable and satisfactory. But as a matter of fact, we now know that the valuations of new houses are practically identical with what they would have been before the war, and that being so there will be no reason for the Railway Company to alter the qualifying figures for free tickets. In the light of what is now known we think the Bangor Urban Council would be justified in making a further communication to the Company with the object of having the status quo preserved.

It is quite evident that there is no danger of the company being inundated with applications for free tickets from very small houses which, by virtue of being built now, might chance to be valued at £15 or over. As a matter of fact, two houses were built in May Avenue recently and were afterwards sold on the understanding that the free ticket would be given. Being valued at less than £15, the purchaser will not be able to get the ticket, so that

Right: McClement's Bus Service, in Holywood, undated

either the house will have to be revalued or the seller of the property will be obliged to purchase the ten year tickets out of his own pocket.'

In November 1922 the *Spectator* reported good news:

'The directors of the Belfast and County Down Railway Company Ltd. have decided to restore the privilege of house free tickets over their system and their decision has created much satisfaction in the towns concerned where it is stated, building operations will be encouraged as a result.'

However the good tidings were not to last for long, as at the end of that year, the *Spectator* reported with regret:

'The Co. Down Railway Co. have been driven by causes which were sufficiently explained by the chairman, Mr Thomas Richardson, at the annual meeting on Thursday to discontinue the free ticket privilege. The announcement will be read with regret by owners of land and others who have especially benefitted from the operation of the grant. The chairman said: – "In view of their falling receipts and the diversion of a large part of their passenger and parcels traffic to privately owned motor cars and to charabancs, the company was not now obtaining from those house free tickets anything like the amount of traffic that it formerly derived and it was not now in a financial position to continue the privilege of free travelling which it formerly did and he had to announce that after the fullest consideration of all the circumstances the directors definitely decided at a Board meeting held on Wednesday, that no further free tickets would be granted for any house in respect of which the prescribed notice of intention to build had not been lodged with the secretary before the 27th instant and notices to that effect would be published and posted up at the various stations that afternoon."
Credit is due to the company for the way in which by the granting of free tickets and other services, they have encouraged the development of Bangor in the past and it is hoped that more prosperous days may return when it may again be reasonable to ask for a resumption of the free ticket in respect of new houses'.

Alas 'more prosperous days' were not to return.

By this time, the railways were coming under competition from buses for the custom of the rural population, especially. By June 1924, Morrow's Enterprise Bus Company provided four services from Bangor to Belfast each day, including one via Crawfordsburn, undercutting even the railway's third class return fare of two shillings and four pence with a price of just one shilling and sixpence. The following year, the rival Bangor Queen bus company was set up. The BCDR was obliged to reduce its fares, and its profits fell accordingly. Goods traffic was also increasingly being sent by road.

As shown in the photograph, one of the Holywood services was operated by Thomas McClements. The Holywood Library Archives have a copy of a Petty Sessions summons against Mr McClements for carrying more than the authorised number of passengers for the seats provided in his 'charabanc'

on a public road in the city of Belfast on 31 January 1925. He was to appear in court less than a month later – justice was speedy in those days!

The company had the interests of the travelling public at heart; for example according to the 1925 Bradshaw's timetables, fast trains from Bangor stopped exceptionally at the Halts to *'take up passengers for Cross Channel Steamers'*.

The 1924 edition of the *BCDR Official Tourist Guide* continued to sing the praises of Bangor as a tourist destination:

'The great attractions of Bangor are its pure air and sea, and its unrivalled facilities for bathing and boating. For gentlemen two excellent bathing stations are provided – at the Pickie Rock on the west side of the bay, and at Clifton on the east side. In both places deep water is to be found at all states of the tide, and there is ample provision in the way of dressing-rooms,

Above: The Hill and Bangor Road at Cultra

spring-boards etc. Ladies have the use of these establishments at fixed hours; and at Ballyholme Bay… a grand sandy beach is at their disposal. Bangor is the headquarters of the Royal Ulster Yacht Club; this club's annual two-day regatta is one of the most important yachting events in Ireland, and attracts all the crack boats in British waters. Three sailing clubs are also established here, and matches take place continually. Boats of all kinds may be had for hire.'

Notwithstanding such promotion, in 1926, the company's Board of Directors even had a preliminary discussion about outright closure of the whole system, or at the most retention of just the Newcastle and Bangor lines. In the following year, the BCDR chairman, Thomas Richardson, was sent to London to plead for amalgamation with the London, Midland and Scottish Railway (which by then owned Northern Ireland's Northern Counties Committee system). This plea was politely considered but declined.

The *Spectator* reported in June 1926 on another tack tried by the BCDR, which clearly came as a shock to many:

'The exceedingly difficult position in which the Belfast and County Down Railway Company has been placed by the diversion of traffic to road vehicles was the subject of a deputation from the railway company to the Bangor Urban Council on Tuesday night. Mr C.A. Moore, the general manager, pointed out various ways in which, as large ratepayers, the company considered that they were entitled to the co-operation of the Council, notably with regard to the levying of charges for the use of public parking places by buses and the limitation of the number of licences issued. He said, almost in so many words, that unless the bus companies are required to pay for the public facilities they enjoy in the provision of roads, stopping places, etc. and thus to some extent put on a par with the railway companies in the matter of running costs, it will be a matter for the directors of the Belfast and County Down Company to consider the closing down of their line. As Mr McMillan remarked in the brief discussion that followed Mr Moore's sensational announcement, this is a new point of view for most people. It is common knowledge that the receipts of the company have been steadily dwindling for the last three years and obviously the resources of a railway*

company are not without limits. But the likelihood of the railway having to stop altogether has never suggested itself to anybody.

The possibility of a cessation of the train services, which have undoubtedly done much to build Bangor up, is a matter of the gravest concern to the public, and the Urban Council will not be accused of prejudice in favour of the company if they give it the most careful consideration, not from the point of view of the company as such, but in relation to the interests of their own town, which are threatened. But, with the greatest goodwill in the world, there is not much that Bangor as a municipal body can do in the present state of the law. Parking places cannot be charged for; the limitation of the licences presents great difficulties, as the only grounds on which further licences can be refused is that already there are enough to deal with all the traffic. Probably there are fully enough of these vehicles to meet the needs at the present time, but it is very difficult to prove that this is the case, and the applicant for a licence has the right to go before the Home Ministry and demand redress. The effect of the discussion at Bangor on Tuesday night will be to ventilate the matter with its unpleasant possibilities but otherwise we do not see that it can lead to any alteration in the present position. The matter is one for general, not local, treatment. The obvious plan for the Belfast and County Down and for other railway companies whose interests are threatened, as they allege unfairly, is to make representations to the Government with a view to having legislation enacted to deal with the points they complain about. The outlook appears to be rather a hopeless one. It may be possible to have powers conferred on licensing authorities to levy taxes on the road vehicles to correspond with the amount of damage they do to the roads and possibly legal sanction might be given for the imposition of parking charges; but the great difficulty in the way of legal action will be the force of public opinion or that large portion of it which benefits from the cheap facilities available on road vehicle services. Governments are slow to move in opposition to the wishes of a considerable section of their constituents.

The railway company claims that the present conditions with regard to road vehicles are a virtual subsidy from the public purse which permits the buses to give cheaper fares than the railway can do and make a profit. The railway also labours under the further disability that it has very little say in regard to the hours and conditions of service of its employees, a result of the way in which the railwaymen are organised. No such disability exists at present in connection with the bus companies, and it will be a considerable time before there is a busmen's union of any consequence. The Belfast and County Down system is peculiarly vulnerable to road competition on the Bangor side and this company has suffered more than most from the new form of transit. As ratepayers the representatives of the company had a perfect right to go before the Council and state their case, but in what way their position can be bettered by Council action it is very difficult to see.'

Perhaps they took the views expressed in this *Spectator* article to heart, as we know the Stormont Government was lobbied by the railway

companies, and legislation in 1927 made it legal for the local railways to operate their own bus services. Accordingly in October 1928, the BCDR both introduced a bus service between Holywood and Belfast and bought up competing private bus companies. Four years later it became a road-haulier too, with lorry services between Bangor and Belfast.

Another of the curiosities of the railway system in Ireland was that for a period even after Partition, orders were still issued from Dublin relating, for

example to arrangements for the Royal Ulster Constabulary. Thus a notice signed by RJ Moore as Superintendent of the Line at the GNR (Ireland) Office dated 1 June 1923 refers to arrangements that had been made by the Government in Northern Ireland to call up the men of the Ulster Special Constabulary for training purposes who were to travel to one of a limited number of centres, two on the BCDR system. The men were to be supplied with a warrant for a return ticket for the cost of a single fare.

Three years later, on 12 July 1926, the Superintendent wrote to advise the operators that bona fide *'emigrants travelling to the ports of Belfast and Londonderry en route for America …'* were to be offered tickets reduced by one-third, on production of the requisite paperwork. (Up to 1953 the GNR remained a private company with no Government funding and thus able to operate north and south of the Border. It was then nationalised by the two Governments, but was not partitioned between CIE and the UTA for another five years.)

In the 1920s, there was again consideration of electrification of the Bangor branch, together with the possibility of an extension from the town to Donaghadee, but the new Northern Ireland Government declined to provide support.

From the mid-1920s, various documents exist relating to dealings between the BCDR and the War Department and indeed other bodies. One Agreement from August 1924 indemnified the company from liability if it was carrying explosives on behalf of the Government. The following year, a further Agreement was reached providing that at all stations where accommodation existed for dealing with horse traffic, that specially reduced charges should be applied for Government horses on military purposes; in return, the company should be liable to no financial risk if delays to its services were occasioned as a result.

Mr Robert Milligan of Priory Park Nursery, Bangor Road, Holywood, florist, entered into an agreement allowing him to use the flower stall at Bangor station for the sale of flowers, fruit, plants and seeds for five years, at a rental of £5 a year.

In 1926 Billy Minnis succeeded Charles Moore as General Manager. As RM Arnold relates, one of Moore's favourite maxims was *'those buffers are intended to show the end of the line, and are not for crashing against'*. One train had run away into Donaghadee, wrecking much of the station, but killing no-one other than an unfortunate cat which happened to be in the wrong place at the wrong time. (As the chapter on accidents shows, one of the Manager's sadly regular duties was representing the company at inquests into fatalities on the line.) Minnis had begun his BCDR service as a junior clerk as early as 1884, and was to continue in harness right through to 1944, an extraordinary record. (He too had a Helen's Bay connection, being captain of the Golf Club and having his picture hung there.)

The company's finances deteriorated quite fast from the mid-1920s. According to the *Railway Year Book* for 1925, the BCDR had recorded a profit of over £36,000 in 1924. The company had 30 locomotives, 214 'passenger vehicles', and 703 goods vehicles. It owned no less than 47 houses or cottages for railway servants. A total of 3,831,409 passenger journeys were made on its 80 miles of track.

In February 1925 Belfast to Holywood rail fares were reduced to three pence. And in 1927, temporary one-year salary reductions of 10% were imposed on BCDR staff, which was later extended. The *Spectator* reported it this way:

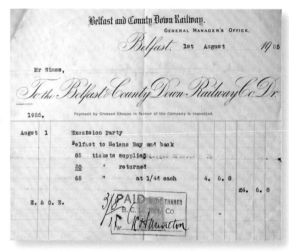

'After many delays, which were not within the control of the Directors, the company's application for reclassification of the railway as a class 3 railway was heard by the Irish Railway Wages Board in October, and a finding was unanimously arrived at, as a result of which the salaries and wages of all members of the staff (excluding shop men) have been subjected to a reduction of 10% for a period of 12 months as from 1 November 1927.'

That same year, the Directors announced with regret that they were unable to recommend the payment of a dividend on either the ordinary stocks or most preference stocks of the company. The *Spectator* reported that the company had lost over £11,000 in 1926. The article added that the cause was two-fold – road competition and the 1926 miners' strike which had greatly increased the cost of coal. Nevertheless two bridges had been renewed and signalling improvements put in train (as recorded in the chapter on that topic).

In 1927 the *Spectator* reported the death of a faithful servant of the BCDR, who had clearly been a familiar face between Holywood and Bangor for two decades:

'The death occurred on Monday morning of Mr Robert T. McCammon at his residence, Maretta 79 Bloomfield Road, Belfast. Deceased had been in failing health for some time and had been confined to his home for the past six weeks. He was well-known and highly respected having been with the Belfast and County Down Railway for over 35 years. He started his railway career at Ardglass in 1892 later going to Newcastle and Downpatrick. For the last twenty years he acted as guard on the Bangor line. Deceased leaves a wife, two sons and a daughter to mourn his loss.'

There were other challenges too of one sort or another to the viability of the Bangor line.

In the 1930s, a substantive proposal was worked up to close the line and make it into a roadway – this was entitled *Roadway or Railway between Belfast and Bangor*, written by TI Lloyd, 1933, printed by the *News Letter*. The book did recognise that while the theory might be fine and that buses did have advantages, one of the issues was the narrowness of the track, as compared to the width of a roadway, even in those days – let alone the dual carriageway that now exists. Fortunately, nothing came of that idea.

Nor too did a plan to electrify the Bangor line, also in the 1930s.

The 1930s were the era of the famous slogan – 'Bangor and back for a bob', a 25% reduction on the regular fare, beginning with third class excursions. (A 'bob' was of course one shilling in pre-decimal coinage. Although as DB McNeill recalled when addressing the Bayburn Historical Society, during a Bangor water shortage in 1933, it was rechristened by some wags as 'Belfast and back for a bath!')

Seasonal business could still be good, both from Bangor and to it, as the following *Spectator* articles from July 1929 and 1930 respectively record:

Above: BCDR Receipt for a Sunday School Outing to Helen's Bay, 1 August 1925

'No fewer than six trains were required to convey to Newcastle on Wednesday the people who wished to take advantage of the County Down Railway Co.'s Wednesday afternoon trip. Over 5,000 passengers were carried and the number of trains was a record. At Bangor station alone nearly five hundred tickets were issued for the Wednesday excursion to Newcastle.'

'Abundant proof of Bangor's popularity as a centre for day trippers was afforded by the dense masses of people who were brought by train and bus on Monday. The trains carried something like 15,000 people or rather less than travelled by rail a year ago, but the aggregate traffic must have been even larger than on 13th July, 1929. It was a most orderly crowd. An interesting incident in the morning was the arrival of 2,000 excursionists from Lurgan. These were the Royal Black Preceptories of Lurgan area together with their lady friends and followers. It is an amazing fact that for thirty years past the Lurgan "black" men have made Bangor the venue of their annual outing. A very orderly and respectable company they were and one which redounded to the credit of the Orange Institution as a community of law-abiding people – the substantial backbone of the country.*

I pass on a word of commendation and congratulation to Sergeant W. O'B. Armstrong, head of the constabulary in Bangor. Sergeant Armstrong succeeds, without ostentation or fuss in preserving order and discouraging such unruly spirits as might bubble over to the disturbance of the peace in the excitement of holiday time. The fact that there were no serious accidents and scarcely an arrest is the best vindication of effective police methods in Bangor.'

(The Lurgan Royal Black Preceptory continued to travel each year to Bangor by train, until the end of the Belfast Central Railway connection in 1965.)

There were also summer excursions from Great Northern bases, crossing the Lagan, and on to Bangor. Similarly one could travel extensively from Bangor, to resorts elsewhere. One promotional leaflet proudly offered the opportunity to journey to Portrush over no less than three of Ulster's railways.

The Irish Railway strike of 1933 did not affect the BCDR, as its workers had already suffered the 10% reduction in wages – the same over which the GNR and NCC employees took strike action.

The Northern Ireland Government asked Sir Felix Pole (formerly Manager of the English GWR) to review public transport in 1934. His report led to the Road and Railway Transport (Northern Ireland) Act 1935 which created the Northern Ireland Road Transport Board (NIRTB) and which in turn took over the BCDR's fleet of buses and lorries. (Casserley criticises the NIRTB for running services in direct competition with the railways rather than as feeder services as had been promised.) Pole concluded that the population of Northern Ireland was too thinly spread for railways to succeed in the long term, though his report did note that the BCDR 'derives the greater part of its revenues from passenger traffic on the Bangor branch'. He recommended the pooling of receipts by Northern Ireland's railways.

One small crumb of comfort for the beleaguered railway companies was the agreement reached at this time with the Pigs Marketing Board for pigs to be transported by rail to slaughterhouses, for one shilling and three half-pence per pig, whatever the distance. (Unfortunately – from the pigs' standpoint – there was no provision for return tickets.)

By the late 1930s, the BCDR was making an annual loss; no dividend had been paid on the ordinary stock since 1926, and the locomotives and rolling stock were obsolete. Crosthwait had managed to order one diesel from Harland and Wolff – not for use on the Bangor line – and two new bogie carriages, but the BCDR was left well behind its local competitors in terms of travelling comfort.

And what were the headquarters of the company like, at Queen's Quay? Sinclair Duncan's father had begun a lifelong service of the BCDR as an indentured clerk, before the First World War. His father would bring his son into the office occasionally, when he was working overtime in the

Belfast and County Down Railway.

Spend Six Hours at
Beautiful Bundoran
DELIGHTFUL STRAND :: MAGNIFICENT SCENERY

On TUESDAY, 19th JULY,
Attractive Through Excursion
To BUNDORAN
BANGOR Train departure 8-40 a.m.
HOLYWOOD " " 8-55 a.m.
Returning from BUNDORAN at 6-45 p.m.

Exceptionally Cheap
Return Fare - 6/-

Express Corridor Train with Refreshment Car attached will run via the Central Railway at Belfast, enabling the journey to be made without change of coach.

Belfast, 27th June, 1938.

W. F. MINNIS,
General Manager.

R. CARSWELL AND SON, LTD., QUEEN STREET, BELFAST. (1212)

Above: Summer Flyer for a BCDR Excursion to Bundoran from Bangor and Holywood, courtesy of Victor Corrie.

1930s. Sinclair recalls '*banks of high sloping desks at which the clerks worked on stools, and massive typewriters with violet carbon paper*'.

In terms of traffic on the commuter lines, Sinclair observes that up to the Second War, it was not uncommon for people working in Belfast to travel home to stations such as Bloomfield, Knock, Dundonald or Holywood, for lunch, before returning to the city for the afternoon's labours. He remembers weekly updates from his father on the company's traffic receipts for the previous seven days – while there were occasional improvements in passenger revenue, that for goods was invariably declining. He adds that, given the seaside business, the company was unusually dependent on good weather; while the pre-booked trains were always full on 12 July whatever the elements might have in store, the volume of passengers on the annual holiday on the following day could be hugely reduced if it rained.

It should also be remembered that until the 1960s many people worked a five and a half or six day week; thus there were also more 'rush hour' trains out of Belfast around 1pm on Saturdays.

The Second World War

The Second World War saw a resurgence of activity on all Northern Ireland's railway lines. To meet the needs of Belfast's industry at this time, the first train left Bangor at 5.05am, while trains left Belfast for Bangor at 6am taking home weary workers who had completed the nightshift.

At this time, the Ministry of Home Affairs and the Northern Ireland Government was responsible for the railways. It paid the BCDR over £2000 to provide air raid shelters and even for the '*obscuration of fireglow from loco fireboxes*'. The company did not however obtain the military protection for Crawfordsburn viaduct that it requested owing to other demands for such resources.

Rightly Crosthwait saw an opportunity to try to upgrade some of the BCDR's elderly locomotives and rolling stock. Two of the 1909 engines needed reboilering, and were also given new fireboxes.

Emergency surcharges were introduced by the BCDR from 1 January 1941, '*to meet increasing operating costs, arising out of the present emergency*'. A 10% increase in the charge was applied to the following range of items (which seems extraordinarily eclectic): bath chairs, street organs, perambulators, sewing machines, motor bicycles and cars, returned empties and even corpses! However the following page contained the exceptions to the rule which were exempt from the surcharge in the meantime, including the accompanied luggage of music hall artistes, newspapers, hunting horses, packs of hounds and police sources, and finally '*hearses, coffin cases (not returned) and empty coffins*'. Passenger fares, however, were not increased – it was cheaper to travel alive than dead.

The BCDR's manager, Mr Minnis, made arrangements from early 1941 for a greater number of locomotives and carriages to be held overnight at stations away from Belfast. As a result of this foresight, the two main air raids of the Blitz bombing of Belfast in April and May 1941 did comparatively little damage to BCDR rolling stock, although unfortunately many of the records were lost, particularly those relating to the BHBR era. (The absence of BHBR and BCDR papers is very obvious in comparison to the wealth of

Above left: BCDR Engine No 27 (with Holywood Motor) in Holywood Station, 1939, courtesy of Charles Friel. *Above top right:* Notice of Emergency Wartime Surcharges on BCDR Traffic Rates imposed from 1 January 1941. *Above bottom right:* 1942 Third Class Weekly Season Tickets including the Bangor Line, courtesy of Victor Corrie.

material on most of Ireland's other historic lines, held in the base of the Irish Railway Record Society outside Heuston station in Dublin.) Sadly both a guard and a signalman died in the vicinity of Queen's Quay, the latter in his signal cabin.

On the other hand, the Blitz contributed significantly to the company's ticket sales, with many Belfast residents finding temporary lodgings away from the city to which they would travel by train. A significant number of wooden dwellings were erected within walking distance of stations along the Bangor line. Another source of additional income was those assigned to Northern Ireland for reasons connected with war work. One example was the author's father-in-law, a Royal Navy Commander, who was posted to Belfast for 18 months to supervise the fitting of the engines into naval ships being built by Harland and Wolff. He took lodgings in Bangor and commuted daily.

Again, many employees of the company wished to volunteer to serve, and this aspect is recounted by Arnold:

'Traffic to the County Down countryside so increased that the BCDR was soon in dire straits for staff, having to employ boys on footplate work after only a few weeks cleaning.'

The normal progression for an aspirant engine driver was to spend some considerable period, years even, as a cleaner before graduating to the

Above: No Spitting Notice, courtesy of Con Auld
Above right: Notice dated 1 June 1948 of Day Fares on the Bangor Line

fireman's role and eventually maybe to driver. At the other end of the career spectrum, some no doubt stayed on longer than they might otherwise. The BCDR staff register has an entry for instance of one 68 year old fireman based at Queen's Quay in 1943 who was recorded in the accident book. The same accident book register has one James McClements working as a temporary porter in Holywood station in July 1942, aged just 16, while John McClune sustained injury as an acting fireman in the same year, also aged 16.

Richard Whitford points out that during the war, trains were even run in the middle of the night, for example at 3 am. As already noted, the public timetable shows the first train leaving Bangor departing at 5.05 am, with the first leaving Queen's Quay in the opposite direction just 10 minutes later. The working timetable issued on 5 June 1941, was provided to BCDR staff with handwritten additional notes. It shows that two engines were now kept overnight at Bangor.

But some things about human frailty remained unchanged. Coakham records an early incident of 'rail rage' which featured in the BCDR minute book of this period. Most regrettably, blows were struck, in a first-class compartment of all places, when a lady wanted to have a window opened, and a doctor wished to have it closed. Alas history does not record the outcome of the spat!

In the summer of 1944 Mr Minnis retired. The BCDR approached the Great Northern Railway (GNR) with a proposal (probably a plea) that the position of the BCDR General Manager would be abolished, and that the GNR would act in an advisory capacity. Traffic departments of the two companies were to be gradually merged, in anticipation of a reduction of traffic after the end of the war and the need for further economies.

In October 1944, the BCDR experimented on the Bangor line with the use of a Great Northern Railway diesel railcar from the Dublin suburban

services. Looking ahead, at a BCDR Board meeting on 8 January 1945, management favoured introducing additional stock, but 48 hours later the accident at Ballymacarrett (covered in its own chapter) was to have sweeping implications for the future of the company, setting all such ambitions to naught.

In the wartime years, (compensation for Ballymacarrett apart in 1945), the company had made a profit. However in 1946 the BCDR as a whole showed a net loss of over £40,000, although the Bangor line itself made a profit of over £25,000 in the first seven months of that year alone.

The writing was thus pretty clearly on the wall by this stage. A meeting of the chairman and deputy chairman of the BCDR with the Stormont Prime Minister and the Minister of Commerce was proposed, at which the company envisaged putting before them a proposal to close down the BCDR except for the Bangor branch. Action was deferred by the Minister while advice was sought from financial consultants.

On 5 March 1948, it was announced that the BCDR would be sold to the NIRTB for a total of £486,000. Six months later, in September of that year, the Ministry of Commerce announced that the County Down Railway would be taken over by the newly-formed Ulster Transport Authority in company with the NIRTB.

Above: Memorial to BCDR Staff who fought and died in the First World War (at Belfast Central Station)

Chapter 8

The Post-War Years

Into the Ulster Transport Authority

In 1946, with the horror of the Ballymacarrett accident still in people's minds, the Northern Ireland Government announced its intention to bring together under one public management system the Northern Ireland Road Transport Board, the BCDR, the NCC and the GNR. The proposals were published as a Bill in 1947 and were implemented in 1948 under the Transport Act (Northern Ireland).

On 30 September 1948, the independent life of the County Down Railway was extinguished and it became part of the Ulster Transport Authority (UTA). This was just over a month after the centenary of the opening of the Belfast to Holywood line had been marked.

The last ever entry in the BCDR minute book is dated 1 November 1948 which recorded a meeting of the Directors to sign off the half yearly accounts to the end of September. A loss of £85,288 was shown in red, and their final decision was that no dividend could be paid!

For the first year or so the County Down system continued to operate much as before, although commuters on the Bangor line benefited from the replacement of the old six wheeler coaches with newer NCC bogie stock.

However this could not last, and in 1949 changes began to be introduced.

Under the Northern Ireland Act 1948, a Transport Tribunal was created to hear appeals against proposed line closures. All the local authorities affected appointed lawyers to plead the case for retention, but not only were their efforts to little avail, the legal costs fell to the ratepayers. To be fair, the Tribunal did produce a report later recommending reopening the Comber line with a reconnection over the Lagan to the Great Victoria Street terminus. (This proposal which would have seen Bangor and, possibly, Comber trains running into a new four-platform station fronting Durham Street, close to but separate from Great Victoria Street station.) This was however ignored.

From 15 January 1950, all services on the BCDR south of Comber were to cease, although the line to Donaghadee survived for a further three months up to 22 April. Goods services on the Bangor line ceased in 1950.

Richard Whitford and Ian Sinclair note that until November 1957, a few trains continued to operate from Belfast only as far as Holywood.

Ivor Graham notes that the private railway companies sought to maximise their income, through for example, requiring passengers to buy tickets for their dog(s) and bicycles. A bicycle ticket might be sold not to a particular station but on the basis of train travel not exceeding, say, ten miles. As the UTA did not require separate tickets, dog owners were one category of traveller likely to have been glad to see nationalisation.

In 1957 a further attempt was made to close the Bangor line and replace it with buses. The *Spectator* covered the debate at some length. Fortunately this proposal too was not proceeded with; one factor seems to have been

Above left: Way Out Sign, courtesy of Con Auld
Above right: Track being re-laid at Bangor, March 1961, EM Patterson, courtesy of Charles Friel

the recognition that no less than 50 new buses would have been needed to provide an equivalent service.

As set out later some of the intermediate stations on the line were closed. At a meeting between UTA managers and Holywood Urban District Council in November 1957, Councillor Dunn, the chair:

'Told the UTA representatives that they considered it a grave injustice to the people of Holywood to close the halts at Kinnegar and Marino… transport had been nationalised for the convenience of the public… [and] was subsidised by the people's money, and had it been an independent concern, it would have been in liquidation long ago.'

The UTA said that before the four halts had been closed, just 557 stops per week had been made at them. In responding to criticism at another meeting a member of the Northern Ireland Parliament said that the UTA was an independent body, but they were *'killing the goose that laid the golden egg by these actions'.*

In spring 1961, some track was re-laid at Bangor, (as shown in the illustration).

In July 1963, Henry Benson, an accountant with Coopers & Lybrand, reported to the Minister of Home Affairs on *'Northern Ireland Railways'.* At that time, the annual rail engine mileage on the BCDR section, constituted less than a third of the total mileage in Northern Ireland. On the other hand, compared to the NCC and GNR sections, it was the only part making even a modest profit. (When provision for depreciation was taken into account, the railway system in Northern Ireland made a loss of just under £500,000, in both 1961 and 1962.) The average age of the steam locomotives across the system was 30 years, and of diesels just four years less, while that of the carriages was 39 years.

(Particularly worryingly, the average age of the passenger brake vans was the highest, at no less than 62 years.)

As early as paragraph 67, Benson made his position clear:

'I think it will be helpful if I state shortly at this early stage in my report the conclusions which I have reached as a result of the whole of my enquiries as this will make it easier to appreciate and assess many of the matters which are dealt with in the ensuing paragraphs.

68. I recommend that as soon as it is practicable to do so the entire railway system should be reshaped so as to operate fast diesel passenger only services on the commuter lines in and out of Belfast and on the main line between Belfast and Dublin. The Dublin service would operate to the highest standards on the lines of the present "Enterprise" service whereas the commuter services would provide austere, but not uncomfortable, travel facilities for passengers between the main population centres in the Belfast area on the following commuter lines:

>*Belfast – Larne Harbour*
>*Belfast – Portadown*
>*Belfast – Bangor….*

70. The whole of the remaining railway system should be closed.'

Benson did graciously accept that closing any part of the railway system would be unpopular in many quarters, but he could not resist cattily pointing out that:

'Many of the persons and organisations who supported the continuation of the railways in their present form apparently did so for sentimental reasons only, notwithstanding that they themselves do not use the railways.'

Continuing his theme of austerity, Benson was clear that the stations, including the termini, should be designed for the sole purpose of providing a means for passengers to embark or disembark from the trains with facilities for selling and collecting tickets. The maintenance costs for the permanent way and the other railway assets should be reduced to a minimum.

CARRIAGES:		
Corridor	117 55	35 43
Non-corridor	172 35	38 48
ADD: Surplus carriages		
TOTAL CARRIAGES	207	39
OTHER COACHING VEHICLES:		
Passenger brake vans	7	62
Bogie brake vans	9	41
Parcel vans	6	46
Bread vans	11	48
Fish vans	3	47
Covered vans	40	20
Horse boxes	6	32
Fruit vans	3	61
ADD: Surplus vans	85 5	34 53
TOTAL OTHER COACHING VEHICLES	90	35

Above top: The 1963 Report on Northern Ireland Railways by Henry Benson
Above bottom: An Extract from the Benson Report highlighting the average age of the Rolling Stock in Northern Ireland

Ironically, many years were to pass before the one positive 'recommendation' in his report was implemented, namely that the traffic service on the Bangor line would be greatly improved if some trains could be taken via the link line from Queen's Quay station to the Great Victoria Street station.

One might say that his approach to staffing matters was from the perspective of a bean counter; he anticipated that nearly half of all railway staff would be made redundant. He added:

'Morale generally is poor and, as a result, the standard of work is suffering… This is leading to a loss of efficiency and in the supervisory and administrative positions it is particularly unfortunate as management of a high order is required when an organisation is in difficulty.'

Benson was clearly struck by the scale of the ambitious plans for the development of faster roads across Northern Ireland at that time. Had he had his way, Derry/Londonderry and indeed all stations along that line, would have lost their rail service some 50 years ago. That is of course outside the ambit of this book, but for the benefit of Bangor line passengers without their own internal padded seats, we are fortunate that his miserable strictures about austerity have been consigned to the history books.

Billy McCormick recalls that the Benson report caused a sensation when it came out, as one might well imagine. In some ways, it was even more dismissive of train travel than the more infamous report of Dr Beeching which led to the closure of so many lines in Britain. On the other hand, Sir Henry – and later Lord – Benson recalled subsequently in his autobiography that he had felt that Stormont wanted him to recommend the closure of the entire railway system, but he was not formally told this. What a mercy.

In line with another of Benson's recommendations, in 1964 first class travel was ended on the Bangor line diesel sets.

Charles Friel points out that in the 1950s there were day excursions between Bangor and Dublin, worked latterly by diesel locomotion, which survived up to the point when the Central Railway which had linked the Great Northern and County Down lines was closed by the UTA, (and the so-called 'Shaky Bridge' over the river Lagan was subsequently taken down). It was on 31 July 1965, that the Central line was severed when its bridge over Middlepath Street was removed in connection with road

improvements. This was to be the end of the last regular service steam excursion train to Bangor, from Lisburn. It was to be a further 11 years before a connection was restored.

The post-Benson Era

By the late 1960s, Holywood was becoming a road traffic bottleneck, especially in the rush hours. Consultation on the various alternative schemes led to the creation of the bypass which further severed the town of Holywood from its original seascape. (Interestingly, this is one of the most pressing issues that the current Masterplan for Holywood is seeking to address.)

The creation of the bypass had implications for the railway line; on the climb from Holywood up to Marino, it was necessary to resite the railway embankment a short way out to sea. The scheme was publicised in 1967, but work did not begin for three years, with the new section of railway line finally coming into use on 28 March 1971.

In May 1967, railway staff came out on strike in support of their Managing Director, John Coulthard, who was being dismissed for saying that he was not in place to administer the last rites to the Northern Ireland railway system. It was a measure of the respect in which he was held. (His successor had first joined the BCDR as a boy porter in 1929.)

In April 1968, new legislation took effect, and the Northern Ireland Railways Company Limited (NIR) came into existence. The assets and

Above: *Last Steam Passenger Train at Bangor Station, 28 July 1965, EM Patterson, courtesy of Charles Friel*

responsibilities of the former Ulster Transport Authority were transferred to a Holding Company.

The Troubles inevitably posed major challenges for those operating railway lines in Northern Ireland.

On 27 November 1971, a bomb exploded in Queen's Quay station, causing damage to the concourse and its glass roof. Specifically on the Bangor line, in October 1973, a bomb exploded on the 12.20 down train at Marino, badly damaging a diesel trailer and two railcars.

Richard Whitford recalls that – for a signalman – bomb alerts that affected the normal running of the timetable were the biggest problem. Another colleague recalls that during the UWC strike in 1974 there were bomb scares in the Sydenham area, and the police and Army were often called out to check the signalling, accompanied by NIR engineers.

The Central Station at Maysfield opened in 1976, with the closure of the historic Queen's Quay station. On Saturday 10 April 1976, the last train left for Bangor from Queen's Quay and on 12 April Bangor trains ran into Central Station, with the renewal of the bridge across the river Lagan. This finally enabled all the rolling stock and motive power from other parts of Ireland to run freely on the surviving fragment of the County Down system to Bangor.

What impact did this have on the Bangor line?

One answer may be found in an article in the *News Letter* of 21 March 1977 which was headed *'new rail line boosts resort's tourist trade'*. The article stated optimistically that:

> *'Bangor seems set for a 'boom' summer thanks to Belfast's new Central Railway system… The Bangor Tourist Development Association have gone all out to bring the attractions of the resort to the attention of people who previously had scarcely given North Down a thought, either for holidays or day trips'.*

The Association directed its 'come-to-Bangor' campaign in mid-Ulster, Londonderry and 'Eire'. It was trying to get over the message that Bangor was worth a visit all the year round. The article noted that until about six years previously there had been a lot of tourist traffic from Glasgow and this had fallen off to a trickle. However all was not lost, for Bangor retained *'the greatest of all natural attractions – the safe blue sea'*.

There could be other challenges, of an operational nature too. In 1979, the NIR engineer noted with concern that an over eager passenger had opened the door of a train prematurely, before it reached the down platform at Helen's Bay. The door had struck the parapet of the bridge over the historic Carriage Drive. To prevent a recurrence, remedial action was required to lower the parapet wall slightly and skew the decorative stonework of one of the pinnacles. As the bridge was historic too, listed building consent was required. (It seems slightly ironic that this issue arose nearly 30 years after the first automatic doors had been introduced on the line!)

The upgrade of the Bangor line in the early years of the current century is covered in the final chapter.

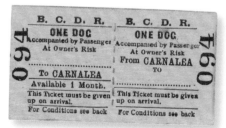

Above left: *RUC officers searching the line near Carnalea Station in 1977, courtesy of Spectator Newspapers*
Above right: *BCDR Dog Ticket to Carnalea, courtesy of Ivor Graham*

Chapter 9

Locomotives and Rolling Stock

Early Steam Power

The author is indebted to Desmond Coakham for much of the information in this chapter. (More detail, including a full range of magnificent photographs of locomotives and rolling stock is to be found in his uniquely researched and authoritative 2010 publication.)

The first locomotives acquired by the Belfast and County Down Railway were four 2-2-2 tender engines purchased from Bury, Curtis and Kennedy of Liverpool in October 1846. (The term 2-2-2 is shorthand for describing the wheel arrangement of the locomotive. The first 2 indicates there is one leading carrying axle with a wheel either side. The second digit indicates the number of driving wheels; in this case one wheel on each side. The third digit indicates the number of wheels supporting the back of the locomotive; again, in this case, there is one axle with two wheels. As a general rule, the driving wheels are the middle wheels and are always a larger diameter than the carrying wheels fore and aft of them. On the BCDR (as on almost every railway in the world), locomotives became larger as time went by and the number of wheels increased. Later BCDR locomotives had either 4 or even 6 driving wheels which were connected by coupling rods visible on the outside of the wheel. The driving wheels could be anything up to six feet in diameter, with the others roughly two-thirds that size or smaller.)

Engine No 3 had the misfortune to fall into the dock at Liverpool on its way to Northern Ireland. After some years' service engine No 2 was rebuilt at an engineering works on the Queen's Island in Belfast, one of whose partners was CS Lewis's grandfather.

We do not know the exact design of these first locomotives, but it is most unlikely that the driver and the fireman would have had any protection from the elements.

These engines were found to be uneconomical on the Holywood branch, so William Fairbairn and Son of Manchester were contracted to deliver a 2-2-2 tank engine at a considerably lower price, in May 1850.

Tank locomotives were so called because their water supply did not come from a separate tender immediately behind the engine, but was carried either in tanks which stood either side of the boiler or, in the case of a saddle tank, in one tank carried on top of the boiler.

The BCDR chairman, WR Anketell, was responsible for the procurement in 1858 of the next generation of 2-4-0 tank engines with an innovative design by Joseph Beattie and built by Beyer, Peacock & Co of Manchester, which had been founded just four years earlier. Some of the technical details sound almost lyrical – '*the firebox was divided into two separate parts by a transverse mid-feather and a hanging bridge on the crown*'. These two engines used coal, whereas the earliest locomotives on the BCDR's Holywood line had been coke-fired. The coke was initially imported, though a special works at Queen's Quay was set up for some years, before the next series of engines used coal. Sir John Macneill reported that Beattie's patent coal-burning engine had cost only half as much to run as the other engines.

A year later, a new engine was constructed by Beyer Peacock specifically for the Holywood line. This was a smaller 2-4-0 side tank. No 8 in the BCDR inventory, it was working a BHBR train when it derailed in the Belfast yard in March 1866.

The Vulcan Foundry of Earlestown, Lancashire next provided a total of seven 2-4-0 saddle tank locomotives to the BCDR and the BHBR between 1864 and 1876. The class were affectionately called '*Badgers*'. The first arrived with the BCDR in January 1864, and the type was chosen by Domville (the locomotive superintendent of both companies) for working the BHBR, two engines obtained on hire-purchase arriving in May and June 1865. The BCDR remained responsible for paying the quarterly instalments to the manufacturers, recovering the money when it could from the BHBR. At least the crew had some embryonic protection with a weatherboard in front.

Above: *Renumbered BCDR Engine No 20 at Downpatrick, 1905; (originally BHBR engine No 6, 2-4-0ST, built in 1876 by the Vulcan Foundry), Belfast and County Down Railway Museum Trust*

Coakham has done some fine detective work to clarify some of the confusions of this period. An agreement was made in October 1865 between the BHBR and the Midland Wagon Company, under which the latter was to supply on hire-purchase 60 coaches and 'Birmingham tank engines'. He believes that only one of the intended four engines was delivered before the first agreement failed, with the crash of the British bank Overend and Gurney, leaving three still in the hands of their makers John Fowler and Co of Leeds, two of which were subsequently acquired by the BCDR.

In 1870, the BHBR purchased two 2-4-0 side tank engines from the Yorkshire Engine Company of Sheffield, thus ridding itself of dependency on BCDR motive power. (This was the first to have an enclosed cab for the crew.) While these worked the Bangor line under BHBR management, ironically after the 1884 BCDR takeover, they were replaced by the latter's own – older-design – Badgers.

Interestingly the cost price of new locomotives did not change hugely over the intervening years, although if one discounts inflation, they probably did become a good deal cheaper comparatively, as technology improved. Thus the 1846 Bury engines cost £2,150 each, whereas the much larger 0-6-0 Beyer Peacock which included a separate tender purchased in 1878 cost just £20 more. It is also interesting that the BCDR clearly made a point of seeking several competitive tenders on each occasion, and this led – as shown above – to a variety of different manufacturers supplying the company. With hindsight, one wonders whether in practice that might not have been a false economy, not least as there would have been only a limited interchange of spare parts.

In the 1880s, the BCDR purchased five 0-4-2 tender engines from another new company, Sharp, Stewart and Company of Manchester. Curiously these were converted to tank locomotives at the turn of the century when they replaced the Badgers. Indeed two of this class inaugurated the push-pull service on the line to Holywood.

In addition to external purchases, the company also set up its own workshops at Queen's Quay, if not to create entirely new locomotives, at least to make the maintenance, repair and overhaul of the existing engines easier.

One other observation seems fair comment – the new technology appears to have been more reliable than one might, with hindsight, have expected. That may in part be as a result of brief breakdowns and mechanical failings not being recorded in detail, either at the time or in subsequent expert accounts such as that of Desmond Coakham. That author does record that on the BCDR the average life-span of a locomotive was about thirty years which is longer than one might expect. On the other hand it is the greater length of service of the early 20th century engines that balances the comparatively shorter lives of those built in the mid-19th century. And this greater life-span in the later days, may well have been, in part, from the lack of capital available to BCDR management from the 1920s on, with which to purchase more modern replacements.

In 1889/90 the BCDR considered further options for the Bangor branch. This time the managers tended to favour the newer 'compound' engines, but when Robert Miller, the locomotive superintendent was sent to England to look at various alternative models, he strongly advised retaining the 'simple' engines with trailing bogies. Interestingly, the Directors on the company's Locomotive Committee, which included at least two experts in engineering – James Barbour and William Pirrie (clearly a man of strong opinions) – overruled the

Above left: BCDR Engine No 2 0-4-2T, built in 1880 by Sharp Stewart, Desmond Coakham Collection, courtesy of Andrew Crockart
Above right: BCDR Engine No 7, 2-4-2, at Holywood Station, 1949, Desmond Coakham, courtesy of Andrew Crockart

locomotive superintendent. Accordingly an order was placed with Beyer Peacock for four 2-4-2 compound tank engines. Engineer Culverwell also had a view on the matter, urging that:

'The best type of engine for working the Bangor traffic would be an 8-wheel with the four centre wheels coupled…. The tanks should be side tanks and not saddleback.'

These engines proved not very effective on the Bangor line, being stiff on the curves and their axle boxes running hot. Culverwell commented on a trial with a different leading bogie (i.e. a total of four leading wheels) conformation:

'I have travelled on the front of the engine from Belfast to Bangor and the bogie rode very well, the driver of this engine seemed very pleased with it.'

One is quite impressed that a senior manager paid proper attention to the views of an operational expert!

In their final form, these compound locomotives which had become 4-4-2Ts weighed over 60 tonnes each, and were withdrawn in 1920.

In 1890, the BCDR Directors were clearly feeling flush, as they ordered another three 2-4-0 compound tender engines from Beyer Peacock.

In 1893, the company secretary was instructed to write to Beyer Peacock commissioning a further one engine with the same power as the previous 2-4-0s. The letter provides some fascinating insight into a Board of management that was clearly getting very exercised about comparative minutiae of technical details they should properly have left to their operational experts:

'There has been considerable difference of opinion as to whether your figures of dimensions etc… are exact equivalents of those of the 1892 compounds. My Directors prefer to throw the whole onus of this decision on you, and you will require to be very particularly accurate in this, because the results of our test will be communicated, by desire, to several other companies who know of this experiment by us.'

This proved to have marked the last wag of the 'compounding' tail amongst the BCDR Directors.

This locomotive, No 6, which first entered service in 1894 had something of a charmed life. It was this one that hauled the Royal train on the main line in 1897. In 1929 JL Crosthwait marked her for scrapping. However she was still around 10 years later at the outbreak of war, when additional locomotive traction was required. She was given a new boiler, cylinders and repairs to her tender, and reappeared in February 1943, repainted in what Coakham describes as dark olive green livery, lined out in scarlet and white. No 6 regularly headed the Saturdays only Golfers' Express to Newcastle, reaching a top speed of 60 mph between Dundonald and Comber, and taking just the hour to make the journey from Belfast. No 6 was taken out of service in 1950, and scrapped six years later – her total mileage was an impressive 1,545,510.

Later in the 1890s, a further six 2-4-2 tank engines were acquired from Beyer Peacock which was by now becoming the preferred manufacturer. Three of these in their later years were regularly used for the Holywood railmotors (which required the handling of only the bogie auto-coach and two six-wheeler carriages), and sometimes in the late 1940s on the full Bangor line, though they were really under-powered for the main line. One unfortunately and perhaps prematurely ended 53 years of faithful service in a collision with the tender of another locomotive! RM 'Mac' Arnold referred to one aspect of their performance:

'Any regular traveller on the Bangor line… knew well the explosive sound as they shot past on the other line.'

He is unusually complimentary about these locomotives – *'surely one of the merriest designs of engine ever to run in this country'.*

The kitty was not yet exhausted. Before the end of the century, Beyer

Above: BCDR Engine No 20 (renumbered 220 by the UTA), 4-4-2, from Belfast, approaching Crawfordsburn January 1951, EM Patterson, courtesy of Charles Friel

Peacock were given a contract to build first five bogie tank engines of 4-4-2 design, and then a further three which arrived in 1909. When JL Crosthwait joined the company, he ordered a further four which were delivered in 1921. (It should be recorded that the total number of locomotives at any given time on the BCDR never rose above 30.)

These bogie tank engines did yeoman service between the wars, though the additional strain put upon in the Second World War, meant that Crosthwait reported in January 1943 that eight of the 12 had cracks in their mainframes. Repairs were effected, and all 12 were still at work when the Ulster Transport Authority took over in October 1948.

Indeed they carried on into the early 1950s. One fine story is told of a tank engine with a light train out of Queen's Quay bound for Bangor, being

waved off by the guard at Sydenham. Alas by the time the guard turned to climb on-board, the train had left the station. The quick-thinking guard walked up the road where he was able to flag a lift in a passing sports car. Despite going the longer way round, the guard was delivered to the platform at Holywood station before the train steamed in!

The 4-4-2 engine No 30 which was one of the earliest, built in 1901, was saved from scrap. It was put aside for preservation at Queen's Quay and given sanctuary in the Transport Museum first at Witham Street, and

subsequently transferred to the splendid gallery at Cultra. Arnold notes that after the Second War, No 30 worked the important 8:20 am ex-Bangor train. He was particularly impressed by her reliability after nearly 50 years in harness.

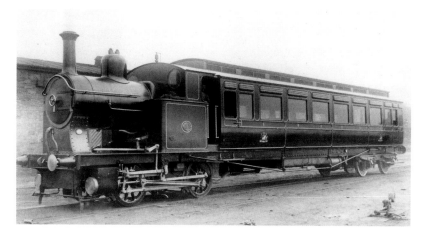

Arnold states that in his view, in these 4-4-2 locomotives, 'the BCDR had in 1904 the five finest passenger tank engines in Ireland'.

As noted earlier, the railmotors introduced on the Holywood line in 1905 were ordered from Kitsons of Leeds. The power units were 0-4-0 tank engines and the single carriage to which each engine was physically linked, had a pressed-steel under frame which made it significantly stronger than the six-wheeler carriages which were predominantly wooden.

The railmotors were said to be popular with the BCDR management and the Board, though they were not so popular with some passengers who found that just two doors for 72 passengers led to slow unloading at Queen's Quay. On other lines, railmotors were said to have an annoying vibration from the engine and suffer from fine coal dust everywhere.

The original engines were worn out by the end of the First War, and the carriages were given spare front bogie wheels and then reused with alternative engines and usually one or two additional coaches, though the push-pull facility was retained in the new configuration.

It was the carriage from railmotor No 3 which tragically did the damage when it ran into the 'flimsier' rear carriage of the stationary Bangor train in the 1945 Ballymacarrett crash (see Chapter 12).

Above left: BCDR Engine No 30, 4-4-2, built in 1901 by Beyer Peacock, preserved in the Ulster Transport Museum, Cultra, Collection Ulster Folk and Transport Museum
Above right: BCDR Railmotor No 1, Desmond Coakham Collection, courtesy of Charles Friel

The 'Baltics'

Apart from one other 0-6-0 engine commissioned from Beyer Peacock in 1904, (reusing an earlier tender), and subsequently two others which survived until the 1950s, the next – and final – main series of steam locomotives purchased by the BCDR were the 4-6-4 'Baltics'.

The locomotive stock was feeling the strain in the latter years of the First World War. Culverwell reported to the Board in August 1917 that he and Mr Miller were agreed that

> *'The proper type of engine to be next delivered… should be a 4-6-4… The 4-6-4 is the perfection of the tank type, and if it now be adopted I have no hesitation in saying that every department of the railway, traffic, loco and permanent way will be amply satisfied for 20 years to come…. I think all would be agreed that both in winter and summer there are constantly trains on the Bangor branch which are amply heavy enough to justify the margin of power now aimed at.'*

The locomotives were to be no less than 80 tons in weight.

Beyer Peacock had built its first Baltic tank for the Dutch State Railways in 1913. Interestingly Culverwell corresponded with a considerable number of contacts in both Irish and British railways over the detailed design of the Baltics; his consequential 'picky' correspondence with Beyer Peacock clearly exasperated their management!

BCDR Nos 22 to 25 were delivered in summer 1920, at an average cost of just over £6,000 each. Alterations to platform clearances at several Bangor line stations were required to accommodate their large outside cylinders.

The *Spectator* recorded in August 1920 that:

> *'Four new powerful tank engines have recently been delivered to the Belfast and County Down Railway Company by Messrs Beyer, Peacock and Co. Gorton, Lancashire. The engines, which are to be used for the passenger service on the Bangor line, are of the 4-6-4 type – bogies in front and rear*

> *and six wheel coupled. They are of the latest design and in the trials they have given every satisfaction.'*

Alas, however the Baltics proved to have a vast appetite for coal. RM Arnold sympathises with JL Crosthwait who had had the Baltics forced on him at the start of his tenure in office and was no doubt obliged to listen to demands for economy throughout his service with the company.

The Baltics were taken off duty during the winter months in the 1930s to reduce coal consumption, at a time when savings were essential. However, during the Second World War, money came in to pay for the extra coal, and the Baltics were worked hard.

Arnold begins his 1969 book by describing the effect of Baltic No 24 heading the 8:20 am train from Bangor to Belfast:

> *'When this train had been jammed tight with some 800 passengers, the gross load was at least 240 tons and every note of the Baltic's exhaust as she rasped her way under bridge 49 and up through the cutting towards Bangor West could be heard distinctly from our house at Ballyholme, over a mile away.'*

Arnold was also an inveterate timer of individual steam trains. For example, the express would rattle through Helen's Bay station at 50 mph before, in his words, being extended over the Crawfordsburn viaduct as the half mile bank (i.e. rise) steepened from 1/107 to 1/70. 60 mph was very rare indeed, even with a non-stop train on the down direction, though coming back to Belfast, in the pre-UTA days, BCDR drivers might take the embankment approach down to Holywood at 60 mph, notwithstanding the overall speed limit being 5 mph less. Times in this era ranged from 20 minutes for a non-stop train through to those outside the peak hours which stopped everywhere taking around 33 minutes for the full journey.

He notes that in the BCDR days, departures from Bangor were often at 15 minutes or 45 minutes past the hour. In the last full year of steam, 1952, no less than 38 trains were run in each direction on a weekday, as well as services from Belfast to Holywood and a couple more going as far as Helen's Bay only.

Above left: Engine No 22, 4-6-4 built in 1920, approaching Bangor, 1937, courtesy of Charles Friel
Above right: Print of the Beyer Peacock Baltic Class, courtesy of Edythe Kennedy

Arnold had no hesitation, in his book *Steam over Belfast Lough*, in describing the triumphs and foibles of the drivers and their colleagues, mostly with affection and respect. However, he was hardly tactful in referring to one fireman's '*long scrawny neck adorned with carbuncles and boils*'.

While Baltic No 22 was kept back with an eye to potential preservation at the Belfast Transport Museum, all were auctioned for scrap in 1956.

The BCDR's steam story comes close to its end with a dock-side shunter (No 29), and three 4-4-2 tank engines, the design of which owed a good deal to JL Crosthwait. (Again Beyer Peacock submitted the successful tender.) The last of these did not arrive until early 1945 when it was put straight on to hauling Bangor business expresses.

To complete the picture, brief reference should be made to the diesel-electric locomotives, which the BCDR was one of the first to operate in these islands, especially on a passenger service. No D1 was procured from Harland and Wolff, in 1933, at a cost just over £4,000, with a second ordered four years later from the same firm which had her trial run to Bangor on 24 May that year. According to Coakham, there were a number of both teething and subsequent mechanical troubles, although management estimated a significant saving in annual running costs over steam locomotion. Curiously the second, and ostensibly more developed of the two, gave

the more trouble. It was returned to Harland and Wolff in 1944 in return for a compensatory cheque from the shipyard company. (Interestingly, Ian Sinclair notes that this second one, No 28, later went to the NCC/UTA before ending her days as station pilot at Great Victoria Street. She was not scrapped until 1973 – the last BCDR loco in service – so whatever the reliability problems in BCDR days, she seems to have improved with age!)

The UTA management did allocate three of their 2-6-4 'Mogul tank' engines (which were also nicknamed 'Jeeps') which worked on the Bangor line for a few years, before being replaced by diesel traction, as the following section relates.

Casserley records that right to the end of steam working, the BCDR maintained the excellent practice of allocating two pairs of drivers and firemen permanently to each engine. In his view this resulted in much rivalry between the various teams in keeping their charges well up to scratch, and the engines usually presented a very well-kept appearance.

It should be recorded here that when the UTA took over the BCDR stock, 200 was added to the original number allocated to each locomotive, (thus for example No. 23 became No. 223) as can be seen in a number of the illustrations both in this chapter and elsewhere in the book. The UTA also sent several sets of carriages which brought previously un-experienced comfort to the Bangor line. They ran in sets of eight carriages and were often split into 4-coach rakes for the lighter services.

Above left: BCDR Diesel D1, built in 1933 by Harland and Wolff, at Ballynahinch, Desmond Coakham, courtesy of Andrew Crockart
Above top right: WT Class Engine No 10, 2-6-4, at Carnalea, March 1951; (this only operated on the Bangor line for two years under the UTA), EM Patterson, courtesy of Charles Friel
Above bottom right: UTA MED on trial at Bangor January 1953, EM Patterson, courtesy of Charles Friel

The Multi-Engine Diesels and their Successors

After the steam era, the Bangor line was famous in the 1950s for initiating the use of Multi-Engine Diesel (MED) trains, some years ahead of their consideration in Great Britain.

This was an initiative of the Ulster Transport Authority (UTA), aimed at improving the railway's economic position. The Bangor branch, now devoid of goods services but, retaining heavy passenger traffic, was considered the ideal line on which to try out the idea.

Colm Flanagan observes that this was a very imaginative approach by those running the local railways to sustain the viability of the system, given the Government's unwillingness to provide any investment at that time. He would go so far as to say that for a period Northern Ireland was a world leader in this technology. Had it not been for the diesels and their comparative success, it was more likely the system would have been closed.

The first trials were with borrowed Great Northern Railway railcars, following which the UTA constructed an experimental three-coach diesel railcar in 1950-51. According to Coakham, the two power cars, Nos 6 and 7, had AEC engines slung under NCC 1930s stock, remodelled internally, with no Second class. Curiously, Nos 6 and 7 ran with an intermediate steam-age carriage. They went into service in August 1951.

Following the success of their AEC railcar, the UTA further developed the concept and brought into service in 1952 its prototype MED, this time using Leyland engines. In addition power-operated sliding doors were fitted – another first for the Bangor line and indeed unique in the British Isles at that time. Ian Sinclair explains that the significant difference between the MEDs and the earlier AEC railcar was that trains could be coupled together with up to four power cars plus unpowered trailers and all the engines be controlled from any of the driver's cabs. This was a first, probably in the world, and is a feature of all diesel railcars today.

The UTA built a further 14 similar three-car trains during 1952 and 1953, so that by the end of 1953, all services on the Bangor line were covered by railcars. Speeds and timings on the line showed an immediate improvement, (although the early MEDs still struggled to crest the bank out of Holywood above 30mph). It was the first line in the British Isles to be completely dieselised.

The late Bill McAfee, who became the UTA's Chief Mechanical Engineer, told Sinclair that the development of the MEDs was a continuation of the pioneering work done by the NCC's engineers at York Road in the 1930s and that engineers came across from British Railways to look at the MEDs. These were then used as a model for the "Diesel Multiple Units" (DMUs) built for BR in its modernisation programme of the mid-1950s.

Northern Ireland was leading the world in diesel railcars at this time!

There was first-class accommodation behind the driver, and then open plan seating for third class – second class notionally being phased out, as the train sets were introduced. Coakham does record that for any passenger 6 feet tall or more, the seat spacing in third class was akin to torture. The MEDs were built at the UTA's Duncrue Street works.

In 1956 the engines were upgraded, thus allowing an additional trailer in each set. The interiors were however fitted out in comparatively Spartan style, rather like bus seats of the era.

Above left: Driver Walter Geary in MED cab at Bangor, January 1953, EM Patterson, courtesy of Charles Friel
Above right: UTA Workshops at Duncrue Street, July 1949, courtesy of Roy McComb

The MEDs ran on the Bangor line up to the late 1970s, being replaced with diesel-electric railcars, class 80, once the new connection across the river Lagan had been made with the rest of the system in Northern Ireland, via Central Station. The out of service MEDs were initially taken to the old Nutts Corner airfield, where some served as sheds for a couple of years, and were then interred in the flooded Crosshill Quarry near Crumlin. One major flaw that had been discovered was the use of blue asbestos insulation in the engine sections (and perhaps elsewhere), which raised significant health issues for staff working on the MEDs and some of the later railcars used elsewhere in the system.

The author remembers talking to the late George Smyth who lived beside the station in Helen's Bay, who had been Works Manager at York Road and then at Queen's Quay, after 40 years in the business. He had pointed to a number of his former colleagues who had been working on the railcars at York Road and had sadly developed ill-health as a consequence in their later years. George also told how on a few occasions some officials came over from BR, later in the 1950s, and said 'Oh, you have the same type of trains as us'. George replied 'No, you have the same type as us, we had them first!'

Further to the class 80, a number of 450 class units were built in the mid-1980s on British Rail Mk 1 coach under-frames, reusing engines from the previous class 70 units. Finally, in 2004/05 the service to Bangor was the first line in Northern Ireland to benefit from the arrival of the Spanish-built CAF diesel multiple units which provided a new level of comfort and safety.

Rolling Stock

It would be wrong to gloss over rolling stock entirely. However it is a subject that usually excites little enthusiasm, saved from the most devoted aficionados. One factor which is striking, though not surprising given the shortage of funds from which the company running the Bangor line for most of its private sector existence suffered, is the old-fashioned nature of the carriages, with correspondingly less by way of modern safety features.

The BCDR placed its first order for coaches (with four wheels only and four or five compartments internally) with Joseph Wright of London who was about to move to Birmingham where the carriages were constructed.

Coakham cites a lovely report by a Dublin-based locomotive superintendent in 1876 who examined the four first class carriages of this era which the BCDR were offering for sale; he found that:

> 'They are a very old type, small size and very low roofs, so passengers must take off their hats or stoop well down when they enter the carriages.'

Initially guards and breaksman travelled outside, though in January 1855 it was decided to dispense with 'the breaksman on the Holywood line', a carriage having been altered to allow the guard to operate an internal handbrake. (Coakham reminds one that 'break' was the original, correct spelling, as the purpose was to break the speed of a vehicle.)

In June 1863, the BCDR Manager estimated that four Firsts, two composites, three Seconds and two break vans would be required to work the Bangor line. (A composite carriage has compartments of more than one class.) A year later a contract was placed with the Railway Carriage Company of Oldbury for eight composites and two passenger vans. A trial run revealed that the 'birdcage' lookouts (on top of the roof) fouled some of the over bridges on the BHBR. Once the Bangor line was opened, it was found that the BCDR had considerably underestimated the demand for carriages. By 1867, the BHBR had the use of a further 50 coaches, nearly all by courtesy of the Midland Wagon Company. (One of the Oldbury passenger vans went, still with its birdcage roof, to become the office of the 'smallest of small' stations at Carnalea.)

The BHBR carriages were refurbished as soon as the line passed into BCDR ownership. This was preferred to the purchase of new rolling stock, even though BHBR second class carriages were 'bitterly complained of, being most uncomfortably narrow in the seats'. Joseph Tatlow was critical of the condition of the carriages in 1885:

> 'Many were in a sorry condition, particularly those which had been taken over with the Holywood and Bangor Railway.'

He also noted that while first and second class accommodation represented over 50% of the total capacity, no less than 66% of the passengers travelled Third Class. The first six-wheelers were ordered in 1886. Both these and some others built two years later for the third class were still in day-to-day use until taken over by the UTA and scrapped in 1951.

In 1889 consideration was given to acquiring a State Carriage. Tatlow opined that as the distances were so short, he did not 'think that lavatory accommodation... is essential'. The carriage was purchased from the Metropolitan C&W Company for the price of £600. It was used for the first time on 21 September 1889, taking the first Marquess of Dufferin and Ava

and his wife to Helen's Bay, where a carriage awaited them for the drive to Clandeboye House.

The Carriage Committee of BCDR Directors concluded in the early 1890s that more modern designs were required. They replaced 30-year-old carriages which had been condemned by the superintendent as 'quite rotten'. The new wood was certainly well preserved – the mahogany for panelling had been stacked and drying for four years prior to construction. It was only three years before the end of the 19th century that the first bogie carriages were acquired.

The Royal Saloon was acquired in 1897 for the tour of Ireland carried out by the Duke and Duchess of York (later King George and Queen Mary). The *Belfast News Letter* waxed lyrical about its interior decor for its second Royal usage, to Bangor in July 1903. There were rose-pink Axminster carpets, the six easy chairs were covered with French striped green silk, and the furniture included two Sheraton tables. The 'ladies' boudoir' was upholstered in rich gold freeze velvet and the smoking room retained its crimson morocco. (It will be recalled that after the First World War, it was recycled for the Golfers' Saloon. It also served, according to the late Michael Williams, a pupil of Rockport School in the late 1920s (and later Deputy Headmaster), as the carriage of choice for boarders travelling to the school at the start of term, which delighted the boys as they could sit around the tables and play cards! They disembarked at Craigavad and walked to the school whilst a horse and cart came from the school to collect their luggage.) The coach body is at Downpatrick.

By 1903, carriages – of all classes, though still six-wheelers – were being constructed in the BCDR's own Queen's Quay workshops. These featured regularly on the Bangor line. In 1920 JL Crosthwait was asked to submit a sketch for a bogie carriage with lavatories. The Board was prepared to entertain just two of these for the long journeys to Castlewellan and Donaghadee.

In terms of comfort and ornamentation, by 1893, horse hair had been replaced in second-class, while third class seating remained bare wood until 1905. Photographs in first class compartments were introduced, at Joseph Tatlow's suggestion, in 1886. 20 years later they made their appearance in second-class, along with mirrors. Further class discrimination was entertained when the no spitting injunction was introduced, as this was never provided in first class accommodation! This originated from a request by the National Association for the Prevention of Consumption (Ulster Branch) in 1901. Interestingly, until the 1930s, on the BCDR, it was normal to regard compartments as non-smoking unless labelled 'smoking'. Oil lamps provided illumination for the first decades, though Pope's gas lighting was introduced in the 1890s. Electric lighting

did not appear until after the First World War. Individual hot water foot warmers were supplied by the 1890s, though the first use of steam heating does not appear until 1919. By the time of the 1905 Rule Book, conventional alarms which acted on the vacuum brake had been introduced.

The BCDR regular practice, where possible, was to separate third class from first class by interposing second class accommodation, either in the form of individual coaches or composites.

In 1938 two new bogie carriages arrived on the Bangor line. While the company tried to purchase some more, this was not possible in war time, so it made do with acquiring four, much older, reconditioned bogie carriages from the NCC in 1943.

As Victor Corrie has observed, with a few exceptions (primarily the Baltics and these bogie coaches), trains on the BCDR at the end of the Second World War looked much the same as they had at the end of the First. Certainly six-wheelers still constituted the vast majority of the passenger accommodation. Denis Grimshaw observes that the BCDR liked to maximise the numbers accommodated in a six-wheeler. Coakham records that between 1920 and 1923 the BCDR built at the Queen's Quay carriage workshop 14 third class six-wheelers, all with seven compartments

Above left: Interior of the BCDR Royal Saloon, courtesy of the BCDR Museum Trust
Above right: Bangor Station, August 1950, with UTA No 218 arriving: note the six-wheeler coaches, HB Priestley, courtesy of Charles Friel

UTA Carriage Workshop, with Staff, courtesy of Roy McComb

per carriage, rather than the more usual six or less. This extension of the body beyond the wheelbase, added to the rocking sensation when travelling on the Bangor and other BCDR lines.

Roy McComb worked as a coach-trimmer for the UTA, serving a five-year apprenticeship from 1953. He recalls that on occasion, he and his colleagues would work on refurbishing a carriage or a compartment, while it was travelling on the Bangor line. This would involve covering the seat or redoing the floor.

The non-passenger accommodation on the line is also of interest.

The first horse boxes were acquired by the BCDR as early as 1858, with the stock steadily increasing thereafter up to 1916 to meet the demands of the hunting and racing fraternity. The standard 4-wheeled horsebox, such as the one illustrated, had three stalls for horses in the middle with a compartment at one end for the accompanying groom(s) and another compartment at the other end for saddles and other kit. As noted elsewhere, they were kept quite busy on the Bangor line.

For the first 18 months, the Holywood line had no goods traffic. Then in autumn 1849, the Board concluded they were missing valuable business. Accordingly they instructed John Godwin to act, and he swiftly obtained a quotation from Thomas Firth, the Belfast coachbuilder, for cattle and open wagons. Coakham records that Thomas Firth became the BCDR locomotive superintendent in 1854, so presumably the range of wagons he supplied had given satisfaction. By 1865, the BCDR had just on 180 assorted wagons in use across its system.

Learning this lesson, ten open wagons were ordered from the Rail Carriage Company, in Oldbury, for the opening of the Belfast, Holywood and Bangor line, though they were always BCDR's stock. When the BCDR took over the Bangor line in September 1884, this had grown to a total of 17 wagons.

By this time much of the original stock was becoming decrepit, and Berkeley Deane Wise, the engineer, was permitted to purchase at auction 29 wagons from the Londonderry and Lough Swilly railway which had changed the gauge on its line. By the mid-1880s, there were nearly 400 BCDR wagons. (Ballast wagons were used to carry the materials to repair the permanent way.) His successor, Culverwell, was authorised to purchase a proper six wheeler ballast wagon – elsewhere this book records the sad fate of a milesman who was thrown off a make-do ballast wagon in 1882.

In the 1920s, JL Crosthwait gained permission for the construction of nine rail-carrying wagons, to his own design. However, from then on, there was a serious decline in the company's goods traffic, with little incentive or indeed spare cash to modernise the stock. When the BCDR was taken over by the UTA in 1948, some of the trucks had been built in the 19th century, and the average age of passenger brake vans was over 60 years.

Above: BCDR Horse Box, Desmond Coakham, courtesy of Andrew Crockart

Chapter 10

Signalling

Beginnings

Signalling is something that the travelling public usually take for granted, that is until something goes wrong. Yet it is a crucial part of the operation of any railway line, and much is due to the successive generations of signal engineers and signalmen who have striven to ensure a safe and timely service.

Again, in this chapter, the author is indebted to Desmond Coakham's research, as well as to Richard Whitford's expertise. Signalling uses terminology that can readily baffle the layperson.

Coakham recounts that 'policemen' were among the early employees of the company, when there were very few signals to operate and much walking between points at the Belfast terminus.

The earliest signals were of the semaphore type, and in 1852 the BCDR agreed terms with the Magnetic Telegraph Company for the use of two wires, for the transmission of the signal control systems along the route.

There were no signal cabins in the very early days. The BCDR minutes record a Board decision:

'to enquire if any sentry boxes are for sale at the Barracks, and if not to get estimate for providing 12 boxes for the switchmen.'

At Ballynahinch Junction, the employee who looked after the water tank was required to be pointsman also and *'must have the switch lever in his hand as each train approached the station'*. A derailment there in 1885 seems to have been caused as a consequence of the inability of any man to hold a pair of points with a long train passing at a speed of 25 mph.

Berkeley Deane Wise patented his train staff in 1886, being a variation on the 'staff and ticket' system that permitted two or more trains to pass in the same direction between two stations on the single line, the last one carrying the staff and each of the others in possession of a ticket declaring that the staff had been seen. (Wise devised metal tickets, inserted in the

end of the staff and released only by the stationmaster at the starting end of the section.)

In August 1887 Joseph Tatlow recommended the staff be used between Holywood and Craigavad. Wise's staff was also ordered for Helen's Bay, being extended to Bangor by 1891.

Following the Armagh disaster of 12 June 1889 in which 88 persons lost their life, block working and continuous brakes for passenger trains became statutory obligations under the Regulation of Railways Act which had been speedily passed in the same year. This required installation of these systems, as well as that of signal and point interlocking. (Had the trains concerned in the Armagh accident been fitted with continuous brakes,

it is highly unlikely that either part would have broken loose and run so far. Moreover, if the line had been operated on the absolute block system, it is unlikely that the following passenger train would have been allowed to leave Armagh until the section occupied by the special Sunday school excursion train had been signalled clear.)

The need to keep signalling equipment up to date could never be ignored. For example, Culverwell advised the BCDR Board in December 1916:

'The signal frame at Holywood is the oldest one on the line and consists of 19 levers…. an up-to-date arrangement would require about 40 levers… most of the material… and all the levers will be from the former Belfast frame.'

The signal gantry and signal cabin at Queen's Quay were the largest in Ireland! There were at one time no fewer than nine signal cabins

Above: Craigavad Signal Cabin, McCutcheon Collection, NIEA

joiner) at each end. An electric current was applied to the rails at one end (on much of the Bangor line batteries were used in these early days) and this energised a relay at the other end of the section. When a train entered the section, the circuit was shorted out through the wheels and axles and the relay "dropped". This was a fail-safe arrangement because if a rail broke or the power supply was lost, the relay would again drop as though the section was occupied by a train.

Even on this issue the BCDR had to be different! To distinguish these automatic upper quadrant signals, which unlike the upper quadrant signals used at Larne Harbour or in Great Britain, used standard lower quadrant arms but with the red and green lenses reversed, the flat outer end of the arm was cut to a point.

Automatic signalling between Ballymacarrett Junction and Holywood came into operation in November 1926. Coakham records that this is where the 'stop and proceed' practice began:

'Working of Caution Signals: signalman must stop train two minutes before using signal. Trains must wait two minutes at Stop signals before proceeding cautiously.'

The following month the required waiting was increased to four minutes in falling snow and fog. (This practice was at the heart of the disastrous Ballymacarrett crash in 1945.)

The Bangor line was one of the first to install automatic signalling from 1926 onwards. This was taken on to the Holywood to Bangor West section around 1932, the part from Craigavad being controlled from the Bangor station signal cabin.

The BCDR decided for most of this section on the use of the 'Banner' signal devised by WR Sykes Ltd., which had been in use elsewhere for some years. Adopting the classic BCDR make do and mend approach, the

from Queen's Quay to Bangor, including Craigavad, Helen's Bay and Carnalea on the stretch from Holywood. (This facilitated trains terminating at the first two of those stations.) Hence the decision to reduce the number, as an economy measure, by introducing automatic signalling.

As we shall see later on, BCDR management were clearly not averse to re-using redundant equipment. Following further discussions, a grand five-arm shunting signal was erected at Holywood.

Automation

In 1925 the lower quadrant semaphores at Tillysburn were converted to upper quadrant and electric motors fitted, allowing them to be remotely controlled from the signal box at Sydenham, and Tillysburn box closed.

In 1926 the signals at Sydenham were similarly modified but this time they, and the signals at Tillysburn, were converted to fully automatic control (and Sydenham box closed), being worked by "track circuits". The track circuit is an arrangement whereby the sections of track are electrically isolated from each other, in those days by using a wooden fishplate (rail

Above top left: Carnalea Signal Cabin, July 1967, EM Patterson, courtesy of Charles Friel. Above bottom left: BCDR Ticket permitting the train to proceed, courtesy of James Nicholas Swan at Tickets Please. Above right: Approaching Holywood Station, July 1965, EM Patterson, courtesy of Charles Friel.

engineer selected spare signal posts, made out of either lattice iron or timber for suitable locations between Cultra and Bangor. A trial automatic Banner signal was erected for testing at Craigavad. No semaphore signals were used thereafter for the main running signals although semaphores were retained to control shunting and wrong-line working. (At Helen's Bay and Craigavad there were also full-size "wrong line" starter signals at the Belfast ends of the down platforms to facilitate trains from Belfast which terminated there. In addition, both stations had several miniature "dwarf" semaphore signals for shunting purposes, mainly in and out of the goods sidings. Holywood also had a "wrong line" semaphore starter on the down platform and would have had a number of other semaphores, dwarf and possibly also full-size, to control shunting movements, access in and out of the "bay" platform and the goods yard.)

The introduction of the Banner signals allowed a third signal box, Carnalea, to be closed and allowed Holywood, Craigavad and Helen's Bay boxes normally to be left "switched out", with the Banner signals at those stations then working fully automatically, or "switched in" as required for shunting or trains terminating in which case the signalman worked them like any semaphore signal. An A appeared in a small window on the signal to indicate if it was under automatic control.

The Banner signals were circular in which an arm swung through 45 degrees. They worked automatically, though the 'Down and Up Homes and Starters' at Holywood, Craigavad and Helen's Bay could be manually controlled by levers in the respective signal cabins. (Richard Whitford notes that Banner signals were more normally used in Britain for repeater rather than main signals.)

It may be worth adding for completeness that by the 1930s, normal practice would have been to use colour light signals as automatic signals. However they required powerful bulbs to be seen in daylight or times of poor visibility and this necessitated a mains power supply. It is understood that Banner signals were selected as much of the line beyond Holywood was remote from a mains supply and they could be operated by battery.

On the Bangor line, the Banner signals were normally "on", ie: at red or "stop". They were "approach controlled" which meant that when a train entered the section ahead of the signal, if the section beyond the signal was clear it would switch to an "off" or "go" indication. This was because the signal was worked by an electro-magnet which only drew current when the signal was "off", so this saved on battery power.

In the Second World War, one BCDR signalman never showed up for his shift – he had been killed 100 yards short of the signal box by a German bomb dropped in the 1941 Blitz on Belfast.

One of the improvements made in the wake of the 1945 Ballymacarrett crash was the installation of telephones at key signals, communicating with Bangor and Ballymacarrett Junction signal boxes. Illuminated panels were also then provided in these cabins to indicate the position of trains on the line. "P" sign signals were also added to the automatic signals; if a driver phoned in from a signal at "stop", if the section ahead was clear the signalman would switch on a light in the "P" sign signal (a black P on an orange background) to give the driver permission to proceed at caution.

Written guidance was regularly issued from headquarters. One such was the UTA Notice No 64 issued on 24 April 1959. It provides a good description of the system then in use:

'The working of trains on the section between Ballymacarrett Junction and Bangor is governed by automatic signals with the provision at Holywood, Craigavad and Helen's Bay to operate the running line stop signals manually if necessary…

Above left: Banner Signal outside Carnalea, December 1952, EM Patterson, courtesy of Charles Friel
Right: Extract from UTA Signalling Guidance on Single Line working Helen's Bay/Bangor

Automatic signals and semi-automatic signals not being worked manually are identified by an 'A' sign.

Semi-automatic signals are those which normally work automatically but may, when necessary, be worked manually, in which case the 'A' sign does not appear.

Manually worked signals (in addition to those referred to in the preceding paragraph) are provided at (a) Ballymacarrett Junction and Bangor to control entrance to and departure from the section governed by automatic signals, (b) at Holywood and Helen's Bay for up trains leaving the down platforms and (c) at Sydenham level crossing to indicate the position of the gates.

The automatic signalling was renewed in stages in the 1970s by colour lights with the last semaphores, in Bangor, being replaced in 1998.

The last signal cabin on the line, at Bangor, which had been designed by Culverwell, was closed in 1988. It was finally demolished in 1995, just short of its centenary. No trace remains.

Some Personal Recollections

Richard Whitford served as one of the last signalmen in the cabin at Bangor station, before he became station inspector. The photograph vividly shows the working interior.

The signal frame in Bangor had come from Magherafelt where it was no longer needed after 1950, although at that station there would have been only something like 10 train movements a day, compared to 50 or 60 daily in Bangor. (The frame is now in use on the heritage line at Downpatrick. It must be most unusual if not unique for being used at three separate locations.)

The shifts for a signalman were long, from 6 am in the morning until 2 pm, and then from 2 pm until midnight. In the latter years of the cabin's operation, no relief was provided during a shift. The first train out from Bangor would leave at 6.50am in the morning, but often before then there would be shunting in the station area.

Signalmen would be provided with a copy of the 'working timetable' – this was very different to the version made available to the public, including a wide range of additional information, such as the goods trains, lists of speed restrictions, shunting arrangements etc.

Signalmen had considerable authority and discretion. For example a train from Belfast to Bangor could be stopped at Craigavad or Helen's Bay if operationally this was required.

Above left: *Approaching Bangor Station, McCutcheon Collection, NIEA*
Right: *Helen's Bay Banner and Siding Semaphore Signals, Desmond Coakham, courtesy of Andrew Crockart*

Richard recalls that one of the pitfalls for which signalmen had to be ready was the occasional landslide or tree fall around Cultra, and on toward Marino.

Up to the mid-1960s there were regular summer excursions to Bangor via the GNR from places as far afield as Monaghan, Cavan and Strabane, in addition to the occasional Dublin excursion. Indeed from 1958 until the line was broken at Middlepath Street in 1965, Bangor had two Sunday School excursions every Saturday, between mid-May and the end of June, from Portadown. Each train was of eight carriages. The Sunday Schools were mostly in the Portadown and Lurgan areas but they came, too, from Dungannon and Annaghmore or from Poyntzpass and Scarva. Fitting them into the normal busy operating schedule at Bangor could be a particularly tricky challenge, as Coakham records.

Above left: *Bangor Signal Cabin, 22 March 1980, with the 9.50 am ex-Central arriving at Bangor, courtesy of Richard Whitford.*
Above right: *Inside Bangor Signal Cabin, on an authorised visit, December 1960, courtesy of Richard Whitford.*

Chapter 11

Accidents and Attempted Murder

Introduction

While it may appear rather ghoulish to rehearse a list of accidents that resulted in personal tragedies, research into the pages of the *County Down Spectator* for the years from 1915 to around 1930 records a depressingly large number of fatalities. Nearly all would strike the modern reader as needless. Some were amongst railway staff, but the majority concerned passengers. For no obvious reason, in this particular period, Helen's Bay station was clearly a black spot.

Apart from the accidents, there is also a grisly attempted murder.

So far as it aids the narrative, the accounts are drawn directly from the *Spectator*. The illustrations in this chapter have been deliberately chosen for their context, rather than as specific to the incidents, as has the historical period selected for inclusion on this topic.

Accidents

Helen's Bay, October 1915:
This has a feature that is common – the assistance given by other passengers, in this case a member of a well-known local family and two soldiers based at Grey Point Fort.

'At the Bangor Hospital on Saturday morning John McClure, 13 Chobham Street, Belfast, a guard on the Belfast and County Down Railway, succumbed to the injuries he received at Helen's Bay station on Sunday

Above: Helen's Bay Station, pre-1918

10 October. After the unfortunate man had been removed to hospital it was found necessary to amputate his left arm and leg, and little hope of his recovery was entertained.

Dr Samuel Wallace, Coroner for North Down conducted an inquest on Saturday last.

Samuel Dalzell, porter at Helen's Bay stated that he was present on the 10th inst. when the 9.43 train from Bangor arrived. When the deceased got out of the guard's van he was in the same condition as the witness had always seen him – perfectly sober. As soon as all was clear McClure gave the signal to start, and turned towards his van. As he attempted to board the train he missed his grip and fell between the van and the next carriage. There were two carriages behind the van. The train was in motion before McClure attempted to board it, which was the usual practice. As soon as the witness saw what happened he shouted that the guard had missed his van. The train did not stop. Some soldiers gave assistance in lifting the deceased from the permanent way.

Agnes Beaney, who witnessed the accident, said that deceased evidently missed his hold on the van. She assisted in his removal to the platform, and rendered whatever help she could.

George Rooney, stationmaster, stated that he did not see the deceased until after the accident, as he was at the head of the train. McClure flashed his green light in reply to witness's signal that all was clear.

Dr George Campbell stated that death was due to shock following severe injuries and loss of blood.

Mr W Tughan expressed the sincere sympathy of the railway company for the widow, children and relatives of the unfortunate man. The deceased, he said, was a trusted servant, and the best evidence of his trustworthiness was the fact that he was on his way to promotion. Continuing, Mr Tughan referred to the valuable services rendered by two soldiers, Corporal Thomas Moore and Private Doyle, of Greypoint Fort. In a letter to the railway company, Dr Killen mentioned that he thought these two men had saved the unfortunate guard from immediate death from haemorrhage, as they had already put on a tourniquet when he arrived, and this was so well done that he had not to remove it until the man reached the hospital. The soldiers remained in Bangor till 4 o'clock in the morning to render any aid they could.

Kinnegar Halt with fast train

No 2 SEC
150TH R E

Royal Engineers at Palace Barracks, 1916

The jury returned a verdict of accidental death, attaching no blame to anyone. They added a rider commending the conduct of the two soldiers, and expressing the hope that their conduct would be brought to the notice of the proper authorities.'

While in January 1916 came news of the compensation paid by the BCDR:

'*On October 10th, 1915, John McClure of 13 Chobham Street, Belfast, a guard in the employment of the Belfast and Co. Down Railway Company met with an accident in the course of his duties at Helen's Bay station, as a result of which he died on 16th October. The Co. Down Railway Company had lodged £194 9s 9d in Court in respect of compensation. Mr James Reid B.L. (instructed by Mr John Graham) applied to the Court for apportionment. His Honour apportioned the money as follows: to the 3 children, £25 each and to the widow, Sarah Jane McClure, the balance and interest.'*

Kinnegar August 1916:

This accident occurred outside the Holywood to Bangor stretch of line, but merits inclusion as it is a particularly poignant case.

'*A painful tragedy occurred on Saturday afternoon at the Kinnegar Halt, Holywood when a fifteen year old girl named Annie Dinsdale who resided with her stepmother at 100 Hyndford Street, Beersbridge Road, Belfast was knocked down and killed by a Belfast and Co. Down Railway train. The deceased was crossing the permanent way with the intention of going to the Palace Barracks to see her father – a soldier belonging to the Irish Rifles – and was killed by the 12.45pm train from Bangor to Belfast which was running through from Holywood to Sydenham, the accident taking*

place about 1.05 pm. The train was quickly brought to a standstill and the mangled body was conveyed to the Belfast terminus whence it was removed in the ambulance to the Royal Victoria Hospital.

In the Royal Victoria Hospital, Belfast on Monday, the City Coroner (Dr. James Graham J.P.) held an inquest concerning the death of the girl named Annie Dinsdale.

Herbert Dinsdale, father of the deceased gave evidence of identification and said his daughter was to have met him at the Kinnegar Halt to go with him to Bangor to attend an entertainment for wounded soldiers. A soldier named Thomas McLean stated that he got off the motor train at the Kinnegar Halt on Saturday last. The girl got off the same motor and started to walk across the line at the back of the motor which commenced to move. Witness shouted at her that a train was coming but she went on. When the train passed he noticed the girl lying on the permanent way.

Hugh McIlroy, driver of the train said he blew the engines whistle when the train was entering the Kinnegar Halt. When the motor train was out of the platform the girl came from the back of it and ran along the line upon which the Belfast bound train was travelling. The train was going at a speed of between 25 and 30 miles per hour. Hugh Bell, fireman corroborated.

James Milligan stated that when the girl was removed from the line she was placed in the guards van where she died a few minutes later.

Dr. H. Tweedie said he was of the opinion that death was due to fracture of the skull. The jury returned a verdict of accidental death.'

Crawfordsburn Viaduct September 1918:

This accident took place on the Crawfordsburn viaduct when a company painter tried to evade two trains passing each other on the narrow way there. (It was to be another 60 years before the viaduct was properly widened.)

Above left: *Grey Point Fort as it looked in the early days, reproduced from a print held by NIEA*
Above right: *Crawfordsburn Viaduct, before it was widened, EM Patterson, courtesy of Charles Friel*

'George Davidson, aged 19, Steens Row Belfast, lies in the Royal Victoria Hospital in a critical condition as the result of an accident on Wednesday morning on the Co. Down Railway. Davidson is a painter on the permanent way staff of the Belfast and Co. Down Railway, and he was working at the viaduct at Crawfordsburn between Helen's Bay and Carnalea. He was standing on the left-hand side of the down line, leaning against the parapet as the 8.10 engine from Belfast and the 8.20 express from Bangor were approaching. When the Belfast engine got close to him he made an attempt to cross the line in front of the engine. The engine struck the unfortunate young man and he was knocked against the carriages of the other train which was passing at the moment. Some of the carriages passed over Davidson's leg and the foot was completely severed from the limb. The stationmaster at Helen's Bay, on learning of the accident, immediately summoned medical assistance and later the injured man was conveyed by train to Belfast and later to the hospital. Davidson was severely injured about the head and had a fractured collar bone, while his leg was so badly mutilated as to require amputation.'

Helen's Bay June 1919:

One of the most poignant accidents occurred as a result of a mother's natural instinct to protect her child from apparent danger.

'Helen's Bay Railway Station was the scene of a distressing fatality on Saturday evening, when a Belfast lady, Mrs Alfred Shepherd, 142 Agincourt Avenue met her death under unusual circumstances.
The deceased lady, accompanied by her husband, Mr Alfred Shepherd, their two children and two lady friends had gone to Helen's Bay for an afternoon picnic. After spending a very pleasant time the party returned to Helen's Bay station to entrain for home. While awaiting the incoming train the two children were playing on the platform. Suddenly the little boy went nearer the edge than his mother thought judicious. Realising the perilous position of the lad should a train come along, Mrs Shepherd ran forward to bring him back.

In her anxiety to reach him she herself approached too near the edge, over balanced and fell on the line with a sickening thud. Many bystanders rushed to her assistance but she was seen to be too badly injured. Medical assistance was telephoned for. The train having arrived, the unfortunate lady was placed in a compartment and brought to Holywood, where Mr Fred Hambleton, stationmaster, had promptly secured medical assistance.
Dr R. A. Shekelton met the train, but found that Mrs Shepherd had passed away, her neck having been broken. The doctor travelled on the train to Belfast with the grief-stricken party and at Sydenham, the train was met by Mr W.F. Minnis, traffic superintendent, who also accompanied them to Belfast. The body was then removed to the home which Mrs Shepherd had left so shortly before in the best of health and spirits. The deceased lady's husband is Mr Alfred Shepherd, the well-known member of the Irish Football Association who represents Fermanagh and the Western Division on that Council. His brother, Mr Fred Shepherd, is a prominent member of Linfield Football Club.

Helen's Bay August 1922:

One of the most tragic fatal accidents on the line occurred at Helen's Bay in August 1922, at the most formal level crossing between Holywood and Bangor:

'Two brothers named John and James Ernest Upton, well-known residents of Helen's Bay were killed at Helen's Bay Railway Station on Sunday afternoon under distressing circumstances.
It appears that the brothers who resided with their mother and sisters at Wynard, Helen's Bay, left home about 2 o'clock in the afternoon with the object of travelling by the train leaving Bangor for Belfast at 2.15. Having a few minutes to spare they walked along the road towards Crawfordsburn instead of going into the station direct. Hearing the approach of an engine and presumably believing it to be that of the train they were desirous of catching, both made a hurried attempt to reach the platform by means of the accommodation level crossing adjoining the goods shed. The younger

Above: *The road from the station down to the beach at Helen's Bay*

brother, James Ernest who was leading closely followed by John had almost got clear of the line when a light engine returning from Bangor came along and struck both of them. James Ernest was thrown clear of the track but the other brother was carried for some distance by the engine, the driver of which pulled up as quickly as possible. [A 'light engine' is a locomotive travelling on its own, ie not pulling a train.]

The terrible affair was witnessed by several persons in the station and assistance was promptly forthcoming. John was dead when picked up but the younger brother was still alive and Dr Gibson of Mountpottinger, who was in the vicinity at the time, did all that was possible for the unfortunate man and made arrangements to have him removed to the Royal Victoria Hospital, Belfast by the 2.15 train, but death took place before the train arrived. The bodies were placed in the waiting room of the station by the police and Dr Gibson broke the tragic news to the bereaved relatives.

Mr John Upton was an Excise officer in Belfast and his brother managed a department in Messrs. Greeves' mill. They were very much attached to each other and were exceedingly popular in the Helen's Bay district where the news of the tragedy caused the greatest consternation. The elder brother was aged about 40 and the younger 35. They were unmarried.'

The inquest, which took place in the Helen's Bay station waiting room, was reported at some length. (The illustration shows the old BCDR sign at the former crossing which was still in place until recently.)

'An inquest on the two brothers, John and Jas. Ernest Upton who were killed by a light engine at Helen's Bay Railway Station on Sunday afternoon, was held on Monday in a waiting room at the station by Dr Wallace, coroner for the district.

The first witness was Dr. Wm. Gibson, The Mount, Belfast who gave evidence of identification…The witness then proceeded to relate how he

had been called to the scene of the accident and described the condition in which he found the unfortunate men. In the case of John, death was instantaneous, but the younger brother lived for about fifteen minutes after the accident.

The station master at Helen's Bay, George Rooney, was next examined and said on Sunday at 2.30pm he was standing on the down platform near the edge and saw a light engine coming round the corner from the Bangor direction. About 100 yards from the level crossing witness also saw the two deceased crossing the line. They appeared to have come from the direction of the county road. They ran over in front of the engine which struck them. One was then on the left-hand side of the engine and the other was in the centre of the track. One was knocked clear of the line and the engine went over the other. The driver pulled the engine up at the platform. It was not intended to stop the engine at the platform.

To the Coroner - The signal at the crossing was down to intimate that a train was coming.

To a Juror - Sometimes the signal was down when no trains were coming. The gates did not work the signals.

To the Coroner - He did not know the rights of the public as regarded the crossing.

A Juror suggested that if the public were not supposed to use the crossing the gates should be kept locked.

In reply to Mr Warnock, witness said there was a fence of tall sleepers jutting out from the side of the level crossing and there were usually several wagons near the place where the accident occurred. These would to some extent obstruct the view of a person looking down the line. On the opposite side of the crossing there was a footpath which was occasionally used by persons going to the up platform. About 100 yards from the crossing on the Bangor side there was a curve in the line.

To Mr A.J. Lewis - The engine whistled twice as it approached the level crossing.

Patrick Owens, the driver of the engine said he left Bangor about 2.15pm. When nearing Helen's Bay he saw the two deceased running across the line. Witness was about twenty yards from them when he noticed them.

Above: BCDR Warning Notice at the Helen's Bay level crossing

He sounded his whistle, shut off steam and applied the brakes bringing the engine to a standstill. Before that the engine had struck the men. One was knocked clear and the other went below the engine.

To the coroner - He was going about 35 miles per hour. As he sounded his whistle the deceased did not look up. The Coroner asked if there was another train about this time.

The Stationmaster - Yes at 2.29.

Mr Lewis said the Coroner had put his finger on the crucial point in the case. The deceased mistook the light engine for the train and were rushing to catch it.

Henry Miskimmin, farmer of Helen's Bay who has a right-of-way over the crossing said he was standing at the opposite gate when the deceased came through the other gate. Just then witness heard the engine whistle and the deceased running to get across the line were caught by the engine.

To a Juror - The deceased did not appear to look if the engine was coming but seemed in a hurry and walked with their heads down.

In reply to the Coroner, witness said the crossing gates were supposed to be kept closed and there were notices on them to that effect.

Mr Warnock in his address to the jury said the row of sleepers beside the gate on the down side of the crossing was about seven feet high and obstructed the view in the direction of Bangor and as there were usually several wagons at that place, a person going over the crossing from the county road could not see what was coming until he reached the second line of rails. He suggested that the company should alter that state of affairs.

Mr Lewis, on behalf of the directors and officials of the company, expressed their deepest sorrow at the terrible tragedy and conveyed their earnest sympathy to the relatives of the deceased. He was not personally acquainted with these young men but he had heard a lot about them and of them it might be said: "They were lovely and pleasant in their lives and in death they were not divided." Continuing, he said the crossing in question was solely for the accommodation of the farmers who had land on the other side of the railway from the county road, and the deceased had no business to use it whatever. They were really trespassers. It was quite clear what occurred. Hearing the rattle of the light engine, they imagined the train by which they were about to travel was approaching and they made a rush across with the idea of reaching the platform before it.

The Coroner and jury associated themselves with the expression of sympathy and a verdict of accidental death was returned.'

Helen's Bay October 1927:

The *Spectator* reported another tragedy at Helen's Bay in October 1927:

'Early on Thursday morning the mutilated body of Mrs Elizabeth Vance (55), of Castle Street Antrim, was found on the permanent way close to the platform at Helen's Bay Railway Station. Up till Thursday evening, when the body was identified, mystery surrounded the discovery as the only clue afforded the police was the return half of a rail ticket from Bangor to Belfast bearing Wednesday's date. The body was found after the departure of the train for Belfast.

The hour at which Mrs Vance met her death is uncertain, but from the appearance of the body death must have taken place some hours before discovery. Part of the back of her head had been torn away and the injuries were such that she could not have survived long after the accident.

Helen's Bay police, who were in charge of the affair, got into communication with the Detective Department in Belfast, in an effort to trace the relatives. As well as the ticket which was in Mrs Vance's pockets there was only a small sum of money.

An inquest was held on Thursday afternoon, before the body was identified, when a verdict of death due to laceration of the brain from being accidentally struck by a passing train was returned.

A signalman in the employment of the B.C.D.R. Company said he was on duty from 6 o'clock on Thursday morning and about 6.40 noticed a woman lying between the up rail and the edge of the platform. He saw she was dead and informed the clerk.

The clerk, Arthur Sloan, said that after seeing the body he informed the police.

The stationmaster, George Rooney, said he was on duty up till about 11.35pm on Wednesday. The last down train passed at 11.32 and the last up train at 11.15pm. He did not remember having seen the woman at the station during that day.

Sergeant S. Irvine, of Helen's Bay, gave evidence of examining the body. He informed the police at Belfast and Antrim, but they could not trace the woman up till then.

Medical evidence showed that death was due to laceration of the brain. There were no marks of violence on the body.'

Craigavad December 1927:

In an article headed 'Fatal Step Forward', the Spectator reported the death of a foreman ganger, Robert McClelland, aged 68, between Cultra and Craigavad. (Alfie Beaney recalls another BCDR employee, Tom Stratford, a linesman – or milesman - who lived in the same row at that time.):

'While working on the Belfast and County Down railway line between Cultra and Craigavad on Wednesday morning, Robert McClelland, The Cottages, Craigavad, was instantly killed by an engine coming from the direction of Belfast.

At an inquest held the same evening by Dr S. Wallace, coroner for North Down, District-Inspector S Nevin represented the police.

WJ Cooley, Strand Street, Holywood stated that he was working with the deceased and J Walsh on the line near Cultra when they saw a train coming from Helen's Bay. Walsh and witness moved to the up line side and McClelland went to the down line side. When the train passed McClelland stepped towards the line again to join them and an engine from Belfast coming round a bend on the line knocked him down, killing him instantly.

The driver of the engine, David Roseman, Madrid Street, Belfast, said he left Belfast at 8.12pm and met the up train at Cultra. He noticed two men on the right side of the line and one man on the left. After passing them, his fireman told him he had struck a man and he pulled up.

The fireman said he saw the deceased step forward and be struck by the buffer.

Dr WD Donnan, who examined the deceased, stated that he found him suffering laceration of the brain due to a compound fracture of the skull. The verdict was that deceased died at Ballycultra from injuries caused by being accidentally struck by a light engine whilst at his work. No blame is attached to anyone.

The late Mr McClelland who was 68 years of age, lived with his wife at Craigavad, the family all being married. He was a foreman ganger and been employed with the Belfast and County Down Railway for over 40 years.

He was held in the highest esteem not only by the officials of the railway but also by his workmates. He was a member of the Orange Institution and was one of the oldest members of Glencraig Parish Church.'

Bangor July 1928:

The Spectator recorded the death of a company milesman that summer:

'The circumstances connected with the death of James McMullan of Belfast Road, who was literally cut to pieces by the 7.20am train from Belfast to Bangor on Saturday, were investigated by Dr Wallace, coroner for North Down and a Bangor jury in the Town Hall, Bangor on Saturday afternoon. The jury found a verdict of accidental death from the terrible injuries received and added that they attached no blame to any person.

Head Constable Maguire, Newtownards, examined the witnesses and Mr John McKee, solicitor, was present representing the Belfast and County Down Railway Company. Mr W.F. Minnis, the General Manager was also present.

Patrick McMullan of 16 Belfast Road identified the remains as those of his father, a milesman on the railway, whom, he said left home at 7.30 that morning to go to his work. He was in good health about 50 years of age and was not defective in his hearing.

Thomas Morrow, another milesman on the line, said the deceased was about 200 yards in front of him as they went up the line to their work. Witness was in the hut getting his tools when the 7.30 train from Belfast went past. He heard the whistle sounded at the usual time as the train was coming to the crossing. He heard a grating noise on the rails as if there was something below the wheels. The train did not stop but went on to Bangor. He proceeded up the line to his work, and some 150 yards from the hut he saw the mangled remains of the deceased. He knew the deceased well. He was in good health and witness had no reason to think he deliberately ran into the train.

To the coroner - He walked that way every morning and knew the train was due.

In reply to Mr McKee, Morrow said the hut was on shore side of the line and he had to cross both lines of rails to get across. The train coming to Bangor was on the line of rails next the shore. The deceased, when witness saw him, was on the other lines, and there was no hut and no reason whatever for McMullan to have been crossing the lines at that particular place.

Hugh Skelly, of Solway Street, Belfast, who drove the engine of the 7.20 train, said that when approaching Bangor he saw the deceased about 100 yards away from him walking up the middle of the up-road. The train was on the down line. He had sounded the whistle just previously when he came through Bangor West Halt. He then lost view of the man, and the first indication he had of anything amiss was a "scringing" below the engine. The fireman called "we have killed one of the milesmen" and looking back witness saw the body being shot out between the second and third coach behind the engine. He did not pull up but went on into Bangor, which was quite close and reported to the station master. He could have pulled up in about 200 yards. He was going at a speed of about 25 to 30 miles per hour. The witness added that if the deceased had been on the road the train was on at the time he saw him he could have made an effort to save him.

In reply to Mr McKee, the driver said he was on the shore side of the engine, and after he got a view of the man the front portion of the engine obscured him from witness's view. When he felt the crash he considered that he could go on into Bangor as quickly as he could have stopped.

Bernard Malone, Kilmood St. Belfast, fireman on the engine, said the deceased was about 100 yards from the train walking on the sleepers of the up line when witness first saw him. "When we came within six or seven yards", said the fireman, "I saw him throw himself across the rails in front of the train. He didn't stumble". He did not know the deceased well - he had merely "passed the time of day" to him - and he never observed anything peculiar in his manner. Witness described how he heard a crash and looking back saw the body being thrown out from below the coaches.

In reply to Mr McKee, the witness said the usual place for sounding the whistle was about two hundred yards from the scene of the tragedy at Thompson's Crossing. Malone said he had his eyes on the deceased continuously for about 100 yards and he saw him leave the up line and throw himself in front of the train on the down line.

A juror remarked that the man might have tripped and the Coroner said it was quite possible he might have stumbled.

Dr S.P Rea, Medical Officer of the Bangor Dispensary District, said the body was completely dismembered. Death must have been instantaneous. The cause of death was shock due to injuries.'

Attempted Murder

Bangor Train Outrage August 1922:
The *Spectator* did not spare its readers the grisly details of an attempted murder that occurred on a train from Bangor to Belfast in the summer of 1922. The story was first reported as follows:

'It appears that Mary Anne Sargeant, a domestic servant, whose address is given as College Square North, Belfast, was the victim of a serious attack while travelling by the four o'clock train from Bangor to Belfast on Thursday.

It is alleged that a man said to reside at Spamount Street, Belfast attacked her in the carriage when the train was between Holywood and Sydenham. Guard McCartney heard her screams at Sydenham and rushing to the carriage found her in a state of collapse with blood pouring from her face and throat. A man ran out of the carriage and made to get away, but Guard McCartney pursued him and brought him back.

He was brought in the guard's van to Belfast, where he was handed into custody. The woman was conveyed to the Mater Hospital where she lies in a critical condition.'

The following week revealed more:

'In the Belfast Custody Court on Friday, Edward Thornton, Spamount Street, Belfast, was charged on remand with unlawfully cutting and wounding Mary Anne Sargeant in a train between Bangor and Belfast on 10th inst. On the case being called District Inspector Spiers said the girl was still confined to hospital and her life was not considered out of danger. Mr Roche R.M. remanded the accused for another week.

He [Thornton] was brought in the guards van to Belfast where he was handed into custody. The woman was conveyed to the Mater Hospital, where she still lies in a critical condition.

Miss Sargeant was engaged as a servant at 4 Ballyholme Terrace and was formerly maid to Mrs James Savage, Ballyholme Road. It is supposed that the attack was a sequel to a disappointed love affair.

When the accused was brought before the magistrates last Friday, Detective Constable McLean said that about four o'clock on Thursday afternoon he was on duty at the city terminus of the Belfast and County Down Railway. On the train coming in from Bangor, he, acting on information he received,

went to the guards van and found Special Constables Wm. Robinson and Albert Beattie in charge of the prisoner there. He then went to a carriage at the rear of the train, in which he found the injured woman lying on a seat. Blood was flowing from wounds on her face and neck…he returned to the guards van and took accused into custody on the charge stated. After cautioning prisoner that anything he said might be used against him, prisoner said "I am going to say nothing; that's the truth." Witness on searching the accused, found on him a railway ticket from Bangor to Belfast, a blood-stained handkerchief, two chisels and a razor blade and handle which were separate. A pair of blood-stained gloves were handed to witness by Robert H. Maltman, Rugby Avenue, Belfast, who was a passenger on the train. It is further alleged that the accused had two suits of clothes with him.'

So did the next edition on 9 September, which recorded the court hearing exchanges verbatim, with the victim having recovered sufficiently to give evidence, and counsel for the accused probing the former relationship between the two:

'At the Belfast Custody court today, Edward Thornton, Spamount Street, Belfast, was charged with the attempted murder of Mary Ann Sargeant at Sydenham on the 20th August last…

Guard John McCartan said he was in charge of the train, which left Bangor at four o'clock. Just as the train reached Sydenham he heard screams of "Murder" and looking out along the train he saw a girl attempting to get out of a third class carriage. She was covered with blood and he ran to her assistance. She called to witness "Catch him; don't let him away."

Witness saw the prisoner get out of the train on the permanent way, and run towards Holywood. Witness caught him within 100 yards of where he left the train. When the prisoner alighted, he dropped a small piece of iron (produced).

After the train left Bangor, witness noticed the prisoner looking out at every station, and at Holywood he alighted, but re-joined the train immediately it started getting into the carriage in which the lady was seated.

Mary Ann Sargeant said the accused got into her compartment just as the train was about to start from Holywood station. Witness was alone at the time and was reading a book. He smiled and said "Hello Mary!" He stood up in the carriage and she kept on reading, taking no notice of him. She knew nothing more until she got a blow on the head. She tried to get up to the [emergency] chain but he caught hold of her. She did not know how many blows she got but the last one on the forehead caused her to fall on her face on the floor of the carriage. He stooped down and turned her over. When she opened her eyes he took a razor out of his pocket. He opened it and she sprang at him to get it from him. He tried to get at her throat with it. He had his left arm round her neck and the razor in his right hand. She caught hold of the razor and broke the handle off it, but he kept hold of the blade. She managed to get it off him just as the train stopped.

The District Inspector - Did he make any further attempts with the blade? Yes he did. When the train stopped I shouted "murder."

How long have you known prisoner? - I went with him for about a year and nine months, but I knew him before that.

Mr Graham- I understand you were to be married to him at one time? - I was to be married to him twice over.

The District Inspector - And something arose to put it off?

Mr Graham - The course of true love did not run smooth.

Witness - Not in that case. Continuing she admitted that during the time of their courtship he had written her affectionate letters and she had replied in similar terms to him.

"Wasn't he very fond of you?" queried Mr Graham, and the witness answered "I do not know."

Do you think the love was all on your side? Did he buy you a watch? - Yes

A locket? - Yes.

A ring? - He got paid for the ring.

Has love to hatred turned now with you? - Yes.

District Inspector - No wonder.

Mr Graham- You were very much in love with him at one time, and you have a wee hankering after him yet notwithstanding all?

There was no answer to this but Mr Graham said - Now, do not look so

scornful at me. When were you engaged to be married first? - I cannot mind any dates at all.

Is it about a year ago or more? - Something like that.

Where were you to be married that time - In St Mary's.

Were your names down? - Yes.

And were not you quite happy and contented in the prospect of marrying him? - Yes but his own were against me.

Were not you very fond of each other, or you never would have arranged to marry? - Of course we were.

Had that to be broken through about a year ago owing to his mother having died a short time before? - We were to get married after his mother died, but his sister came between us and said we should wait until the year from his mother's death would be out.

You still continued keeping company with him? - Yes.

When was the second time you were to be married? - February of this year.

And what place did you select this time? - St Mary's

And were the names down again? - Yes; the names were not down the first time.

What was wrong the second time? - He has got to answer for that; not me.

Do you think it was his fault? - Yes

How long were you at Bangor? - Two months.

Above: *Exterior of Sydenham Station, Desmond Coakham, courtesy of Andrew Crockart*

Did he come down to see you? - He did not come down to see me, but to annoy me.

Did you walk out together? - Yes.

And had a happy time? - We were alright.

Did he not see you for five or six weeks before this time he met you on the train? - He had been annoying me anyway.

Did you not want him? - No.

What was the dispute between you? - That is his fault, not mine.

Was not he always very fond of you and wanted to marry you? - Yes.

Do you not know he is still very fond of you? - That will not mend the marks on me.

Medical evidence was given that the girl had severe cuts on her face, one across the neck two inches long, and scratches; incised wounds on the scalp, on the right hand; bruises on the legs, arms and head and two black eyes. The cuts could have been caused by the razor produced and one of the wounds on the forehead could have been caused by the blunt instrument produced.

In reply to Mr Graham the doctor said when she arrived in hospital her life continued to be in danger for four days. Mr Gray said it was a most cowardly assault and returned the accused for trial to the next Commission, refusing bail.'

The final reporting of the trial took place in the first week of December that year; (clearly justice proceeded at a much faster pace than it does nearly one hundred years later):

'Edward Thornton was put forward at the Belfast City Commission on Saturday, before Mr Justice Wilson for sentence for having maliciously wounded a girl named Mary Ann Sargeant in a railway carriage between Holywood and Sydenham on 10th August.

"In my opinion, this is the most serious and awful crime that has come before me at this Commission" said Judge Wilson, in passing sentence of twelve years penal servitude upon the accused.

Mr Fox, B.L. (instructed by Mr J. Graham), addressing the judge on behalf of prisoner, said he recognised that the man had pleaded guilty to a very serious charge, and he appreciated that his Lordship would give him substantial punishment. There were, however, a few matters it was his duty to lay before his Lordship. Prisoner was a bricklayer's labourer and for the past six or seven years had suffered from insomnia and neurasthenia. A few years ago, whilst engaged in his work, he fell from the roof of a house on which he was working and sustained fracture of the skull. Since then, his physical condition had been seriously aggravated. He was very much attached to the young lady, Miss Sargeant and on the day in question, he had no intention of waylaying her but when he entered the railway compartment he was in a most amiable frame of mind and said "Hello Mary!" She spurned him and he became upset and owing to his neurasthenic condition, lost his mental balance with the result that he did the terrible deed to which he had pleaded guilty. The prisoner had a sister who suffered from epilepsy.

His Lordship - I cannot take that into account at all.

Mr Fox said he would explain. That sister had made an attempt on her life and prisoner had taken the razor out of her way. He (counsel) suggested that there was no premeditation on the prisoner's part. There were certificates from two doctors showing he had suffered from insomnia and neurasthenia, was neurotic and easily excited. At the time he was not in normal health and not responsible for his actions.

The father of the prisoner gave evidence as to the weak physical condition of the son, which, he explained, became worse after his mother's death. His daughter suffered from epilepsy and any articles like razors had to be taken "out of her road."

His Lordship said the prisoner had pleaded guilty to an indictment charging him with maliciously wounding Mary Ann Sargeant with intent to do her bodily harm and disfiguring her. In his opinion that was one of the most dreadful crimes that had come before him at that Commission. The prisoner had known the girl for some time and apparently arrangement had been made for their marriage, but she had broken it off and did not want to have anything to do with him at all. She had got into the train not knowing he was on it, and at Holywood, where a stop was made, he waited until people had got out of the compartment and entered it where she was then alone.

She was reading a book and took no notice of him. Prisoner proceeded with some instrument to hit her a blow on the head and knock her down. She attempted to alarm the guard but prisoner prevented her from doing that. The girl said she did not know how many blows she received. Prisoner then stooped over her and took a razor from his pocket, deliberately opened it and she, apparently anticipating what he was going to do, tried to get it away from him. He caught her round the neck with his arm, she grabbed the razor and in the struggle the handle came off. Prisoner still kept the blade and made further attempts to cut her throat and he cut her on the neck and face, she still continuing the struggle. How she was not murdered by the prisoner one could really not understand. When the train arrived at Sydenham station people came to her assistance and prisoner tried to get away by the other side of the train. It was a most serious and awful crime and the least sentence he could impose was penal servitude for twelve years.

On the announcement of the sentence there was a painful sensation in court caused by some relatives of the prisoner.'

(It is interesting to note that current research at Queen's University and elsewhere suggests that a serious blow to the head, such as that suffered by the attacker some years before, can significantly increase the likelihood of the person undertaking violent acts subsequently.)

Chapter 12

The Railway Disaster at Ballymacarrett

Introduction

Some understanding of the disaster at Ballymacarrett may be obtained from a much smaller accident which occurred on 16 July 1938 at Bangor station. The 7 am train from Belfast had just left, and the 7.15 workmen's train was being formed, with an engine running the empty carriages up to the station buffers. Clearly the driver misjudged the length or speed of the train and ran at speed into the buffers.

The incident was recorded in the following week's *County Down Spectator*, under the headline '*Spectacular crash blocks line, coach driven on to platform*'. What would have constituted the rear carriage of the train, an elderly six-wheeler, was in the words of the newspaper '*shorn off at the running board*'. The result was that the entire body of the carriage was driven over the buffers onto the station concourse, leaving just the bowed

and broken chassis on the line. Fortunately, at that time no passengers had yet congregated on the concourse platform, so there were no casualties.

The accident brought out the fragility of the six-wheeler coaching stock, essentially wooden bodies bolted onto a largely wooden chassis. The debris was '*sawn and chopped and pulled bodily off the line*', observed by a significant number of holidaymakers who stopped to watch it being cleared away. The *Spectator* recorded one watcher who was heard to remark '*in 40 or 50 years of travelling to and from Bangor, he had never known such an accident to occur*'.

A few years later, a much more serious accident, involving two early morning BCDR trains heading into Belfast, gave rise to 23 fatalities, in all.

Early in the morning of 10 January 1945, in darkness and fog, a major accident occurred near Ballymacarrett Junction. Although the site of the accident is outside the kernel of this book, the disaster must feature, not least as most of the casualties were Bangorians. It was the second worst accident in Irish Railway history. In addition, the consequences were disastrous for the BCDR.

The Accident

The story of the Ballymacarrett accident may be told largely in the words of the accounts in the *Spectator* of 13 January (which brings out the poignancy of the tragedy occurring in wartime):

'*Bangor's Heavy Death Roll in Train Disaster*

Nineteen men were killed - fourteen from Bangor - and forty-one persons were injured, a number seriously, in an appalling train disaster on the Belfast and County Down Railway Company's Bangor Belfast line on Wednesday morning when the 7.40 am rail car from Holywood crashed into the rear of the 7.10 am workmen's train from Bangor, which had stopped near Ballymacarrett Junction in response to a signal.

The rear carriage of the Bangor train was completely telescoped and the

Above left: Accident at Bangor Station, July 1938, courtesy of the BCDR Museum Trust
Above right: Ballymacarrett Junction, Desmond Coakham, courtesy of Andrew Crockart

dead and injured were trapped amid a mass of wreckage which was crushed into an incredibly small space by the force of the collision. Both trains were crowded with workmen.

The tragedy is the worst in Ulster since the county Armagh railway accident on June 12, 1899, when more than eighty children were killed in a Sunday school excursion.

As the news of the calamity spread in Bangor the general feeling was one of shocked horror, which increased as the day advanced and the magnitude of the disaster was realised. There was acute anxiety on the part of the relatives of those who travelled in the early trains, and the officials at the Bangor terminus were besieged by enquirers.

The Mayor of Bangor (Councillor Walter Malcolm) has opened a fund with a view to alleviating in some measure cases of immediate distress and hardship among the relatives.

The Casualty List

Dead

C.M. Harvey, 2 Hazeldene Park, Bangor,
(assistant works manager at Sirocco)

Herbert J. Keenan, 39 Donaghadeee Road, Bangor
(foreman plater at Harland and Wolff)

Edward Shaw, Andrew's Field, Groomsport

Trevor M. Crosby, 47 Southwell Road, Bangor,
(worked for Belfast Corporation Electricity Department)

Samuel Stewart, 6 Saunders Street, Belfast

Hawthorne C. Bennett, 7 Grovehill Gardens, Bangor
(storeman at Harland and Wolff)

Wm. J. Wallace, 41 Railway View Street, Bangor,
(plumber's helper at Harland and Wolff)

George Dempster, Hall Street, Conlig,
(Iron Foundry, Harland and Wolff)

George Crawford, Ballycopeland, Millisle,

(Northern Ireland Transport Board)

Stephen Lennon, Southwell Road, Bangor,
(boiler-maker at Victoria Engine Works)

George Moore, 29 Windmill Road, Bangor,
(boiler-maker at Harland and Wolff)

J.H. Muir, 4 Summerhill Park, Bangor,
(machinist at Sirocco)

J. Hawthorn, 2 Arthur Street, Conlig,
(woodworker at Harland and Wolff)

Wm. J. Douglas, 44 Seacliffe Road, Bangor,
(pattern-maker at Harland and Wolff)

Peter Byrne, 3 Mount Royal, Bangor and 123 Upper Abbey Street, Dublin
(Harland and Wolff)

Samuel Wilson, 5 Clandeboye Road, Bangor,
(plumber's helper at Harland and Wolff)

J. McMeekin, Demesne Avenue, Bangor, painter

Robert Stitt, 86 Elmwood Drive, Bangor,
(labourer at Harland and Wolff)

Fred Creed, 31 Holborn Avenue, Bangor,
(pattern-maker at Harland and Wolff)

(A further four passengers subsequently died from their injuries. For those listed above, their occupation has been added from subsequent items in the *Spectator*. Several were members of the Home Guard or contributors to the war effort in other ways. Many were recorded as having additional skills or interests, including one who was a drummer in a well-known dance band.)

The crash occurred at a point opposite the Oval football ground, between the Ballymacarrett and Victoria Park halts.

The 7:10 train from Bangor had been stopped at Ballymacarrett halt when the motor train, the motor coach, two other coaches and an engine at the rear crashed into it. It was very dark at the time. There was a terrific crash followed by the noise of splintering woodwork and cries for help.

The heavy motor coach mounted the chassis of the last coach of the Bangor train, ploughed its way along the entire length and wrecked the last two compartments of the next coach. It finally came to rest on the chassis of the demolished end coach.

The body work of the eight compartments of the last coach was reduced to matchwood. Passengers, woodwork and cushions were strewn over the track. The cries of the injured could be heard above the confusion.

Doctors, nurses and rescue parties worked by the light of bus and ambulance headlamps, and of bonfires of wreckage at the side of the track. Passengers who had escaped injury did heroic work in releasing men who had been trapped.

High tributes have been paid in many quarters to the splendid assistance rendered at the scene of the smash by shipyard workers, nurses, police, N.F.S., railway officials and others in removing the dead and extricating the wounded from the debris, and grim scenes were enacted before the exacting task was completed. The staff of the Royal Victoria Hospital, where the casualties were taken, gave efficient and expeditious service, demonstrating once again the adequacy of this great institution to deal with heavy demands on its resources.

An aspect of the tragedy which leaps to the mind is that a large number of the victims were engaged on work of great national importance, so that it may be said truly of them that they, too, have given their lives while contributing, each in his own way, to the preservation of national and international freedom.

Accustomed as we have become to the dread tidings of death and disaster inseparable from war, this calamity on the home front adds its heavy quota to the vast sum total of human sorrow and suffering through which the world is passing.

The Mayor of Bangor, in conveying the sympathy of the citizens to those who have suffered in the catastrophe, has announced the opening of a fund to deal with cases of immediate necessity, and it is gratifying to learn that the response of the public has been prompt and generous. We commend this fund to the thoughtful and generous support of our readers.

It was a grim sight which met the eyes of spectators as daylight grew stronger. The motor coach, which was only slightly damaged at the end, rested drunkenly on the buckled and bent chassis of the coach. The end of the second coach was a mass of splintered wood, iron-work and personal belongings of the injured.

Breakdown workers were sorting out coats, hats and shoes and piling them neatly on the battered roof of one of the carriages at the side of the track. Pathetic relics of the tragedy were workers lunches and bottles of milk - some of them unbroken. A pair of gloves protruded from the heap of debris, and at another point a scarf dangled from the twisted remains of a luggage rack.

James Hewitt, the guard of the Bangor train, received cuts on the face and head, but despite his injuries, he ran along the track and gave warning to a following train.

In an interview he said that his train was three or four minutes late. "At Victoria Park halt about 200 men got out and then approaching Fraser Street halt, the next halt, we found that the Ballymacarrett signal was showing red and we stopped. We were stopped about three or four minutes and I was about to get out of my van to find out what was wrong, when there was a terrific crash and I was thrown headlong. I hit my head against the side of the van. I jumped out and ran back to find that the Holywood motor train had struck us.

When I realised what had occurred I ran back along the track waving my red lamp and put down a number of detonators as a signal to the next Bangor train, which was by then almost due. In the darkness and with the line blocked it would have been a simple matter for it to pile up on the wreckage".'

A later report described some of the actions in Bangor:

'The pathetic scenes at Bangor railway station on Wednesday when the names of the casualties began to come in were described by a member of the railway staff.

'It was a heart-breaking job to have to break the news to the relatives, but it had to be done and we did it as gently as we could', he said. 'The police of Bangor did all they could to help us by advising us as the names were

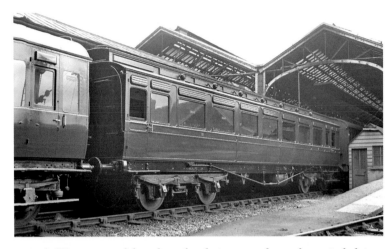

received. We are grateful to them for their sympathy and tact in helping us to handle a difficult situation. The relatives, we are sure, will be grateful too.'

Mr John Todd, a member of the clerical staff at the station, was busy for most of the forenoon in connection with the disaster. When he returned from his lunch the first casualty he received was that of his brother-in-law, George Moore, 29 Windmill Road, who was among the dead.

Mr C.A. Valentine, station master at Bangor, and Mr W. Aicken, assistant station master, called at the homes of the relatives on Wednesday and tendered the deep sympathy of the Railway Company. It added to the poignancy of their mission that in some cases it was the first intimation that the disaster had occurred.

Enquiries at the local police barracks were handled with great consideration and sympathy by the police, for whom the disaster had a personal bearing for reason by the fact that one of those seriously injured and detained in hospital, is James Brown, 19 year old son of Sergeant T.H.E. Brown. He is an apprentice at the Sirocco Works.

A special word of praise is due to the local and city telephone staffs, who were called on to put through numerous calls both from Belfast and Bangor. The operators dealt with the emergency with unvarying understanding and efficiency. Many of those who travelled by the early trains hurried to the telephone to acquaint their friends in Bangor of their welfare. The Post Office telegraph service had also a busy time and rose to the needs of the occasion with their characteristic efficiency. The Bangor Town Hall staff gave able service in dealing with enquiries there. The staff at the 'Spectator' Office were able to acquaint callers with the position as it developed from hour to hour.

Touching references to the railway disaster were made by the Mayor of Bangor (Councillor Walter Malcolm, J.P.) and other members at Tuesday evening's meeting of Bangor Borough Council, and a resolution was placed on record expressing the Council's profound sympathy with those who had been bereaved and the hope that the injured might be granted speedy and complete recovery.

The Mayor said the calamity of the previous Wednesday had cast a gloom over the Borough; they were indeed under the shadow of death. Many of those who lost their lives were engaged on work of national importance. 1945 had been heralded as the year of peace, but those brave men who had been working so industriously towards that end would never hear the peace bells ringing.

The Mayor went on to say that the accident produced wonderful feats of heroism on the part of those who engaged in the work of rescue. He paid tribute, in passing, to those women in the neighbourhood of Ballymacarrett who, without thought of what they might have been sacrificing tore up the linens which they had in their homes in order to place them at the disposal of the injured. Visiting the homes of a number of the bereaved in company with his wife and the town clerk, he was much struck with the heroic bravery of wives and mothers facing an empty and desolate future as the result of the catastrophe. The sister-in-law of one bereaved wife told him there had been so many friends called and they had had so much sympathy shown to them during the past few days that it made them think of the people of Bangor as being one great family. He was touched by that tribute to the prevailing communal spirit.

The Mayor spoke of the appeal he had issued and said it had met with a universal response and he took that opportunity of expressing his thanks to those who had given and would give. He acknowledged the willing service *of the staff in the town clerk's office in dealing with an avalanche of letters and enquiries.'*

The Aftermath

Subsequent actions, to raise funds for the appeal and the formal investigations were also reported in the *Spectator*:

'Capronis announce that, in aid of the Mayor of Bangor's Rail Disaster Fund and with the full co-operation of Bangor Civil Defence Post No. 41, a variety concert will be held in the Grosvenor Hall, Belfast on Monday evening, 29th January at 7:30. Doors will open at 6:30.

A galaxy of Ulster artistes, all of whom are giving their services voluntarily, will contribute to a programme of exceptional merit. To begin with there is the dance orchestra representing the Northern Ireland Musicians' Association of which it may be mentioned, Mr Freddy Creed, one of the victims of the disaster, was a popular member. Individual artistes are James McDowell, tenor; Jackie Wright (comedian), Freddie Sales (comedian), Alfie Donnelly (comedian), Dorothy Beggs (soprano), Billy Brown (accordionist), Holywood and Mitchell (Hawaiian serenaders), Leslie Farr, R.A.F., popular singer from Billy Ternents band; Hazel Bryson, LG.S.M., monologist; Rita Cairns (soprano), Eddie O'Doherty (Londonderry vocalist), Mike Fox (banjoist), Fred McAllister (baritone); The Donavons

(Hill-Billy instrumentalists). Cyril Flenly will compere the show.

Messrs. Caproni in arranging the concert, which is expected to bring in a large amount for the Fund, will have the collaboration of CD Post 41 with a sub-committee consisting of Messrs. T. Henderson, A.R.P. Officer, W. McKelvey, Divisional Warden; and H.T. Page, Senior Warden.

Admission is 3s 6d and 5s and tickets are on general sale in Bangor and Belfast.'

'The inquiry was opened by Mr R.D. Duncan, B.Sc., M.Inst.C.E., Inspector of Railways in Northern Ireland in the Clarence Place Hall, Belfast. After hearing statements he decided to take the evidence in private despite a protest from a solicitor appearing on behalf on some of the next-of-kin.

Mr Duncan said that the inquiry concerned the worst railway accident in Northern Ireland since 1889, thus terminating a period of over 55 years of comparative freedom from mishap. An inquiry such as that was held primarily from the technical aspect in order that the Ministry of Commerce might be advised as to the cause of the accident and of any measures which should be adopted in the interests of public safety to prevent a recurrence. It was in no way a court for the determination of legal responsibility. Witnesses were not examined on oath, nor was he (Mr Duncan) bound by the strict law of evidence. The inquiry was, therefore, in addition to, and independent of, any proceedings before a coroner or magistrate.

Mr Duncan added that he must, therefore, consider whether if he heard in public the statements of some, or all of the men who might be concerned, it would be likely to prejudice them from that point of view. Just as important, the object of hearing the whole, or part, of any evidence in private was to obtain the frankest statements possible from those concerned without their feeling apprehensive that they might be prejudiced at any subsequent court proceedings. Statements on behalf of relatives and the public generally would not normally be permitted, but he did not entirely close the door, provided he was satisfied that the subject matter would assist him in attaining his object.

Above: *Railmotor Interior, Desmond Coakham, courtesy of Andrew Crockart*

Mr James Hurst, chairman of the B. & C.D. Railway said that after so long a period without an accident of that nature occurring on their system, their sorrow was all the more acute, for not since 1871 had a similar type of accident taken place and then two people lost their lives.'

Various other managers then gave evidence on behalf of the Company, including its Engineer, John Crosthwait. This included details on the signalling arrangements which were automatic from Bangor West to Ballymacarrett, but there was a manual signal at Ballymacarrett Halt's outer home signal, and this signal had failed. The signalman had realised this and had left his box in an attempt to hand signal the train but had heard a collision before he could do so.

The position was well summarised by Edward Patterson. The Holywood railmotor had already stopped at the Sydenham automatic stop signal and under the then rules had waited for two minutes before proceeding with caution to Victoria Park Halt where it stopped to set down passengers. It then ran on towards the junction, but the red tail-light of the stationary Bangor train was not visible until the leading coach of the rail motor was only about 30 yards distant.

The BCDR practice of *'stop and proceed'* in which trains halted at automatic stop signals for two minutes and were then permitted to proceed, allied to the fact that the driver was neither required nor able (in the absence of such facilities) to telephone the signalman was in retrospect clearly a highly dangerous procedure. The speed of movement between signals was left to the driver's judgement.

The *Spectator* reported on the case against the driver of the second train. He was:

'Isaac McQuillan (38) of Jocelyn Street, Belfast who had 21 years' service with 2 ¼ years' driving experience. He was controlling the train from the driver's compartment of the rail motor-coach which was leading.

McQuillan appeared at the Belfast Custody Court on a charge of manslaughter of Samuel Wilson, Bangor, one of the 21 persons who lost their lives as a result of the crash.

District-Inspector A.H. Kennedy deposed that when arrested and charged

the accused said: "Everyone knows that the signal arrangement was the cause of the accident".

After a trial lasting four days a jury at Belfast City Commission last Friday night returned a verdict of not guilty against Isaac McQuillan, engine driver, of Jocelyn Street, Belfast, who was charged with the manslaughter of Samuel Wilson, Bangor and he was discharged.

The case arose out of a collision on the Belfast and County Down Railway at Ballymacarrett halt on January 10, when 21 men lost their lives.

The jury considered the evidence for an hour and fifty minutes and announced their verdict shortly after 10pm.

Mr Justice MacDermott after discharging McQuillan, expressed his appreciation of the anxious and careful attention which the jury had given to the case and excused them from further jury service for seven years.'

Various changes in working procedures were at once introduced, with telephones being fitted at signals. Patterson recorded that compensation paid by the BCDR to victims and dependants amounted to £75,000 which proved a massive financial burden on the Company, given that following the end of the War that May, traffic on the railways again reduced significantly.

The subsequent action taken by the Northern Ireland Government is recorded in the chapter on the Post-War Years.

Some Personal Accounts

We do have other accounts of the accident and its impact.

In his *'Reminiscences of Old Bangor'*, Alderman Charles Milligan recalled that his first call that day was to the Royal Victoria Hospital as a blood donor on the emergency list. On his way home, he travelled with the Mayor of Bangor who asked him to arrange a public appeal for funds for the families. They consulted the Belfast Lord Mayor, Sir Crawford McCullagh, a former Helen's Bay resident and commuter on the Bangor line, and it was agreed that Bangor should take the lead, as most of those affected were Bangor people. The Fund raised a considerable sum and was administered by Bangor Town Hall staff.

Sinclair Duncan's father was the BCDR Registrar, at the time. Sinclair

observed that the Company was insured for day-to-day incidents such as trips on a platform, but not for a major accident such as this. As noted elsewhere, the financial consequences were devastating for the Company.

Individuals who travelled on one of the two trains that day were Holywood residents Dennis Ogborn and Georgina McKeown. Dennis remembers how cold and foggy it was. He got onto the crowded train at Holywood for his usual morning journey to the shipyard. There had already been one sudden stop at Kinnegar. Then the train stopped again past Sydenham and there was a huge bang, and he was picked up and thrown violently to the other side of the carriage. He was able to gather himself, and recalls then helping injured passengers, carrying them out from the carriages. It was a ghastly scene.

Georgina recalled being involved in the accident. She said 'We were lucky – we were in the middle of the train.' She also recalled injured passengers crying and pleading 'watch my legs'. She was one of those taken to hospital to be checked over.

RM Arnold was not on the 7.10am train from Bangor on that particular morning, though he often did catch it. He spoke many years later to the driver of the first, 7.10 train who observed that ironically he should not have been stopped at Ballymacarrett outer home signal at all, as he had a clear road at the junction. Arnold records that the railmotor driver McQuillan thereafter had a shed job at York Road.

Above: Sir Crawford McCullagh, Lord Mayor of Belfast, and his wife

Chapter 13
Holywood Station

Initially Holywood was served by a temporary wooden building, when the line opened in August 1848, together with a turntable manufactured at the Falls Foundry in Belfast for a price of £350. The first permanent station house at Holywood was not built until 1850. Sadly what was once quite a major station complex has now been reduced to the bare essentials, with just a few stone walls remaining to bear testimony to the bygone era.

As the BCDR's official architect, Charles Lanyon designed Holywood station. Lanyon had come from England as a young man, married an Irish girl and stayed. In 1835 he had been appointed Surveyor for County Antrim where he was involved in the construction of the Coast Road. As noted in the chapter on Holywood in the mid-19th century, a number of other buildings in the town were also associated with his firm of Lanyon, Lynn and Lanyon.

The original terminus was of course built to serve the Belfast to Holywood line which had opened in August 1848. That was at street level in Redburn Square, adjacent also to Marine Parade. After the building of the line to Bangor, the old station was left on the spur, although services from Belfast that terminated at Holywood continued to use it for some time. As the photograph shows, the original, low-level, tracks were in use as a goods yard in the late 1940s, before the goods service ended in 1950. This area was then used as the bus depot, though it has long since gone, replaced by the dual carriageway.

The original junction between the BCDR and BHBR lines was at the Belfast end of the platform.

The gradients for the line to Bangor required the new tracks for the Belfast, Holywood and Bangor Railway to be at a higher level, so that engines could successfully tackle the bank from Holywood to Marino. A platform was built on the up side of the line, referred to in early days as the 'high level platform'. The BHBR covered its through platform with an interesting timber canopy having an elaborate coffered ceiling and a gable at the Belfast end with the company initials in fretwork (see photograph). (One of these historic monograms, which survived in situ until 1973, is now held by the Transport Museum at Cultra.)

Originally there was just a single track between Belfast and Holywood, though this was eventually doubled before the 1884 takeover of BHBR by the BCDR. In 1886, the station was remodelled by Berkeley Wise. He added the down platform, giving it a segmental section canopy roof in – unattractive – corrugated iron, and built a tall signal cabin at the Bangor end. Unusually (though not uniquely in Northern Ireland, and Holywood was probably the first of this design) the signal cabin included at ground floor level an arch to allow passengers to pass through it to access the platform. Passengers then proceeded down a covered ramp to the subway. The splendid cabin also sported overhanging eaves.

It was at this time that a third line of track was added at the station, providing the facility for engines to run round their carriages if the service

Above top left: The old Holywood Station Sign, Desmond Coakham, courtesy of Andrew Crockart Above left: The BHBR Monogram at Holywood Station, 1963, EM Patterson, courtesy of Charles Friel.
Above right: Holywood Goods Yard, March 1949, Desmond Coakham, courtesy of Andrew Crockart

stopped at Holywood. (It was long enough to hold an entire short push-and-pull train there if need be.)

As noted elsewhere, Holywood gasworks had been built in the 1850s very close to the original railway station. For a long time, the gasworks was a good customer of the BCDR, until in the 1950s gas was piped directly to Holywood from Belfast.

Holywood was unusual in providing the only private siding on the BHBR – to service the gasworks at the Belfast end of the station. Coakham records that coal was delivered from the wagons through shutes in the gasworks wall. In later years, the wagons were worked from Belfast after passenger services had ceased for the night.

The 1886 redevelopment was not the last improvement of the station. The *News Letter* recorded on 25 January 1890 that:

'For some time past the Directors of the County Down Railway have been devoting very considerable attention to the improvement of the several stations along their line. Many of them required modernising, and it is satisfactory to find that by degrees objectionable features are being wiped out and the requirements of the public attended to. Holywood has not escaped their attention. The station there has of late been much improved and the several offices brought together in such a way as to offer the greatest convenience to the officials.'

It is interesting to note that the particular improvements were designed to assist the Company's staff rather than the public. One beneficiary was the Holywood stationmaster, Robert McKee, who had started in the role in 1886, the year the station was extensively remodelled by Berkeley Wise.

The *Belfast Telegraph* reported on 3 January 1911 that Mr McKee had slipped and fallen, hitting his head on the line, while crossing from one platform to another at Holywood. He sustained a bad wound to his head and to one of his legs.

In April 1913 the *Spectator* paid tribute in a front page article following McKee's death:

'By the death of Mr Robert McKee, there has been removed one of the oldest and most trusted servants of the Belfast and County Down Railway Company. Born at Bangor, Mr McKee, as a boy, entered the employment of the line forty-two years ago, being first attached to the station in his native town. At that time, Bangor was not the populous seaside resort it has since become, and the traffic on the railway was just beginning to grow. Assiduous attention to duty – a trait which marked him out all through his long career – brought promotion, and Mr McKee was transferred to Belfast. At first he filled the position of guard, but advancement again awaited him and he was appointed assistant stationmaster at the city terminus. For nine years he faithfully fulfilled his responsible duties until he was transferred to a post of greater importance being sent to Holywood as stationmaster. That is almost twenty-eight years ago and never once in that long period did he fail to act conscientiously towards the company whom he served, while towards the public he always exhibited an unfailing courtesy which made him one of the most popular stationmasters on the line. In Holywood especially he was held in high respect and there his familiar figure will be greatly missed. During his years of service in the Co. Down Company he had seen the railway grow from little beginnings into a prosperous concern, with a network of lines extending all over the County of Down. But he had not only been a witness to its expansion; he was one of those who worked for its success. His heart, indeed, it might be truly said, was in the railway and it is to such devoted employees that the Belfast and County Down Railway Company owes its prominence today.

For some time past Mr McKee had been ailing but he stuck to his post to

Above top left: *Holywood Signal Cabin, Desmond Coakham, courtesy of Andrew Crockart*
Above: *Holywood Station showing the Gasworks, CH Hewison, courtesy of Charles Friel*

the last and died in honourable harness. Only a fortnight ago did he lay down duty for the last time. Mr McKee was not a man who sought publicity and apart from his work he took very little to do with outside affairs. He was, however, a man of deep seated religious conviction, a Unionist whose political faith was staunch and strong, and in the Masonic order, to which he belonged, he was one of the most esteemed members.'

Eleven years later, on 9 February 1924 the retirement of another Holywood stationmaster was likewise recorded in the *Spectator*:

'After forty-five years' service with the Belfast and County Down Railway Company, Mr Fred Hambleton, stationmaster at Holywood retires and goes on to reside at Southsea. Mr Hambleton began as a clerk in the passenger and goods department at Downpatrick at the age of 14 years. He became a telegraphist, was transferred to Belfast and in 1886 was promoted stationmaster at Saintfield. After serving at Crossgar, Knock and Comber, Mr Hambleton went to Holywood in 1913. He is a soldier's son having been born in Bombay in 1854. He is a member of the Church of Ireland and a freemason. Married in 1907 he has one daughter.'

In the 1920s, agreements were reached between the company and two separate coal merchants in Holywood – William Dunwoody and Samuel Kingan. They were permitted to lease coal sheds at Holywood station for the storing of coal which they had purchased and which had been conveyed over the company's lines. (Interestingly on the drawing recording the location of the coal sheds, the road running past the station is described as 'Captain Harrison's Road'.)

Holywood signal cabin was to remain a bastion of manual operation long after November 1932, when automatic signalling of the Bangor line had been completed.

The BCDR's bus garage, when it took on running bus services at Holywood, was beside the up platform.

According to an account in the *Spectator* dated 11 August 1961, when the Queen and Duke of Edinburgh visited Bangor and Holywood, two men were *'perched precariously on top of the railway station roof to get a good view'*.

Unfortunately there was a major fire at Holywood station in August

1965 which probably hastened the demolition by the Ulster Transport Authority (UTA) of much of the station buildings. The fire destroyed the stationmaster's house at the north-eastern end of the original station building. Shortly afterwards the coffered roof of the platform cover was removed by the UTA in what McCutcheon describes as an act of *'wanton vandalism'*. A couple of years later the main station building was finally demolished make way for the new road, although since the fire, the interior had lost much of its historical character. Although the fire destroyed the stationmaster's house and booking office, other buildings survived. Tickets were sold temporarily from a wooden hut on the ramp to the up platform. A new booking office was built a year or two later but with the introduction of conductors on the line in 1969, it was soon out of use. The platform canopies were removed in 1973 as were waiting rooms on the up platform; these were replaced by an open brick shelter. On the down platform, the original waiting room was adapted into an open shelter. Although lying disused since 1969, the main station buildings were not demolished until some re-modelling of the station was carried out in 1988.

The last stationmaster at Holywood was Mr Murtagh. He lived in the station house which was still at that stage part of Redburn Square. Billy McGimpsey was another who worked at Holywood station towards its end.

Norma Cooper remembers that every Sunday night people used to congregate at the ticket office to buy their tickets for the coming week. As she worked for the Ulster Transport Authority, she was allowed to travel for half-fare, subject to the proviso that if a full fare paying person needed a seat, she had to give them hers. She recalls too that you had to show your 'age card' to get a reduced fare. Dennis Ogborn was

Above right: Exterior of Holywood Station, August 1963, showing the gasometer in the background, EM Patterson, courtesy of Charles Friel
Right: Ticket Office at Holywood Station, William McCutcheon, NIEA

another who would go to the station on a Sunday to get the weekly ticket in advance, while Patricia's mother went on her behalf.

There was a much-loved confectionery shop at the station. Dennis remembers the big fire there – '*it was a great place to go on a wet day*'. The shop was run, according to one account, by Miss E Cave from 1910 to 1940, again a remarkable continuity of service.

Richard Whitford recalls, as the rare photographs of the interior suggest, that the inside of the station was dark even in daylight, with long passages.

The original line to Marino from Holywood had both a considerable gradient and a curve, with a 40 mph speed limit for expresses coming from Bangor (which in 1945 was reduced to 30 mph). A section was re-laid in 1971-72 when the dual carriageway bypass was put through Holywood, which necessitated the line being moved out towards the shore. It makes this short section perhaps the most photogenic stretch on the whole line to Bangor.

In March 2011, an attractive mosaic depicting Holywood town, coast, woodland and Cultra, made by a range of Holywood residents and pupils, was erected on one wall of the station.

Left top: The covered Ramp to the Down Platform, Holywood, William McCutcheon. **Left middle:** *The Mosaic at Holywood Station.*
Left bottom: *Holywood Station in August 1963, EM Patterson, courtesy of Charles Friel.* **Right:** *Holywood Station, painted by Norman Whitla, courtesy of the artist*

Chapter 14

Stations Along the Line

Marino Station

We are fortunate to have some of the original legal documents relating to the purchase of the land on which Marino station was built. One dated 10 November 1862 refers to '*conveyance of part of lands of BallyCultra, County Down*'; four parties were involved – Henry Russell, Thomas Greg, the Belfast, Holywood and Bangor Railway Company, and John Edward Koch Esquire (who, as we have seen, was the main contractor responsible for the line).

Thomas Greg (also of Ballymenoch, as we saw earlier) had acquired twelve acres of land in Ballycultra in 1830 by a long lease off Hugh Kennedy and his son John, at an annual payment of 82 pounds. 18 years later Greg granted the land to Henry Russell. Interestingly Greg was paid in 1848 the same sum of £1,800 as that paid by Koch in 1862; moreover the annual rent that the BHBR then paid to the Kennedys was the same as that agreed over thirty years earlier. Koch, who was based at No. 1 Threadneedle Street in London, was buying up the land that the Company needed for the construction of the line to Bangor.

The station was originally opened by 1870, on the Belfast side of the road bridge. A new platform and single-storey station house were then built on the Bangor side of the (Scrabo stone) bridge a few years later.

Following the takeover of the BHBR by the BCDR in 1884, the latter's Manager Joseph Tatlow inspected the stations on the Bangor line. He reported that Marino station which then included both station buildings and a stationmaster's house was '*wretchedly small and inconvenient*'.

One of the best-known stationmasters on the Bangor line was Patrick Dowd (or O'Dowd). He served there for many a year. When the doubling of the line between Holywood and Craigavad was completed in late 1900, Marino station was given waiting rooms, and a booking office and other offices all on the new up platform. The single-storey BHBR station house on the down platform acquired an extra storey and became the stationmaster's house, with a waiting room attached.

In August 1907, according to Keith Haines, the *Belfast Evening Telegraph* visited all the stations between Bangor and Holywood; Dowd was awarded first prize for the appearance of the station, with the newspaper stating that the award was much deserved.

It was also alleged in those days that Marino station won the annual prize for the finest floral display as fresh flowers were despatched from Cultra Manor by the Kennedys just prior to the judging!

On 14 Sept 1918 the *Spectator* had an article announcing the retirement of Mr Dowd:

'Mr P. Dowd better known to the residents and subscribers of Marino as "Paddy" is about to retire after 41 years active service with the Belfast and County Down Railway Company and a total of over 50 years' railway service. Born at Randalstown, he spent his younger days amongst the farms. "Paddy", as he was called, and is to this day, was not content with the life that meant being shut off from the universe and his boyhood's desire was to be in touch with the world and its doings. Commencing his railway career in 1867 with the Northern Railway Company at Carrick Junction, which is now known as Greenisland, he served for a period of almost ten years. An opening which occurred in 1877 for a stationmaster at Marino with the Holywood

Above left: A Postcard of Marino Station, posted in 1922
Above right: Marino Station in 1963, courtesy of Charles Friel

Patrick Dowd, the well-known Stationmaster at Marino Station, courtesy of Tony Merrick

and Bangor Railway Company was offered to Mr Dowd and he commenced duties on 21st May. It was in those days an out-of-the-way country station with a booking-office only, and devoid of its now very fine waiting rooms and other offices, its present picturesque flower beds and its shady bowers. To Mr Dowd must be given the credit for the present pretty little station, in which he took a great pride and succeeded in carrying off the first prize for the best show of blooms on twenty-one occasions between 1886 to 1914.

In 1884 the line was taken over by the Belfast and County Down Railway Company and under the new management Mr Dowd's services were looked upon as indispensable and he has enjoyed the confidence and respect of all those who came in contact with him, from the highest to the lowest and no question ever asked Paddy received an abrupt or discourteous answer. During his forty-one years' service he has never had an accident or mishap at Marino – a fact of which he is proud, and rightly so, considering the number of passengers and trains that must have passed through his hands during what is to many a lifetime. Mr Dowd is still well and hearty and but for that not too welcome friend old age, takes a keen interest in the world's doings. His familiar call will be missed by many who have been in the habit of waiting for his signal to acquaint them of their stopping place. He retires with best wishes of all and the company have unanimously awarded him a pension well worthy of his long service. May he live long to enjoy it and a well-earned rest is the wish of all.'

Years later, the *Spectator* carried a letter from Fred O'Neill, of Oldpark Road, Belfast on 18 January 1958 referring to Paddy O'Dowd – 'a kindly soul and well-beloved of all who travelled to town by way of Marino station'. The letter added an intriguing fact tactfully omitted from the earlier *Spectator* article. Paddy found it difficult to get from the down platform to the up side, and so had made for himself a small ladder. He used to climb down this on one side and carry it over the rails and then climb up on the other side.

It is known that Paddy used to go to Sir Daniel Dixon's (at Ballymenoch House) on Sunday mornings to help the former Lord Mayor of Belfast, who then had a disability, to put on his shoes before he went to church. When asked one day what he was doing, Paddy replied 'I am just going up to shoe the Mayor'! (This Ballymenoch House which dated from the 17th or 18th

centuries burned down in 1913, being rebuilt on a slightly different site by Sir Samuel Kelly.) However Paddy, being that kindly soul, did not 'shoo' away the Holywood Scouts who were said to invade the station property when performing their Scout duties in the area.

The last stationmaster at Marino was Sydney Tedford who was transferred there in October 1945, from the same post at Knock. He continued the tradition of floral expertise, as this photograph of the BCDR Directors' 1947 special first prize certificate for stations and flowerbeds recognises. His daughter, May Anderson, recalls that he grew his own bedding plants, and was particularly skilled with dahlias and chrysanthemums. Sydney started his career with the BCDR as a boy porter at the tender age of 14, shortly after the First World War.

On the platform at Marino station were several splendid, large enamel advertising signs; they promoted Sawer's fish, Faulat's shirts, and Virol. (Faulat's was owned by the Faulkner family who lived nearby.) Sawer's fish merchants used to send deliveries by train to their customers; the parcels would travel in the guard's van, and be passed over to the stationmaster. When the author asked May if the customers then collected their fish from the station, she said 'oh no, they sent their chauffeur or gardener to collect it'! Similarly newspapers were sent by train from the Eason's bookshop at Queen's Quay. One of May's morning tasks was to deliver the newspaper to Captain Creighton before she left for school, and then take him his evening paper, after her return. Other newspapers were made available in the waiting-room for patrons such as Mr Ross to read going up to town in the train.

Stationmaster Tedford provided, as no doubt did many of his colleagues, a very personal service – regardless of gender!

Mrs Ross and her daughter Rhona lived on the shore at Cultra, and would cycle to the station to catch the train. The stationmaster considered it all part of his duty to carry their bikes across to the other side of the line in readiness for their return journey. A different service was performed for two local residents (who shall not be named) who were wont to return

Above: First Prize for Marino Station in the 1947 BCDR Stations and Gardens Competition

from Belfast on the last train 'well-oiled', and in some difficulty finding their way home unaided. Sydney would nobly accompany them both, on foot, to their respective premises at Clanbrassil Terrace and near to the Royal North of Ireland Yacht Club!

May recalls that even though the station house was lit by electricity, all the lamps on the platforms remained gas-lit. One of her father's evening duties was to get out the long pole to light them, taking great care not to touch the mantle. It was a thrill to accompany him, even though she was not allowed to wield the lighter herself.

Another of her father's tasks was to ensure a blazing fire by the time the first passengers arrived in the morning. This meant getting up around 5am; her father and his deputy Charlie Aiken had alternate weekly shifts, with the early starter finishing at around 2pm handing over to his colleague who would then be on duty until nearly midnight.

The stationmaster had an old signalling lamp to wave the trains away after dark. This ran on paraffin oil with a wick, and could be switched by hand to show green, orange or red. May recalls that her father was always keen to ensure that the trains ran precisely to time, for example advising the driver that he would need to make up a lost half minute on the next section.

Con Auld went to school by train from Marino station when he was living at Clanbrassil. He recalls that if he was running late any morning, he would 'holler' down to the engine driver asking him to delay his departure until Con had raced down the steps and onto the platform. Usually the drivers would oblige, notwithstanding the stationmaster's strictures.

May recalls on one occasion waiting on the down platform with a friend to go to Bangor. Driver Paddy Fitzpatrick stopped the train at Marino to allow them to get on. A little later on their journey, the guard came up and exclaimed '*I wondered why this express train stopped at Marino, but now I know it was for you, May*'.

Tony Merrick remembers enjoying the warmth from the fire in the waiting room on the up platform.

The station was closed in November 1957 and the up platform buildings were demolished. The station reopened in January 1960. The station house was acquired by the Tedford family, and Sydney later served as an inspector at Bangor with the UTA. May remembers that even though the facilities were pretty basic, with no indoor bathroom and only an outside lavatory, the house had been beautifully well-built in fine brickwork.

A few years ago the upper floor (itself a later addition) was extended over part of the single storey, a job well done and in keeping with the original brickwork and windows.

Cultra Station

Cultra (or Ballycultra – the town at the back of the strand – in full) is more significant historically than may be realised. Its sandstone was quarried in the 12th century and featured in both Carrickfergus Castle and the Priory church in Holywood. The quarry was worked well into the 19th century and blocks of stone from there are found in a number of Holywood's older houses. Owing to coastal erosion a tall wooden pump was erected to keep the water at bay.

Tony Merrick records that there were few houses there at that time, apart from the three hundred acre Kennedy estate at Cultra House, which had been in the ownership of the Kennedy family since 1671, and the Jacobean Farmhill House. Cultra House, which was on the seaward side of the Holywood to Bangor main road, was rebuilt in the 1870s. However in 1850 Surgeon Kelly described the house as:

'A mansion of great antiquity,… few situations can be more imposing or romantic than Cultra… It is over-shadowed by numerous luxuriant oak trees of singularly beautiful form and growth.'

The diplomat, Sir Robert Kennedy, born in 1851, built the magnificent

Cultra Manor (now in the grounds of the Folk Museum) in the early years of the 20th century.

Cultra station is of interest for a number of reasons.

The original station at Cultra was built by the Belfast, Holywood and Bangor Railway Company under clear instructions (incorporated in the Act of 1860 as stipulative clauses) which stated that there should be:

'A good and sufficient passenger station… of ornamental character… constructed and for ever thereafter subsequently maintained by the Company to the satisfaction of the owner of the time being of the Cultra demesne.'

This was so that the building should be in keeping with the high class villas being built by Charles Lanyon on the Cultra estate. (As the chairman of the BHBR, from 1873, Lanyon had a foot in many camps!)

It was also stipulated by the Kennedy family that at least half the trains passing each way daily had to stop at Cultra, under penalty for breach of £10 per day. The Kennedys' permission was additionally dependent on certain trees being spared, which led to curves on the track. From the above account of the house and demesne, one can have a degree of sympathy for the Kennedys.

As we have seen in the chapter on the Belfast, Holywood and Bangor Railway, that company specially erected ladies' bathing boxes by the sea at Cultra. They must have added to the volume of traffic using the station.

Originally, there was a single platform on the down side of the line. The first station building was a small one, in the (mock) Tudor fashion, made of brick with stone dressings. However, badly damaged by a malicious fire in May 1896, it was replaced. The present – disused – station building at Cultra dates from 1897. Designed by the BCDR's engineer GP Culverwell, the dwelling house was a substantial two-storey red brick building, with extensive passenger accommodation adjoining, on the down platform. It was approached by a Company driveway and fronted by a turning area for carriages.

William Seyers records that the bricks for Cultra, as well as Craigavad station, came from the brick field at the top of May Avenue in Bangor, though that may well have been for the original station building.

William Craig was the stationmaster in 1901 – he must have enjoyed the splendid new premises. He served at Cultra until at least 1911. Craig was also a beneficiary of the decision taken by the BCDR that all stationmasters' houses should have three bedrooms. As the original had only had two bedrooms, it was accordingly demolished.

When the track was doubled from the late 1890s, a magnificent covered footbridge was built at the Belfast end of the platforms to satisfy the wishes of the Kennedys and other distinguished clientele of the neighbourhood. Coakham asserts that this was the only one such on the system. Con Auld records that there was

even a private entrance on to the footbridge for the exclusive use of the Robinson family who had built Culloden (now the hotel of that name) in the early 1880s. (Presumably Bishop Welland who then lived in Culloden from 1899 to 1907, and his successors were beneficiaries.)

Cultra was reduced to halt status in 1934, sadly the original footbridge was done away with some time after the Second World War – the film *A Letter from Ulster* shows it very clearly. For a number of years marks showing where it had been on the seaward side could clearly be seen in the brickwork of the station house, and they can still just be discerned. Also around this time the station building became a private dwelling.

RM Arnold recounts one tale in the 1930s from his own experience, concerning Cultra station when the train from Bangor overshot the platform, with the eight coaches slithering on a carpet of leaves:

'Cultra had half a dozen first-class season tickets holders in those days and a couple are on the platform now, so deep in big business conversation that they scarcely notice that their train has come and gone. But No 3's driver is making a very big effort, having stopped his train before the 5 ¾ [milepost], to propel back to the station. This, he finds, is just about the worst job he has ever tried to do with one of these small engines, but eventually inch by inch with tremendous bouts of slipping the last carriage passes under the road bridge up to the platform. At the next stop the guard suggests to his patrons that they change at Holywood from the austerities of this third class carriage with only half a partition between compartments, but these gentlemen, who are known personally by name to every driver and guard on the line and who own some of the largest business houses in the city, are rather enjoying themselves. At Belfast, No 3 is smartly shunted round her train before her crew fall prey to witticisms from the passengers.'

Cultra station did have a brief moment of glory at one point in the Second World War. It featured in the making of the historic documentary film shot in 1942 *A Letter from Ulster*, which was directed by Northern Ireland's most eminent film-maker Brian Desmond Hurst. The film was made about the American troops who had come to Northern Ireland that year to train for the war in Europe. It was based on two large US Army camps at Bellarena (near Limavady) and Tynan Lodge (in County Armagh) – neither anywhere near North Down. However the film-makers wished to have a scene featuring Coleraine station, and for that purpose Cultra was used.

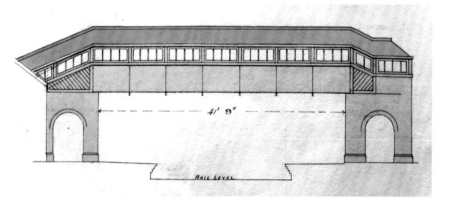

Margaret Smith was then living with her family at Cultra. One day she and her sister and a friend were out for a walk and observed all the activity on the station platform. They were asked if they would mind taking part, being filmed getting off the train at Cultra station. The picture is a still from the original black and white film. Margaret recalls that they neither received any payment, nor did she ever see the full film – just the stills. She also recalls that the guard had to pretend that it was Coleraine station – this was reputed for the rest of the war in some quarters to have been to put spies off! (It is true that station signs were removed as a precaution at that time.)

(For a commentary on the historic film, see http://www.youtube.com/watch?v=rOi4vxcivgc, or www.briandesmondhurst.org).

Cultra station first became an unattended halt in the 1930s. It reverted to being unattended in 1946, and was then closed in November 1957, before it was reopened on 1 July 1978 as the recognised stopping place for the Ulster Folk and Transport Museum. (A photograph, of the derelict station taken in August 1975, shows no up platform at all.) A connection off the down line, just the Bangor side of the station, was created to move

Above: *One of the former Cultra Station gas lamps*
Above right: *Coloured drawing of the Cultra Footbridge erected when the track was doubled, Desmond Coakham, courtesy of Downpatrick and County Down Railway and Andrew Crockart*

the railway exhibits into the Transport Museum before it opened in its new premises.

Denis Grimshaw was chief engineer at this time. He recalls rebuilding the platform on the down side of the line to Bangor to cater for six carriages, whereas due to budget limitations the up platform was only built for three carriages. This was not a problem then as boarding passengers could simply walk through the train to other carriages on the very rare occasions when longer trains stopped at Cultra.

A new footbridge was built at the Bangor end of the platforms, which also gives access to the Museums. The coping stones for the platform edgings were brought in from the disused station at Goraghwood outside Newry to match those which remained from the original station. The station building was sold for £1,000 in 1960, but was vacated in the 1970s.

The historic station building was again purchased, in a state of dilapidation in 2010, with a view to development. It had been entered on the Buildings at Risk Register and was granted listed building status, a few years before that. Plans were submitted for converting the station building into a number of apartments, together with additional housing on the three quarter acre site. A number of objections were raised, sequentially, by the Planning Service, but approval was granted in autumn 2014.

It was envisaged that work to restore the station in line with the plans would begin this year. This will once again recreate the relationship between the station itself and the stationmaster's accommodation.

Craigavad Station

Craigavad was one of the original stations that opened in 1865. Its design is, like several of the others, attributed to Charles Lanyon. The style is Italianate, reflecting the design of the Bangor station.

William Seyers records that the bricks for Craigavad station came from the brick field at the top of May Avenue in Bangor.

Craigavad was – most importantly – a passing place for trains (indeed then the only one) from the very first days of the new railway which of course was only single track from Holywood to Bangor. For all the time of the BHBR it remained the only passing place. After the doubling of the Bangor line, trailing crossovers were laid at each end of Craigavad Station, and were used to reverse those of the 'Holywood motors' that were extended to Craigavad at peak hours. Such was the level of business that a goods platform and siding were also later provided.

The station building was single-storeyed on the up platform side, with the stationmaster's accommodation on the ground floor against the railway embankment.

We know that Bernard Green was the stationmaster in 1905, from the Belfast and Ulster *Directory*, and Alfie Beaney recalls that Reginald Fitzsimons was a porter there, in his childhood.

Alfie remembers farmers from the Craigantlet area bringing in their milk in large metal churns to the station, and on the way dropping off their children to attend classes at the old Glencraig School. There would have been six or seven carts each with several churns, all pulled by horses. (He points out that there was no refrigeration facility for milk in those days, so it was essential to the farmers that they got the previous night's and that morning's milk away to market before it soured.)

Above: Cultra Station with a train for Bangor at the platform. **Above right:** *Craigavad Station from a Belfast-bound train in May 1962, EM Patterson, courtesy of Charles Friel*
Bottom right: *Craigavad Station, William McCutcheon, courtesy of the NIEA*

The local post office was also situated in the station building, being accessed from the platform and managed by the stationmaster. Alfie remembers that the post office was actually in the ticket office – one could buy stamps as well as tickets from the same window.

On 4 October 1940, a masked man held up the stationmaster and got away with 15 shillings and 10 packets of cigarettes, as well as nearly £20 belonging to the Postmaster General. Desmond Coakham records that in the following month the stationmaster resigned through illness and that the post office in the station was then closed.

In 1946, the station at Craigavad was reduced to the status of a halt.

For some years after its formal closure in November 1957 (and its brief reopening for one year from January 1960), occasional trains would stop at Craigavad bringing Girl Guides to their Northern Ireland headquarters at Lorne House, originally the home of Henry Campbell who endowed Campbell College.

The station building at Craigavad was sold in 1976. It has been turned into a charming family home by a succession of caring and imaginative owners. It also proved to be remarkably soundly built, with the original arched windows and high ceilings remaining.

Seahill Station

Seahill station was opened on 4 April 1966. It was established to serve the population of the new development plan which had grown up predominantly in the 1960s.

Initially the station consisted only of wooden platforms made up of sleepers and corrugated iron shelters.

Alfie Beaney remembers Seahill before there were any houses built, other than what was then Rockport School. The only things in Seahill then were 'hares and larks – in the summer we would lie in the grass and listen to them'.

In the 1930s a planned town was to have been sited there, named Port Kennedy, but the War had prevented its development. The same War had seen the creation of a temporary camp at Seahill/Rockport that initially housed American soldiers being trained in Northern Ireland before going on to European theatres of war, and was then used successively to hold Italian and German prisoners of war. The concrete bases for the Nissen huts can still be seen today, and indeed historic keys used to lock some of the wartime accommodation that had been purloined by Rockport schoolboys were rediscovered in 2014, buried in the undergrowth in the school grounds.

In the Second World War, there was also an important little military factory very close to the future site of Seahill station, known as the Glencraig workshop, managed by Charles Hurst, which produced Bofors gun recoil gears and aircraft components. It is known that approximately 45 operators were employed there, mostly men. The location was in what had been a dairy, just up the hill from the station at what became later the Scout Hall.

The tunnel under the line at Seahill is of interest, as if one looks up at the bridge, it can still just be seen where the track was doubled.

Betty Lowry was living in Seahill before the Halt was created. Prior to that, she walked up to the main road

Above left: Exterior of Craigavad Station, Desmond Coakham, courtesy of Andrew Crockart
*Above right: Seahill Station being built, January 1966, EM Patterson, courtesy of Charles Friel. **Bottom right:** Seahill Station in the early days, William McCutcheon, courtesy of the NIEA*

to catch the bus for Belfast or Bangor. But in her words, '*it was great*', when the nearby Halt opened and the railway became the preferred option.

Her father was the postman. He had to be at Craigavad Post Office, at the station, by 6.30am every morning to receive the post for local delivery. Betty recalls that as a result he got to know the individual engine drivers well – the consequences of which are another story!

Stuart Hughes remembers Seahill when the platform was a collection of wooden sleepers. You could get in under the sleepers, and watch the express trains thunder past just a couple of yards away, he recalls. Now into the decimal era, his friends used to put a two-penny coin on the track to see what effect the wheels would have. Of course, nowadays, health and safety, as well as close parental guidance, would never permit such activities.

Helen's Bay Station

Helen's Bay was unique on the line as having an ostensibly private station, built for Lord Dufferin who had his seat at Clandeboye House, some three miles away. Clearly he had a hand in the selection of the architect

and indeed in the design. (Some of the illustrations relating to the station are by kind permission of the Marchioness of Dufferin and Ava, to whom the author is most grateful.)

Benjamin Ferrey played no other part in the construction of the line from Holywood to Bangor as far as records show, though he was involved in formulating other architectural proposals for Lord Dufferin. (Lord Dufferin took the title of the Marquess of Dufferin and Ava in 1888. More information about him can be found in the book *Twixt Bay and Burn, a History of Helen's Bay and Crawfordsburn*.)

The cover of Twixt Bay and Burn has a lovely painting by Norman Whitla of a Baltic Tank engine at the head of a train coming into Helen's Bay station, set in the 1930s. It shows off Ferrey's gothic design to good effect.

Benjamin Ferrey was the youngest son of a draper who became Mayor of Christchurch. He went to London to study under Augustus Charles Pugin, alongside Pugin's son, Augustus Welby Northmore Pugin (who later designed the interior of the Palace of Westminster and Big Ben).

Augustus Welby Pugin designed a number of stations on the Churnet Valley Railway in Staffordshire, notably Alton where he worked for the 16th Earl of Shrewsbury to enlarge Alton Towers. That Ferrey had learned his trade

alongside Pugin may have been a factor that influenced Lord Dufferin to ask him to take on the design of the new station which was originally named 'Clandeboye'.

Ferrey started his own architectural practice in 1834, in London. Some of his earliest work was in the design of the new seaside resort of Bournemouth. The business grew rapidly, with Ferrey designing and restoring or rebuilding many Church of England parish churches. Charles Eastlake in his *History of the Gothic Revival* described Ferrey as '*one of the earliest, ablest, and most zealous pioneers of the modern Gothic school*' and said his work '*possessed the rare charm of simplicity, without lacking interest*'.

The best description we have of Helen's Bay station in its heyday comes from the book 'Helen's Tower' by Harold Nicolson. He describes in a passage concerning the homecoming of Lord Dufferin in 1889 after five years abroad:

'*The station at Helen's Bay was in those days (and indeed until the advent of the motor-car eliminated the train journey from Belfast) one of the most fantastic in the United Kingdom. Just before entering the station the train crossed a high bridge which spanned the two and a half mile avenue between Clandeboye and the sea. The station itself did not, at first sight, differ from*

Above left: Helen's Bay Station, 17 April 1948, Henry Casserley, courtesy of Charles Friel
Above right: Translink Planters tended by Helen's Bay Residents

the other stations of the Belfast and County Down Railway. There were the same long low buildings, the same weather-boarding painted a faint pink, the same 'approach' where the jaunting cars waited for possible passengers, their drivers standing up upon the footboard waving expectant whips. Yet the last door on the left opened upon a little corridor which in its turn led to Lord Dufferin's private waiting-room. This room was, on the whole, the least successful room that I have ever known. It managed to combine the atmosphere of a room which is used too little with the atmosphere of a room which is used too much. It had about it all that sense of the provisional, the transitory and the promiscuous which we associate with public waiting-rooms; its solitary window looked out upon the platform; and its silence was disturbed by the passage of trains, the shuffling of passengers, and the cry of the porter, which (for he was of County Down) was both loud and long. At the same time it exuded the musty depression of something deserted and forlorn: the key with which the stationmaster opened the door rasped in a rusty lock: dead flies innumerable lined the mantelpiece and the sill; the window, which looked out on to the platform and the lives of men was blurred with dust. These contrasts were rendered all the more disturbing by the disparity which existed between the proportions of the room and the furniture which it contained. In construction and design it was nothing more than a little room in a country railway station. Its furniture, however, and ornaments were those of a Victorian parlour. There was a circular table in the centre covered with an Indian cloth. The five chairs which were arranged around it had blue cushions embroidered with a coronet. There was a little red carpet with a criss-cross pattern and vague black flowers in each diamond square. There was a hard sofa in a corner and three cold Spode vases on the mantelpiece. There was an enormous composite engraving of the House of Lords in 1862 with a key-plan hanging framed below it. There were also (for some unfathomable reason) three billiard balls in a little box with a glass top. And there were four, or it may have been five, Landseer engravings in frames of light-coloured wood.

Yet there were stranger things to come. Having rested in the waiting-room, the visitor was then conducted back into the corridor and down a flight of steep stone steps which led to the level of the avenue. On reaching the bottom he was startled to find himself in a large pentagonal forecourt. The walls of this Propylaea were constructed of black granite irregularly morticed together with thick cement. There were a large number of turrets, pinnacles, barbicans, embrasures, machicoulis, ramparts, merlons, battlements, and arrow-slits. The avenue passed through this outer ward at right angles to the railway line. To the right there was a high portcullised gate-way which led down to the sea. To the left an even more imposing feudal arch disguised the railway bridge. Each of these two arches was decorated with a large coat of arms – dexter, a lion with a tressure flory counterflory or, sinister a heraldic tiger ermine.

Today, the avenue, the forecourt, the waiting-room, and indeed the railway station, are seldom used. The tressure of the lion has become more counterflory than ever; some of the balls have dropped from the coronets; and the arrow-slits are hidden in ivy. But on that August morning of 1889 the whole outer ward glistened in welcome. The carriages were waiting at the door of the staircase; the agent and the tenants formed a mounted escort; Lord Dufferin, accompanied by Ronald Munro Ferguson, his impending son-in-law, drove in happy triumph to his home.'

The arms associated with the Marquess of Dufferin and Ava can still be seen engraved on both sides of the stone bridge adjacent to the station, (though they have decayed through previous neglect). The Carriage Drive

Above: The Dufferin and Ava coat of arms on the railway bridge, Anna Masefield

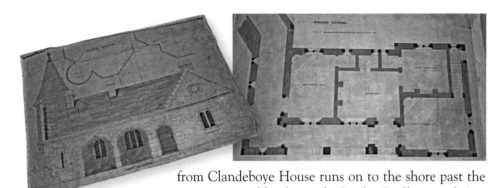

from Clandeboye House runs on to the shore past the station, now as a public footpath. In the Dufferin and Ava Archive at Clandeboye, are original documents relating to the architect's designs of the station and the bridge, drawn on linen. A drawing on a scale of 1 to 10, signed on the back *B. Ferrey*, is entitled '*Lord Dufferin's Private Station*'.

Although the station was originally called Clandeboye, it was later renamed Helen's Bay. The Clandeboye Archive contains a sketch of the station, with the name change in pencil, in the Marquess's own hand.

The late Margaret Garner, an eminent local historian, said that the then stationmaster (and postmaster) Andy Moreland was reputed to have buried the Clandeboye sign with his bayonet and had it renamed Helen's Bay. That is probably apocryphal – Nicolson gives Dufferin the credit for the name change. It had clearly happened before 1886, as Bassett's *County Down Guide* of that year refers to its being '*formerly called Clandeboye*'. Coakham records that it was renamed in August 1885, with Lord Dufferin paying £10 towards the change. A little later the stationmaster was given a cottage in the station forecourt.

In its busy heyday as a station, there was – on the seaward side – a signal

box, a goods siding, a small hoist on the platform, coal facilities and a hut. The original signal box was later used as a parcels office; the gap in the down platform for the rodding can still be seen today.

The siding was added, according to Coakham, following enquiries made to the BCDR's Manager Joseph Tatlow in 1887 by house-builders in Helen's Bay about facilities for bringing in construction materials. The station also served the local farming community – the siding was also where cattle could be loaded onto wagons for the market, and indeed horses (see below). Interestingly, just two years later, an excursion platform was opened, with the siding prolonged to form a loop which could be used to pass ordinary trains.

Under pressure from the Board of Trade, the BCDR added an up platform at Helen's Bay, with subway access in 1894. Culverwell erected one of his waiting sheds on the up platform at the doubling of the track (which was replaced by a brick and concrete shelter in 1973).

The working timetable for BCDR staff dated 1933, provides some information about the arrangements for horse boxes to be loaded and unloaded at Helen's Bay station. For example, the 9:25 am train departure from Helen's Bay on the Tuesday morning could take on board hunting horses only. It is curious to think that this was a normal passenger train that would have had to be backed into the siding so that the horses could be loaded or unloaded while the passengers patiently waited. (Arnold confirms that he had been on passenger trains which shunted off a wagon at Helen's Bay.)

Terence McKeag recalls that, in that era, a wealthy solicitor, Morris McKee, who lived near Rockport, kept horses which he raced at the Downpatrick course. The horses were led along the highway to Helen's Bay station where they were entrained. It was a three day operation, with the journey to Downpatrick via the Comber line on the day before the races, two nights stabling at the racecourse, and their return the day after the races.

Hunting horses too were sent to meets by train. Terence recollects that some local horses knew their way home so well, that once they had been disembarked at Helen's Bay station, they would find their own way back to Crawford's farm at Sunnybrook, near the Ballyrobert Road.

Alfie Beaney recalls that Walter Crozier kept around six hunters at his premises up the Ballymoney Road. His groom, Tommy Stratton, would ride them to Helen's Bay station where they would be put on the train that morning to travel to, say, Ballynahinch, for the meet of the County Down Staghounds. The groom travelled with his charges in the horsebox; the riders would travel by motor car.

Above left: The Front Elevation of Clandeboye Station, drawn on Linen, courtesy of the Dufferin and Ava Archive
Above right: Architect's Plan of Clandeboye Station, courtesy of the Dufferin and Ava Archive. **Bottom left:** *Helen's Bay Signal Cabin, Desmond Coakham, courtesy of Andrew Crockart*

The dangers associated with loading horse boxes are graphically illustrated in this drawing from a book (in Kay Coulthard's collection) promoting safe working on railways.

Brian Patton's father was a manager of some of the small local factories that were set up to manufacture munitions in the Second World War. He recalls that the factory at Ballyrobert produced a variety of munitions (albeit without explosives) which were transported in a trailer behind an old Morris 10 car to Helen's Bay station where they were loaded onto a wagon in the siding. Once a week, the previous six days' production would be transported to Belfast by train – usually amounting to one and a half wagon loads.

The station and its employees have featured prominently in the life of the village over the years. Helen's Bay regularly won second prize as the best-kept station, behind the picturesque Marino. In 1964 the Helen's Bay track maintenance gang received the UTA award for the best kept section of permanent way in the district.

The Station Square is effectively the centre of Helen's Bay and there have always been shops and services there. Mr Thompson was posted here, from Bangor, as stationmaster in 1884. His daughter ran Thompson's Hotel where the Helen's Bay Post Office stood before it in turn was replaced by town houses.

In 1921, an Agreement was drawn up between the BCDR and Mr Michael Boland:

'As you are aware, Mrs Mundell, the previous tenant of the house and shop you now occupy, had an agreement with my company in regard to certain advertisements painted on the wall of the building forming part of her tenancy and which overlooks the property of this company close to our Helen's Bay station… If you are desirous of the advertisements being allowed to remain exposed to view, a similar agreement may be reached.'

The document was actually addressed Mrs Boland, at the *Sunbeam Temperance Hotel*, Helen's Bay (which, ironically, is now an off-licence).

Margaret Garner recounted several tales of the railway from her childhood in a big house on Craigdarragh Road in the village. She recalled how her mother used to take a short cut over the iron gates outside the station. To climb she had to gather up her petticoats and get on the first carriage. The driver always tooted in appreciation. Her uncle, Robert Workman who lived in Craigdarragh House itself, used to walk to church on Sundays along the railway track.

The railway played a vital role in community life over the years. In the Second World War, one naval vessel coming into Belfast harbour 'accidentally' depth-charged a shoal of fish. Some of the catch was put on the BCDR train and one local resident cycled to Helen's Bay station to collect it. Mr Rooney the stationmaster met him with a broad grin, saying 'I have a wee minnow here for you.' The 'minnow' was reputedly nearly four feet long and frozen solid; its new owner (and shortly thereafter consumer) had to walk home pushing it on his bicycle.

Residents of Helen's Bay recall that there used to be a compartment in one carriage in the train coming from Bangor reserved for the Helen's Bay gentlemen, which the stationmaster would unlock to let them in. (To be fair, in terms of gender equality, there also seems to have been a similar arrangement for the ladies.)

Paddy Buckler and Richard Gilmore also remember the welcoming open fire in the station, along with the large table on which parcels and the many other items sent by train were set out, labelled for collection.

Another familiar Helen's Bay resident and station official was Harry Parkhurst. The photograph shows the cottage, 3 The Square, that became home to Harry and his wife Rita through his BCDR railway employment as a porter in the 1920s and eventually to an extended family with nine children. (In later years, the house has been beautifully extended to accommodate smaller numbers

Above left: Beware the dangers of Horse Boxes, courtesy of Kay Coulthard
Right: Harry Parkhurst and members of his family outside their railway accommodation at Station Square, Helen's Bay, courtesy of Irwin Parkhurst

of residents on the same site). Harry and his family were a well-known feature of Helen's Bay as, in addition to his railway duties, Harry became a highly successful greyhound trainer and owner with many major victories throughout Ireland's greyhound venues and coursing tracks. He also tended to a number of the gardens in Helen's Bay as, with so many mouths to feed, extra income was a necessity.

George Rooney had been stationmaster for several decades before; Harry Parkhurst retired at Christmas 1966. The Residents Association arranged a local collection to mark his service.

For several decades since, access to the station building has been denied to railway travellers, as it has played host initially to various restaurants, including the popular Deane's on the Square (run by Haydn and Michael Deane) which gained a prestigious award in 1997. Since January 2012 it has been home to the Deborah Harper Make-up and Beauty salon. The salon has very skilfully restored the building – largely to its former glory – for which it won the 2013 Conservation award from the Railway Heritage Trust; this is marked with a plaque on the wall adjacent to the platform.

The station has even had a ghost story set in it – perhaps not surprisingly given the number of unfortunate incidents at this location over the years (some of which are recorded in the chapter on accidents).

Despite the many changes over the years, including the demise of the BCDR as a separate entity and the closure of its station building to passengers, the railway has in practice turned Helen's Bay into a popular commuter location – just as the early developers of the branch line intended when they offered those free tickets to incoming residents

Crawfordsburn Station and Viaduct

The railway reached Crawfordsburn via a five – arched sandstone viaduct faced with Scrabo stone. Designed by Sir Charles Lanyon, it remains a fine sight. Tradition has it that, years later, a youngster fell off the viaduct but was saved from death by his clothes catching in trees on the way down.

There is a fine account of the laying of the foundation stone in the local paper on 3 October 1863. As well as Lanyon and a Director of the line, Lord Dufferin, Major John Sharman Crawford and the chairman of the Belfast, Holywood and Bangor Railway Company, Robert Ward of Bangor Castle attended. Those present were 'entertained to a splendid déjeuner' at Crawfordsburn House. The foundation stone was removed in 1990, after the centenary of Lanyon's death. A Victorian cache of Belfast newspapers and coins placed there in a hermetically sealed bottle 127 years before by Major Sharman Crawford was revealed.

The original sandstone parapets were replaced in wrought iron lattice-work, when the track was doubled between 1897 and 1902. The BCDR engineer Culverwell strengthened the weight-bearing upper section, and placed new girders that projected 6 ½ feet on either side to provide a planked walkway, with lattice girder railing. However, just 12 inches of room remained between the outer rail of each line and the edge of the original structure (which was sadly insufficient to ensure the safety of railway staff working on the viaduct, as recorded in Chapter 11). The work began in July 1899, and by 6 December of that year the Carnalea to Helen's Bay double line section was inaugurated. The total cost of the work on the Crawfordsburn viaduct was just £2,000.

Further work was done on the viaduct in the early 1980s, under Denis Grimshaw. Given the lack of space between the tracks and outside them, the viaduct needed to be widened, by six feet, now with a lattice parapet made of steel to match Culverwell's original. Precast concrete slabs were placed on top of the original deck which

Above left: *Crawfordsburn Viaduct from the Glen, July 1967, EM Patterson, courtesy of Charles Friel*
Above top right: *Approaching Crawfordsburn Viaduct, August 1964, EM Patterson, courtesy of Charles Friel.* **Above bottom right:** *Crawfordsburn Viaduct, John McEwen*

136

raised the track by some 18 inches, thus helpfully reducing the scale of the dip that had previously existed. The work was achieved with minimal disruption to the running of the service, with closure on just four Sundays, through the use of temporary crossovers at Crawfordsburn and Craigavad.

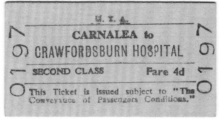

The station (a real halt, with bare timber platforms) that served Crawfordsburn hospital, and by extension the village over the years, was opened in September 1965. It was originally named Crawfordsburn Hospital Halt, and was closed to passengers in 1997/8,

ironically just before the major redevelopment of the nearby Crawfordsburn House. All evidence of the platforms has since been removed.

Originally the bridge over the railway at the eastern end of what became in 1971 the Crawfordsburn Country Park had two arches, with the bridge replaced and the track realigned under Denis Grimshaw's custodianship as Civil Engineer for Northern Ireland Railways.

Carnalea Station

Carnalea was not a station on the original line which opened in May 1865. (Although it is recorded that Koch had plans to build a hotel here originally. There was said to be a grand avenue of trees from the station to the sea, as its only manifestation.)

As on other matters, the *News Letter* is an important source of information. An article dated 12 October 1869 records, under the following heading, that:

'Holywood and Bangor Railway
This company have selected a site for a station in the townland of Carnalea, on Mr Ker's property, midway between Bangor and Crawfordsburn (sic) stations. We understand that several villas will shortly be erected in the immediate vicinity, and that the requisite approaches will be forthwith constructed.'

This again demonstrates the consequences for housing development of the opening of the railway.

It is recorded that one of the fine 19th century houses in Carnalea was built to house the family of Daniel and his wife Frederiké Jaffe (who had moved in 1852 from Hamburg to Belfast) and their nine children. These were the parents of Otto (later Sir Otto Jaffe) and his siblings. Daniel was a prosperous linen merchant, a business which Otto then developed. Their house dates from the 1870s.

The advent of the railway also encouraged the erection of week-end bungalows in the vicinity.

*Top left: Crawfordsburn Hospital Halt, January 1966, EM Patterson, courtesy of Charles Friel. **Above middle left:** Poster depicting the Attraction of Crawfordsburn Country Park, courtesy of the NIEA. **Above middle right:** UTA Tickets to Crawfordsburn Hospital Halt, courtesy of Ivor Graham. **Bottom left:** The former two-arch bridge between Helen's Bay and Crawfordsburn Hospital Halt, EM Patterson, courtesy of Charles Friel. **Right:** Carnalea Station Sign, Desmond Coakham, courtesy of Andrew Crockart.*

Carnalea station was actually built in 1873 according to EM Patterson, although the first station building was an old wagon body of which remarkably a photograph exists.

Following the takeover of the BHBR by the BCDR in 1884, the latter's Manager, Joseph Tatlow, inspected the stations along the Bangor line. He called Carnalea 'the smallest of small stations… The whole accommodation being an old railway carriage, but it seems to serve the purpose of the place'.

McCutcheon states firmly that the main station buildings at Carnalea closely resembled the station at Cultra, built in 1897, and were probably built at the same time, replacing earlier accommodation. The station had itself become a passing place for trains the year earlier. A subway was built for passengers to access the down platform.

There was for many years a splendid private footbridge over the line, from Bridge House toward the shore, originally number OB 43 and then OB 368, also known as Lepper's Bridge. (The bridges on the Bangor line were renumbered after the line was reconnected via Central Station; OB 368 is the 368th bridge from Dublin.) Probably erected shortly after the track was fully doubled, around 1904, it was removed by the NIR in the 1990s. A foundry in Glasgow seems to have supplied the iron-work which included cast iron columns. The photograph by McCutcheon shows the intricate wrought iron latticing.

An early station master at Carnalea was William McDade. He was station master there, according to the *Belfast and Ulster Directory*, including the years 1904 to 1907. It is clear that he served for many years in this post.

A book by David McKnight, entitled '*We have an Altar*', records that for some years, on every Tuesday evening, with the help of his wife Annie, McDade organised Methodist meetings at his home beside the railway track. The sessions were held in the Ladies Waiting Room, but were often so popular that people sat all the way up the main staircase. It was in that station house that the story of Methodism really began in the vicinity of Carnalea.

From its opening on 29 June 1935, Methodists later worshipped officially in the church on the corner of Crawfordsburn and Bellevue Road, now Killaire Park. (This church was opened by Millicent Harte, one of the founders of Glenlola School in Bangor, who was just moving then to live in the first house built on Sheridan Drive in Helen's Bay.) By the 1980s, the local Methodists shared St Gall's parish church, just across the way from their former place of worship.

McKnight's book tells us that for a while after the station house, services were held in the Beresford Café, until McDade discovered a clause in the lease which prohibited religious meetings and dancing.

Intriguingly, the religious connection continued. Mrs Simpson, who was married to a Methodist Minister, was the youngest daughter of the last stationmaster at

Above left: The Original Station at Carnalea, c.1880, courtesy of the BCDR Museum Trust. **Bottom left:** *Carnalea Stationmaster William McDade and his wife and 12 children, courtesy of Elizabeth Porter.* **Above right:** *The Private Footbridge at Carnalea, William McCutcheon, courtesy of the NIEA.* **Bottom right:** *Carnalea Station, Desmond Coakham, courtesy of Andrew Crockart.*

Kennedy Stewart, the Hon. Secretary of what was then the Royal Belfast Golf Club at Carnalea, concerning a fence erected by the Golf Club to prevent trespass, part of which was on BCDR land. For this, the Club paid an annual rent of one shilling!

The Carnalea signal cabin was closed completely in late 1932.

On the down platform, the former Culverwell waiting shelter and low level signal cabin have long since been demolished. Sinclair records that there have been no less than four replacement shelters in subsequent years.

As early as 1946, the station at Carnalea was reduced to the status of a halt, as a cost-saving measure, though it continued to be manned. The station house was initially sold for £703.

As shown in the illustration, the station house remains a fine building to this day, though only one of the two trees has survived. The adjacent single storey building which contained the waiting rooms and the ticket office has long been demolished. The present owners redesigned the premises, with what had been the 'back yard' as a double storey extension with a metal spiral staircase.

Freeman Wills Crofts, the NCC railway engineer turned crime-writer (and nephew of former BCDR engineer Berkeley Deane Wise) partly set one of his novels 'Man Overboard!' in the vicinity of Carnalea station.

Carnalea. Visiting the station house in her later years, she recalled that there had in her childhood been two magnificent large lime trees in the front garden between which she loved swinging in a hammock.

According to an account in the *Spectator*, dated 14 August 1914, ie at the very start of the First World War, earlier that week two men of foreign appearance were spotted by two local lads, making sketches in the vicinity of Carnalea. The lads notified the stationmaster who communicated with the police with the result that the men, who indeed turned out to be German spies, were arrested at Sydenham.

In August 1919, an Agreement was made between the BCDR and

*Top left: A light engine running backwards to Bangor through Carnalea Station, August 1964, EM Patterson, courtesy of Charles Friel. **Bottom left:** Trains passing at Carnalea, Middlemass, courtesy of Charles Friel. **Top right:** Carnalea Station Platform, Desmond Coakham, courtesy of Andrew Crockart. **Middle right:** Carnalea Signal Cabin, July 1967, EM Patterson, courtesy of Charles Friel. **Bottom right:** The Station house at Carnalea as it now is.*

Bangor West

The station at Bangor West, by Bryansburn Bridge, was opened in 1928.

After the First World War, Bangor grew in popularity both as a residential town for business folk, and as a holiday attraction for British visitors. The creation of a new halt, to the west of the town and one mile from the terminus, had been urged by town councillors when BCDR Directors visited Bangor station in July 1923.

However, the halt took five years to materialise. It was formally opened on 2 January 1928. It cost just over £1,000.

The company minute book recorded that it was:

'Being largely taken advantage of by subscribers and other passengers.'

It was a manned halt from the beginning.

One does not always appreciate the effort required, even in those days. An article in the *Spectator* dated 19 January 1929 reported that at the most recent Bangor Borough Council meeting:

'A letter was read from the engineer of the Belfast and Co. Down Railway Company, dated 3rd instant, submitting draft clauses to be included in the Parliamentary Bill safeguarding the interests of the Railway Company where the proposed sewer crosses the railway line at Bryansburn.
The town clerk stated that copies of the correspondence had been sent to the Council's solicitor for his attention.'

Despite the growth of Bangor and the business referred to above, a photograph in EM Patterson's book on the BCDR with a train entering Bangor West halt from Bangor on 1 September 1952 shows how completely rural the setting for the halt appeared still at that time. Nevertheless,

well before this, fast trains between Bangor and Belfast had begun stopping at Bangor West, reflecting the growth in the neighbouring population that the new station was by then serving.

For one senior citizen of Bangor, whose family lived on Shaftesbury Avenue in the 1940s and 1950s, Bangor West halt was the local station. He remembers enjoying throwing sticks into the Bryansburn stream along the way. Like many another boy in that era, he placed pennies on the line to be flattened by the trains. (The old pennies were more amenable to this – of course no-one would dream of such an improper action today.)

After the Second War, there were still many wooden huts and dwellings round the station area, some of which were permanently occupied.

Sinclair records that the original wooden building which housed two waiting rooms and a booking office, was replaced in 1978 with an equally basic brick and concrete structure.

*Left: Renumbered UTA Locomotive 208 at Bangor West on 1 September 1952, EM Patterson, courtesy of Charles Friel. **Above right:** At Bangor West Station in July 1964, EM Patterson, courtesy of Charles Friel. **Bottom right:** An MED at Bangor West Station, July 1964, EM Patterson, courtesy of Charles Friel.*

Chapter 15

Bangor Station

As we have seen previously in the chapter on the BCDR, that company first aspired to bring a line to Bangor. Indeed a contract dated 31 October 1859 between William Dargan and the Edwards brothers for the construction of lines to Downpatrick and Ballynahinch also included a branch to Bangor. The contract even provided for a station to be built at Bangor at a cost of £1,299, and the details of how each stream on the intended route was to be bridged or diverted.

However, the BCDR was not in a position to take forward its Bangor scheme, and the BHBR seized its chance.

As a result, the station at Bangor was built in 1864-5 to a more substantial – and attractive – design by Charles Lanyon, the principal engineering architect for the Belfast, Holywood and Bangor Railway Company. It was described by McCutcheon as a *'substantial pile in red brick with round-headed windows, surmounted by yellow stucco, at platform level and corresponding segment-headed windows, with drip moulds over, at pavement level'*. The

station had an arcaded portico, which was entered from street level up shallow flights of steps.

A tall Italianate tower, a colourful and ostentatious feature in polychrome brick work, dominated the station at the north-east corner and along the timber north-east elevation, where huge lettering proclaimed (later) 'Belfast and County Down Railway' across the face of a projecting high-level canopy. (There was provision for clock faces on the tower, but no money was available for one until 1972!)

Originally the stationmaster was accommodated in the lower storey, at street level, but by around 1890, he was given a separate company house close by. The ground floor contained refreshment rooms, with other passenger facilities on the upper floor.

It is interesting that the architectural style was said to be untypical of Lanyon's practice at that time. Fine mosaic floor tiles were uncovered when the station was demolished many years later.

This splendid station however had initially only one platform.

It is reputed that the spoil, from the excavation to bring the original line to Bangor and the work for the station, was taken to fill in the historic *vallis angelorum* which according to legend was the beautiful valley on the site of the future abbey and town of Bangor where St Patrick and his companions heard a choir of heavenly angels.

As recorded above, in 1884, the BCDR Manager Joseph Tatlow inspected the stations on the Bangor line. He noted that (notwithstanding its splendid architecture) in practical terms it lacked a goods store, siding and cattle 'bank' (to assist loading and unloading livestock).

Coakham records that major work was carried out at Bangor station, beginning in 1889. This resulted in additional platforms, and an all-over roof of Belfast trusses. The goods store (which as noted elsewhere was built in timber, as an economy measure) housed five goods wagons. New refreshment rooms were provided in 1892. It is recorded that engineer Culverwell was the first to sample the grill in the kitchen, having prudently

Above left: Bangor Station, from Abbey Street, Desmond Coakham, courtesy of Andrew Crockart
Above right: Bangor Engine Shed, Desmond Coakham, courtesy of Andrew Crockart

brought some chops with him for the purpose! (This was no doubt an early example of quality-control.)

We know an unusual amount about not just the names but also the characters of the early stationmasters at Bangor from William Seyers' *Reminiscences of Old Bangor* which was first published in 1932.

According to Seyers, the first to hold the post was William Smith –

'A tall dark man with a nice manner and was well liked. After a good many years he got religious and thought it was not right to work on Sunday, so he gave in his notice and left… A little Englishman called Brown came next. He only stayed a few years when he left and went to England. He was killed at the station he went to. Wilson, who came next, took ill and was not long there. Boyd, who followed, was a nice man. He was in love with a Miss Bowman… a tall, handsome, good looking girl, who took ill and died. He left, it is said, of a broken heart.

Jimmy Thompson came next and was there until the change from B. H. and Bangor to the B.C.D. Railway Co. [in 1884] when he was transferred to Helen's Bay. He was most obliging and liked by everyone. He built a nice home at Helen's Bay where his daughter had a restaurant and dance hall.

Robert Cavan came from Holywood in place of Mr Thompson. He was a favourite. He had lost one hand, but had a stump in which he could use a fork etc. He married a Bangor lady, but she died…. He left Bangor to go to be goods manager at Belfast. Charles O'Neill, who came next, was only about six months, when he went to Dublin under Mr Tatlow, manager of the Great Southern Railway.

Mr Matthew Scott, who came next, was about 15 years in charge of Bangor station, and was respected by all. When he was transferred to Ballynahinch, the travelling public was sorry at his departure.

Mr John Walsh, who came in Mr Scott's place, was a very cool, quiet going gentleman. I have experience of him before as he was here a few years as clerk under Mr Cavan. He made a host of friends, was well liked, and retired after about 25 years at Bangor and is now a popular bowler on Bangor green. Mr C.A. Valentine is now carrying on the good work with the assistance of Mr W Aicken and the good staff'.

(It is interesting to note that Messrs Valentine and Aicken were still in post at the time of the Ballymacarrett rail disaster in 1945. Alfie Beaney recalls that Valentine was a very nice man; he was a local Councillor, and playing fields in Bangor are named after him.)

On 23 December 1919, an Agreement was drawn up between the BCDR and Jacob O'Neill of Dufferin Avenue in relation to a car stand at Bangor station. In return for an annual payment of £65, O'Neill was permitted to rent a car stand with space for eight motor cabs or cars within the enclosure at the main entrance to the station. O'Neill was required to:

'Provide a sufficient number of motors or well horsed and properly appointed cabs or cars for the use of passengers arriving or departing by all trains'.

We also have an obituary for Matthew Scott, from the *Spectator* dated 6 March 1937. He had retired in 1925, having served 18 years in stationmaster at Ballynahinch, after his time at Bangor. Scott had joined the BCDR as a boy in the manager's office, before being given his first station at Dundrum. He had been made station master at Bangor when

'A new station was built in Bangor to replace the poor accommodation that had existed hitherto; the Directors showed their confidence in Mr Scott by conferring on him the responsible position of station master…

Mr Scott proved himself an ideal public servant loyal to the Company and unsparing of himself in his solicitude for the comfort and well-being of its clients.'

The obituary added that on his transfer to Ballynahinch, Scott had been presented by the chair of the Bangor Urban Council with *'an illustrated address and a handsome wallet of notes, and Mrs Scott had been given a gold watch'*. The obituary also noted that one of their two sons, David had joined the Army under age at the start of the First World War. He had been killed in action with the Royal Flying Corps in France, after being awarded the Military Cross. Stressing the importance of the railways, the obituary observed that *'in these pre-bus times, the railways were in a real sense the arteries of business life'.*

Seyers also gives an insight into the relationship between the local postmaster and the railway station. Describing one postmaster, he said 'Mr McGrath was very energetic and came up to the station to see most of the mails coming in'. There were then two deliveries from Monday to Saturday, and one every Sunday.

The *Bangor Season* recorded in 1885 that 'the rail is fairly cheap, speedy and prosaic. Both rail and road are now available all year round'.

However Bangor station played a role in the history of women's suffrage which was certainly not prosaic. In spring 1914, at the height of the Home Rule crisis, when guns were being secretly landed, there was an arson attack on the station. The *Spectator* carried two articles commenting on the event, the first on 17 April, entitled '*Town Tattle*':

'*The recent attempt to burn the Bangor station overshadows in importance every other event in Bangor during the past week. I am not going to indulge in a wrathful outburst against the perpetrators of this nonsensical outrage. It is beneath contempt; a sample of feminine instability. Such acts of pettiness, however annoying, impress no-one; and to the person who is philosophically inclined they form an index to the temperament of vote mad women. The ordinary, well-balanced woman only laughs at 'militant hen-peckery' of this sort. Such women are the salt of the earth. Men have never set suffragettes a precedent in 'militant hen-peckery'; they have fought and died for their rights.*

Personally, I can scarcely believe that the attempt to burn the station was the work of Bangor adherents to the woman's suffrage cause, although in this respect, several local persons hold different views. But I certainly do believe that there was co-operation of some sort. I am sure, at any rate, the local non-militants deprecate the outrage as much as non-sympathisers; for actions such as these only weaken instead of strengthening the cause. Women who place the family system with all its beauty and humanity before a bickering political life will always shun the 'militant hen-peckers'.

I may say that if the Railway Station had been burned down, I would not have felt particularly sorry; neither I am sure would the directors of the Belfast and Co. Down Railway Company! It would have been a fairly cheap way of getting a new station! In New York there is a fraternity known

as fire-bugs – I suggest this as a suitable trade for militants. We need very badly a new station in Bangor – but there I am sure a hint is all that is required! Bravo! Brave militants you have the interests of Bangor at heart!'

Two weeks later the following article appeared under the nom de plume of '*My Column*':

'*The police have been seen shadowing certain houses in Bangor. The male proportion of the household thought it was their share of Friday night's loot the sergeant's men were after (gun-running into Bangor), but it turns out that the women folk are looked upon as the more dangerous.*

In other words the police have received instructions to keep certain Bangor Suffragettes under the strictest surveillance.

And mind you it is just possible that the burning fiasco at the Station was the work of locals or how else did they know where to find the bucket of tar in the Goods Station?

By the way, it seems the foreman lamplighter while on his return journey after extinguishing the lights, observed two women – a tall and a short one – crossing the wire fence at the back of the stationmaster's house.

That was at about one o'clock on the night of the 'outrage' and presumably they were the Suffragettes making off after laying their mine.

Never thinking of Suffragette outrages, he thought these females had been on a different kind of errand and stood into the shadow of the demesne wall to see if he could identify them.

They crossed Mr Milligan's flower nursery and again climbed the fence at the hut that stands in the South-west corner of the garden. Unfortunately they at this stage noticed the figure in the shadow of the demesne wall opposite.

They thereupon whispered to each other and stood like statues. Without a budge they thus stood for many minutes, and their observer getting tired of the vigil went home. It is needless to say that had he ever dreamt of their mission, the neighbourhood would have been aroused.

And there would have been a fight in comparison with which the famous

Kilkenny cats would have been as nothing. Just imagine the lamplighter and his stick contending with two real live militants.'

The *Spectator* carried a number of articles about German spies in its issue on 14 August 1914, one being about Carnalea (see the section on Carnalea station).

One arrest was Paul Wentzel who was taken into custody on 7 August. He had been living near Bangor since 1910, having been one of a group brought over to try to resuscitate the fortunes of the lead mines at Conlig. His movements caused suspicions and when his wooden shack was searched sketches were found. Separately a German and an Austrian were landed at Grey Point Fort off a sailing ship and taken to Bangor police station. The *Spectator* recorded that:

'Remarkable scenes were witnessed as the men were removed to the railway station en route for Crumlin Road Jail. Huge crowds began to collect in the streets and at the railway station. Nothing in the nature of a demonstration against the prisoners took place, of course, but some slight booing was indulged in by the irresponsible members of the crowd.'

In February 1926, a collision between some coaches being shunted and goods wagons caused considerable damage, including cracking of the main station wall.

Two years later the *Spectator* reported an unfortunate accident at the station:

'While getting out of the 10.30 train from Belfast on Wednesday night on its arrival in Bangor, a young woman, named Mary Agnes Miller, employed as a domestic servant by Mrs Lloyd, Gransha Lodge, Bangor, fell on the platform and sustained injuries to the head. She was taken to Bangor Hospital and, after treatment, was detained. She belongs to Co. Tyrone.'

It is interesting to note that the capital to fund the building of the Tonic cinema in Bangor came when the Northern Ireland Road Transport Board bought up the Tonic bus service that conveyed passengers to and from Bangor station.

Above top: *The original platform at Bangor station, Lawrence Collection, courtesy of the National Library of Ireland.*
Above bottom: *Bangor station c. 1900, Lawrence Collection, courtesy of the National Library of Ireland.*

The Bangor Gasworks Company imported its coal at Bangor Harbour, but the BCDR benefited from the haulage of an average of just over 1,000 tons of coke to Belfast.

Alfie Beaney recalls the importance of the goods trains for the local community. Early every morning, there would be several horse-drawn 'spring vans', pulled up at the station waiting for goods to be unloaded which they would then distribute to the local shops. The pork for Smyth and McClure came by train in barrels, each containing a selection of fillets, steaks and chops.

Bread too came by train. Every day six or seven Inglis vans would wait for the bread, which had been baked in Belfast, to be brought out on large wicker baskets.

In those days, Alfie remembers, passengers didn't have to go up any steps at Bangor station. The concourse was on the same level as the surrounding

area, meaning that there was quite an incline down to the station on the track itself.

In 1946 changes were made to Bangor station, with Culverwell's timber roofing being partially dismantled, some replaced by a steel framework with asbestos-cement cladding.

It was in the 1950s that the stationmaster's accommodation facing Abbey Street was demolished, along with Culverwell's goods store to make room for the adjoining bus depot. Ironically a new, red-brick, goods store was built, but was never used for its intended purpose, the UTA having now decreed

that goods traffic on the Bangor line was to end.

Later, the original station was rendered over and the brickwork detailing cut back to suit. In 1969, a year or so after Northern Ireland Railways took over from the UTA, further alterations were made to the

station. The wrought iron platform barrier was removed and in this area a new building was erected housing a new booking office, platform barrier gates and newsagent. The old booking office, a wooden structure just inside the main entrance from the forecourt was modified and incorporated into the Whistle Stop bar. A new facade was constructed facing the forecourt and Dufferin Avenue which greatly improved the appearance of the station after the 1946 alterations.

Plans were made to introduce a more commercial element into the attractions of Bangor station in 1978. The *Belfast Telegraph* announced on 1 March of that year that:

'The housewife now standing on platform number two is bound for … wait for it…. the grocery section. Plans by the Northern Ireland Transport Holding Company which is planning a £200,000 facelift for the Bangor station, include shops on the ground floor… the bar is to be doubled in size… there is no reason why in the future we should not see the housewife hopping onto the train to come to Bangor railway station or town for her shopping.'

Clearly the Holding Company planned to obtain some rental income to help cut the railway system's overheads. These alterations were in time carried out. The bar was expanded into the concourse (and the original booking office removed), with its own direct outside access. The newsagent was moved to one of the refurbished shops in the ground floor and a greengrocer took over the other ground floor shop. Some years later a further chunk of the concourse was taken over as a further, larger shop unit.

In terms of curious customers, Ian Sinclair records that the circus came to Bangor by train in July 1964. Indeed there is a photograph of Bertram Mills Circus in wagons outside Bangor station. It is recorded that parts of the metal barrier at the station had to be cut open to allow the animals to

Above top left: Bangor Station, from the corner of Main Street, courtesy of Charles Friel. **Above bottom left:** Bangor Station, as revamped by the UTA, October 1956, EM Patterson, courtesy of Charles Friel. **Above bottom right:** At Bangor Station, August 1961, EM Patterson, courtesy of Charles Friel.

pass through, and then had to be re-welded after the circus had departed.

The current edifice was the first combined rail and bus centre to be completed in Northern Ireland following the integration of the two operations in 1995. Napper Architects were appointed in 1997 to develop the project. As the blurb on the station wall, put up after completion, has it:

'The building attempts to return the sense of place which had been lost after the numerous alterations to the existing station. The building is modern, dynamic and forward looking in nature reflecting Translink's desire to take public transport into the next millennium.'

Left: *At Bangor Station, June 1952, RF Fullagar, courtesy of Charles Friel.* **Right:** *Labourers in a cutting between Bangor and Bangor West, undated, courtesy of North Down Museum.*

Chapter 16

'Six and Out' - Memories and More

This chapter is a miscellany for which the author makes no apology. His regret is rather that time did not permit him to gather still more fascinating stories and personal accounts of the very many ways in which people have been affected by the railway.

No book of this kind would be complete without some recollections of those who had the privilege and fun, as boys, of spending time at stations and on railways. Railways have also, from their beginning, provided a source of amusement for satirists and others of a poetic bent.

One of Percy French's best-loved songs was about the tardiness of the West Clare Railway, *Are ye right there, Michael, are ye right?* And the Ulster lines were not exempt from critical scrutiny. The McCutcheon archive includes a 'topical song' composed by Mr E Radcliff and sung by the Radcliff and Mr Percy French on 22 February 1899 at – where else? – the Railway Benevolent Institution (Irish Branch) Smoking Concert in Dublin. The song pokes fun at the railway barons and financiers. It suggests that

> 'The Clogher Valley Railway is a noble enterprise,
> And one on which financiers have got their weather eyes,
> And Rothschild wants to have it if they'll run to Ballybay,
> But I hear the first refusal has been offered Jimmy Gray.'

Railway cognoscenti will be familiar with the unique Lartigue monorail. In the Radcliff and French song it is joined up with the BCDR thus:

> 'Another scheme we hear of which is quite upon the cards,
> Is to run the Lartigue Railway in Tralee to Newtownards,
> The great advantage of this route, as any map will show,

Is it taps the Cattle traffic from the Fair of Ballinasloe.'

Sometimes railway travel could promote charitable actions, rather than financial speculation. The *County Down Spectator* carried a report in 1921 headed '*Not a secret society*':

> '*Unique amongst the organisations of Bangor is what is known as "the 9-15 Club" consisting of a number of gentlemen who foregather in the train that leaves for Belfast every morning at that hour. Talk about Free Masons or Buffaloes! Candidates for membership of "the 9-15 Club" are subjected to a searching scrutiny and the fact of any man being admitted to its privileges may be taken as satisfactory evidence that he is a man of honour and a jolly good fellow. The social activities of the Club are not confined to the period of their daily pilgrimage to the City. They meet from time to time in their off hours for fellowship and self-improvement. Typical of these periodical gatherings was one held in Thompsons Café, Bangor, under the presidency of Comrade R. E. Morrow when a lecture on Tom Hood was given by the genial and versatile Comrade Wm. Graham and appreciatively received by a full turnout of the Comrades and their friends.*'

In December 1922, the *Spectator* reported that the Comrades brought festive cheer to many young Bangorians:

> '*That unique organisation, the "Comrades of the 9-15 Club" brought Christmas cheer to over 1000 Bangor young people on Friday afternoon.*

> *As is well-known locally, the club is confined to thirty members who are Bangor residents with businesses in Belfast who travel to the city every morning in a specially reserved saloon carriage on the 9-15 train. The journey is whiled away each morning with regularly organised series of lectures, and debates with occasional musical interludes.*

> *The entertainment which took place in the Picture Palace, was entirely organised by the comrades themselves and an appropriate programme of special pictures was shown.*

> *At the close, a large bag of cakes and sweetmeats, the gift of Comrade Sir Thomas Wilson was handed to each child. The children showed their*

appreciation of the entertainment provided by three rousing cheers for Comrades Wilson, Morrow, Rogers, Malcolmson, J.M. Whyte, the popular secretary and others responsible for the organisation of the treat.'

The BCDR locomotive superintendent John Crosthwait moved with his family to Helen's Bay in the early 1930s. His daughter, Edythe, remembers the telephone ringing at night – he had an extension in the bedroom, then a rarity – for example to report a derailment, which often seemed to happen at Ballynahinch Junction. The family enjoyed free train travel – in the case of his wife, for life. Mr Crosthwait was happy to see visitors thronging Helen's Bay beach as it meant more business for the railway, but Edythe has less fond memories of going out with sacks along with other local residents to pick up the vast quantities of litter left behind. She still treasures the engine whistle fashioned into a table lamp that her father was presented with on retirement. After retirement, the guard of an evening down train would leave in the late edition of the Belfast Telegraph at Helen's Bay station for him.

RM Arnold records that on one occasion, learning that a BCDR clerk had a seriously ill child at home, Crosthwait had a cylinder of oxygen sent immediately to the sick-bed.

Sinclair Duncan's father had joined the BCDR before the First World War, as a 16-year-old indentured clerk, serving a five-year 'apprenticeship'. Apart from service during the two Wars (in the first of which he gained two Military Crosses), his father spent his entire career with the company, serving as Registrar in its later years. Although he was poorly paid, there was the great benefit in those days of free or 'privilege' travel for the family on all Irish railways, and concessionary travel on the mainland and indeed in north-western Europe. As Sinclair puts it poetically:

'We were in Killarney when our school-mates hadn't got as far as Killinchy, and, in 1938, in Paris when my friends might have got to Portrush. Free travel also led to summer picnics at all the resorts on the County Down system and – the greatest of all thrills – free seats in the grandstand at Comber station for the spectacular TT races.'

His father was held in appropriate respect; stationmasters would hold the train for him, and even Sinclair, as his son, would be given halfpenny bars of chocolate by the same officials.

Boys will however be boys! Sinclair feels able to share, all these years later, that his school chums enjoyed nothing better in the autumn than throwing chestnuts down from carriage windows onto the open-topped trams below while the train was crossing the Holywood Arches. A more dangerous pursuit in the old six wheeler non-corridor coaches, – and one that he prudently chose not to attempt – was to exit from the compartment while the train was travelling comparatively slowly up the Ballymacarrett bank, then to walk along the running board, using the handholds provided, and re-enter the carriage in another compartment. No doubt if they were observed, the signalman at Ballymacarrett would telephone ahead to the next station, but by then all the boys would be safely back in the carriage, sitting angelically to defy even the sternest examination.

May Anderson's recollection is that she did not get entirely free travel on the BCDR lines, although her father did. One favourite family jaunt was to take the train to Ardglass; her father would bring his bicycle in the guard's van, and when they reached their destination, he would cycle off to catch fish for the family dinner.

Alfie Beaney lived at his grandfather's smithy on the Devil's Elbow on the Holywood to Bangor road. He remembers how local residents living close to the railway bank would be concerned if there was a spell of hot dry weather in the summer; Sparks could often fly up the locomotives' chimneys and set light to vegetation on the railway banks. There would be dozens of fires along the bank, he recalls.

Above: *The Lamp, made from a locomotive whistle, presented to John Crosthwait on his retirement in 1945, courtesy of Edythe Kennedy*

On the other hand trains were of practical help to farmers when working in their fields adjacent to the route. Having no watches in those days, certain trains would mark the passing of the day and the time for, say, the lunch break, or to bring the cows in for milking.

Alfie remembers living at Glencraig in the pre-bus era: 'we travelled to Belfast or Bangor by train – always third class'. The first-class compartments were usually kept locked, he recalls. As most readers over 60 will themselves recall, (at least those who travelled on other lines), windows in the pre-diesel area were raised and lowered by means of a strong leather strap. To open the door of the carriage or compartment to get out, it was usually necessary to open the window first, and then to reach out to turn the door handle from the outside. (This emphasised the innovation in the 1950s of the first UTA MEDs with their automatic sliding doors.)

Alfie observes the changing noise made by the line. In his youth it was very much 'clickety-click, clickety-click' he remembers. The noise of an engine once saved him; walking back from the grounds of Craigdarragh House along the track towards Glencraig late one evening as a time when no scheduled service was running, he fortunately just heard the sound of a light engine travelling fast along the tracks immediately behind him – 'I wasn't long getting halfway up the bank, I can tell you'.

We have noted elsewhere that the signal frame at Magherafelt was subsequently moved to Bangor. Clive Henderson, the son of the bank manager at Magherafelt shortly after the Second War, recalls going to the station many afternoons, as soon as he had got out of school. One favoured location was the signal cabin, where he would be allowed to handle the levers – 'pull that one, sonny' – being a regular invitation.

Magherafelt had a busy goods yard, and Clive recalls often travelling on the foot plate of the shunting engine. On other occasions he would be in the guard's van, and told to wind the brake on as the buffers were approaching. However, at the age of 12, his embryonic career came to an early end. He was out helping with the shunting in the yard, on his own, and pulled the lever to switch the points. Alas he had done so prematurely, with the result that the last seven goods wagons were all derailed. He still has nightmares of the man who should have been working the points racing in desperation towards him, but arriving just too late.

One Holywood resident of long-standing recalls travelling to Bangor by train, during the Second World War, for the family summer holiday over the Twelfth fortnight:

'We packed all we needed into one case. If there was something vital that we had forgotten, my Dad would go back to Holywood by train to get it.'

She added that even in those days some neighbours thought it odd that her family was not venturing further afield for their summer break.

Many is the story that can be told about wartime rationing and measures, mostly illicit, to obtain much-needed supplies of comestibles and clothing from the Republic of Ireland. For many getting to and from the border by train was the only option, especially given the scarcity of petrol.

One Holywood senior citizen recalls how her family moved for safety from Belfast to Bangor after the first raid by the German bombers in 1941. When need arose, the entire family would set off by train from Bangor on a weekend, to travel by train to Warrenpoint (not all of course on BCDR track) where they would cram, with many others making the same pilgrimage, on to a small boat to cross Carlingford Lough to Omeath, where the precious goods could be bought. Many ingenious techniques were adopted to escape the attention of the customs officers on their return. If shoes had been purchased, they had to be scuffed before getting back to Northern Ireland so they did not appear new; sheets on the other hand could be wound round the body, under the outer layers of clothing. And of course, hiding precious small items under the baby in the pram was a common dodge. The smugglers were not always successful, and tales abound of unlucky passengers obliged to return home shoeless or without their new winter coat.

Elizabeth remembers going on the railway from Holywood to Bangor on Sunday school outings. The party would go to Bell's Bakery in the morning, en route to the station, to pick up their buns and sandwiches for the day.

Of course, not everybody used the railway, even when the opportunity was available. For example, James Russell remembers being told about a woman who lived in Holywood who walked all the way to attend obligatory jury service in Downpatrick, and reckoned she was going to arrive in time if she got to Comber before the sun was up.

Anthony Shillingford recalls how helpful were the station staff at Helen's Bay. His parents would send his heavy school trunk across to England ahead of the new term, as Luggage in Advance. It always arrived safe and sound, and in good time, having travelled via a number of separate railway systems.

Helen McCormick has a less happy memory of one incident on the crossing by Glenholme farmstead in Helen's Bay. At that time, her family had one Jersey cow, their pride and joy. Alas one day she was struck by a train while on the track, although fortunately her calf escaped. The lucky calf was promptly christened Miracle, and lived to a ripe old age.

Norman Whitla recalls that during the Second World War, he used to go down to Bangor station to watch the trains. The station was particularly busy then with increased traffic. One evening he was watching a big Baltic tank engine taking on water when the driver asked him if he wanted a ride. The fireman lifted him over the fence and up onto the footplate, and Norman recalls that he had a happy time all evening while shunting. He was invited to try to use the reversing lever, but physically found himself unable to shift it. Times were very different then, when a chance encounter could provide a lifetime's memory for a small boy. As Norman puts it, '*that was when smoke and oil got into my veins*'.

Norman recalls that No. 12 engine (built in 1904) was for many years kept in the little engine shed at Bangor overnight, in order to haul the first train on the morning from Bangor to Belfast. The man who looked after it was a friend of Norman's father, so now and then, for many a happy hour, as a little boy, he could climb all over No. 12. (The cover picture shows No. 12 in the glory of her BCDR green livery.)

He was also a witness of the aftermath of the incident on Sunday 16 April 1944 when No. 13, pulling a load of goods wagons, over-ran the buffers at Bangor station wrecking the ticket collector's box. Norman recalls being told of the excitement as he came out of Sunday school and rushing to the station to observe engine No. 5 pulling the infamous 13 back onto the tracks. Desmond Coakham noted that John Crosthwait was directing operations in his bowler hat.

Billy McCormick notes that the Bangor line was famous for the 4-6-4 Baltic tank engines. They were '*fine looking machines but not very efficient*'. It was most impressive for one to watch them start from Holywood, working up the bank to Marino and Craigavad. On the other hand, the Multi-Engine Diesels were efficient but not particularly interesting, in his view.

May Anderson echoes the impression of the effort that the firemen in particular had to make to maintain steam pressure in the engines coming up the bank from Holywood. On one occasion her father was returning on a special train that was not due to stop until it reached Bangor, but it was making such heavy weather of the slope that he was able to hop off the train as it passed Marino. Indeed Norman Whitla remembers twice being on steam trains before dieselisation when the engine was unable even to get to Marino, and – travelling in the compartment nearest the engine – he could hear the fireman frantically shovelling more coal to raise the steam pressure sufficiently for the engine to be able to move on again in a great hissing and clanking.

On the other hand Norman recalls the great speed attained by the non-stop Belfast to Bangor trains hauled for a couple of years at the start of the UTA era by the NCC engines. He can vividly describe the fierce jolt that passengers in the old six-wheeler carriages experienced just after Crawfordsburn viaduct and the sharp left-hand bend there.

For all the noise made by the trains, May says that she quickly became used to living right beside the tracks. When the family first moved to Marino station, she had difficulty sleeping, but quickly became 'acclimatised', so much so that when passengers would ask her if the train they were hoping to catch had already left, she genuinely would not know.

One of her father's favourite stories was the curious tale of the dog being sent unaccompanied on a train. Unfortunately it managed to slip the leash which was being held by the porter at Sydenham and – enjoying its freedom – race along the platform. The despairing porter was heard shouting '*stop that dog, it's a parcel*'!

Richard Whitford recalls a colleague, the local bus manager, who attributed misfortune to lunar influence. When one female passenger

Above: Baltic No 25 puffing into Marino Station on 9 September 1933, courtesy of Charles Friel.

complained that her bus had gone the wrong way, he told her 'that's because there's a full moon today'; the explanation was accepted at face value. Things did seem to go wrong more often at that time of the month.

For many years we have become blasé about train travel. Hannah recalls travelling on the old BCDR from Queen's Quay on a Girls Friendly Society outing to Helen's Bay once a year. Even though it might rain all day, she fondly described it as 'the trip of a lifetime'.

Romance too was a product of BCDR operations. One resident recalls that her parents first met when her mother stepped onto Holywood station platform after a long journey from Fintona. As a precursor to today's social media, the mirrors in the facilities at Holywood station were put to use to note burgeoning relationships, if one could afford the lipstick with which to make the mark.

Perhaps the last word in this chapter should belong to Dennis Ogborn who tells the following tale. George Reid ran a paper shop in Holywood High Street. He was also a Holywood cricketer of renown – a fine wicketkeeper and a swashbuckling batsman. George preferred not to have to run too much, so he was wont to hit boundaries. One day, playing a home match, he really clouted the ball, farther than ever before. The ball sailed so far through the air that not only did it clear the boundary, it landed in a railway truck which happened to be passing on the track at that time. The cricket ball indeed ended up in Bangor, before it next touched the ground.

As the umpire might have said: 'Six, and out!'

Above: Bangor Station Staff, c. 1935, with Stationmaster Valentine in the centre, North Down Museum.

Chapter 17

Now and the Future

One local businessman who uses the train service regularly, both for himself and his family, describes the Bangor line as '*probably the best railway line in Ireland*'. He could well be right – we do not always appreciate what is on our doorstep.

The consultation paper published by the Department for Regional Development in early 2013 contained an interesting perspective on railway services in Northern Ireland. It recalled that a report produced in 2000 on the future of the network had recommended the '*Consolidation Option*'. This '*sought to turn around the decline in railway use by prioritising new investment on services and facilities which offered the best opportunities the passenger growth*'.

Locally this included prioritising the Bangor line along with other Belfast commuter services.

In January 2001, the Department for Regional Development approved a project by Translink to completely re-lay the Belfast to Bangor railway line. The project had an approved budget of just under £15 million, although as the subsequent Northern Ireland Audit Office report criticised, the eventual cost was over double that, despite certain reductions in the specification such as re-laying all the track between Belfast and Holywood, and not strengthening the sea defences at Holywood. (The initial notion that some trains might run at speeds of 90 mph on the line was also jettisoned.) The final settlement with the contractor was for £23 million – a far cry from the prices paid in the 19th century!

In the event, the upgrade was completed some months behind schedule, with the full timetable being reintroduced in July 2002. The Bangor line has benefited from new rolling stock manufactured in two tranches - the first in 2004/05 and the second some seven years later. Much of these developments were materially assisted with EU funding.

The Audit report acknowledged that the Belfast to Bangor line was busy, carrying nearly 2 million passengers a year. The consultation paper produced by the Department for Regional Development in January 2013 recorded a significant increase in the passenger usage of the Bangor line to over 2 ½ million – a 90% increase from the figure 10 years previously which would suggest that the Government's faith in the investment had been rewarded.

Independent research findings published in November 2014 showed the highest ever passenger satisfaction for Northern Ireland Railways. There had been an overall passenger growth of 8% on the railway service across Northern Ireland, with an increase of almost 6% on the Bangor line. This was coupled with overall Bangor line passenger satisfaction levels of 90% – the highest in the entire network. (This was a far cry from the 1872 Memorandum to the People of Holywood and the vociferous criticism of the service levelled by that town's clergy, as recorded in Chapter 4.)

David Graham, then the route manager for Northern Ireland Railways, rightly recognised the importance of the service provided to the customers and the excellence of the staff:

'*We are delighted with these results. Our customers are telling us we're getting things right… In particular it is great to know customers think our staff are really helpful – credit is due to all my colleagues who work hard to provide such a great service… Punctuality, value for money and train cleanliness ratings are all very high. This is why so many more people are choosing to use the train, year on year.*'

Top right: *The 2014 approach to the eternal problem of leaves on the line.* **Lower right:** *Modern units on the line at Holywood.*
Opposite page: *Postcard showing the contrast with the old Cultra Post Office on the main Belfast to Bangor Road.*

The Bangor line has come a long way in 150 years. The *News Letter* recorded similar sentiments when the new service began in May 1865:

'All the trains were despatched with the utmost punctuality and the numerous travellers seemed greatly pleased with the excellent arrangements of the company'

It added:

'We congratulate the inhabitants of Bangor on the opening of the new line of railway which will very much increase the popularity of that pretty and convenient watering-place.'

The railway has indeed played a central role in the development not just of the two towns of Holywood and Bangor, but also along the whole route, very much as foreseen by its early promoters. It continues to this day to provide an important communications artery. We must be most thankful that none of the occasional proposals to close the line or tarmac over it ever gained sway. Without the railway, the shape and development of modern Bangor would have been very different.

We are also fortunate that the Railway Preservation Society of Ireland, which celebrated its 50th anniversary in 2014, runs seasonal steam excursions to Bangor – a wonderful reminder of past splendours.

One imaginative assessment of the future development of the railway system across the island of Ireland was published in 2004 by the Irish Academy of Engineering which envisaged the network as it might look in 2050. As well as fanciful notions of two tunnels connecting the island with Great Britain – one of which would have broadly reprised the Donaghadee to Portpatrick Tunnel first proposed in the 1880s – it noted *anticipated* developments around Belfast; these included a 12-minute interval light rail service connecting the International Airport through Belfast city centre to Newtownards, with plans to complete a figure-of-eight, bringing Lisburn and Bangor into the loop! Trains, it suggested, would run on hydrogen fuel cells.

Attractive as some of these proposals are, it seems likely that funding for major capital projects will always be constrained. The ambition and energy (and indeed willingness to fail) of the private sector in the Victorian era has given way to a much more sober, risk-averse and audit-conscious climate which inevitably limits the scope for progressive development.

One cannot predict what is to come in the longer term with certainty, and it is most unlikely that in another 150 years the railway will look much as it does today, but in the near future, the Bangor line will surely remain a key part of our national infrastructure and a vital artery for the communities along the route into Belfast.

Above: Bangor-bound Train on Crawfordsburn Viaduct, John McEwen.

Bibliography and Further Reading

- *A Statistical Account, or Parochial Survey of Ireland, Volume 3*, compiled in 1819

- *Ordnance Survey Memoirs of Ireland, Parishes of County Down II, 1832-4, 1837, North Down and Ards*, edited by Angélique Day and Patrick McWilliams, published 1991, by the Institute of Irish Studies, Queen's University Belfast

- *The Life of George Stephenson*, Samuel Smiles, 1881

- *Bradshaw's Railway Manual, Shareholders' Guide, and Official Directory for 1885*, published by WJ Adams and Sons, Manchester, 1885

- *The General Classification of Goods (including a list of the Railway stations and junctions in Ireland)* published by the Irish Railway Clearing House on 1 December 1888

- *The Belfast and County Down Railway,* by H Fayle, reprinted from Railway Magazine, 1906

- *Fifty Years of Railway Life,* Joseph Tatlow, London, 1920

- *BCDR Official Tourist Guide to County Down*, third edition, published by McCaw, Stevenson and Orr Ltd, Belfast 1924

- *Roadway or Railway between Belfast and Bangor,* TI Lloyd, News Letter, 1933

- *Helen's Tower,* Harold Nicolson, Constable & Co, London, 1937

- *Danger Ahead, the Dramatic Story of Railway Signalling,* Richard Blythe, Newman Neame, London, 1951

- *Coastal Passenger Steamers and Inland Navigations in the North of Ireland,* Transport Handbook No. 3, DB McNeill, on behalf of the Belfast Transport Museum, 1967

- *Steam over Belfast Lough,* RM Arnold, the Oakwood Press, 1969

- *Victorian Bangor, an Essay in Local History,* edited by Grenfell Morton, 1972

- *Outline of Irish Railway History,* HC Casserley, published by David and Charles, 1974

- *My Bangor from the 1890s,* Charles Milligan, published by Spectator Newspapers, 1975

- *Twenty-five years gone,* RJA Pue, printed by Wm Sweeney, Reid and Co, Belfast, 1975

- *Holywood as I remember it,* Two Talks delivered to Holywood Gaelic Society 1977 by BR Geddes

- *The Industrial Archaeology of Northern Ireland,* William McCutcheon, Her Majesty's Stationery Office, 1980

- *The County Down,* RM Arnold, published by Irish Steam Scene, Whitehead 1981

- *The Belfast and County Down Railway,* Edward M Patterson, David and Charles, 1982

- *The Belfast, Holywood and Bangor Railway,* Ian Sinclair, published by the North Down Heritage Centre

- *Clandeboye,* Ulster Architectural Heritage Society, W & G Baird, 1985

- *We have an Altar – Fifty Years of Methodism in Carnalea,* David McKnight, Belfast, 1986

- *Buildings of Holywood,* Tony Merrick, published by the Holywood Advertiser, 1986

- *Railways in Ulster,* Grenfell Morton, Friar's Bush Press, 1989

- *The Quiet Shore, a Book of Poems and Paintings,* Tom Kerr, published in 1994 by Pretani Press, Bangor

- *Irish Railways Past and Present Volume 1,* Michael HC Baker, Past and Present Publishing Ltd, 1995

- *Belfast and County Down Railway, an Irish Railway Pictorial,* Desmond Coakham, Midland Publishing Limited, 1998

- *Bangor, An Historical Gazetteer,* Marcus Patton, published by the Ulster Architectural Heritage Society, 1999

- *Holywood Co. Down, Then and Now,* Con Auld, printed by the Spectator and Chronicle Newspaper Group, March 2002

- *Along UTA Lines, Ulster's rail network in the 1960s*, Ian Sinclair, published by Colourpoint, 2002

- *Forgotten Houses of Holywood, Co. Down*, Con Auld, printed by the Spectator and Chronicle Newspaper Group, March 2003

- *Diesel Dawn: Ireland's Contribution to the Development of the DMU, 1931-1967*, Colm Flanagan, published by Colourpoint, 2003

- *A Vision of Transport in Ireland in 2050*, The Irish Academy of Engineering, September 2004

- *Rail Runabout, a look at Northern Ireland Railways from 1975-2005*, by Sam Somerville, published by Colourpoint, 2006

- *The Upgrade of the Belfast to Bangor Railway Line*, the Northern Ireland Audit Office, March 2007, The Stationery Office

- *The Belfast and County Down Railway*, Desmond Coakham, published by Colourpoint Books, 2010

- *Twixt Bay and Burn, a History of Helen's Bay and Crawfordsburn*, (editor Robin Masefield) published by the Bayburn Historical Society, 2011

- *Future Railway Investment: a Consultation Paper*, the Department for Regional Development, January 2013

- *A History of Carrickfergus Gasworks*, Brian McKee and Helen Rankin, published by Carrickfergus Gasworks Preservation Society Ltd, 2013

- *Journal of the Irish Railway Record Society*, February 2014, No. 183, published by the Society, Heuston Station, Dublin

Acknowledgements

With grateful thanks to all the following individuals and organisations, who have helped so much in a variety of ways, especially through sharing their expertise and memories, and in many cases illustrative material. (My thanks too to many others who have also given great assistance, but who are not named here):

Individuals:

Clare Ablett
Jim Aiken
May Anderson
Lola Armstrong
Thelma Armstrong
Alan and Irene Aston
Mark Atkinson
Con Auld
Alfie Beaney
Leanne Briggs
Paddy Buckler
David Campbell
Norma Cooper
Victor Corrie
Kay Coulthard
Andrew Crockart
David Crowe
Roger Dixon

Sinclair Duncan
Stephen Dunlop
Doug Ferguson
Colm Flanagan
Hugh Forrester
Charles Friel
Samantha Gallaher
Richard Gilmore
Ivor Graham
John Graham
Denis Grimshaw
Arthur Hamblett
Neil Hamilton
Julia Harkness
Clive Henderson
Stuart Hughes
Colin James
Edythe Kennedy
Tom Kerr
Michael and Clare Le Marie
Betty Lowry
Roy McComb
Billy McCormick
Helen McCormick
Brian McCourt
John McEwen
Heather McGuicken
Terence McKeag
Georgina McKeown

Betty McLaughlin
Jean Mann
Rosemary Masefield
Tony Merrick
Sandra Millsopp
Laura Morton
Robin Morton
Rev Canon Ronnie Nesbitt
Dennis Ogborn
Irwin Parkhurst
Jack Patience
Brian Patton
Patricia Perry
Elizabeth Porter
Bob Pue
Hannah Renwick
James Russell
Lynda Shannon
Anthony Shillingford
Ian Sinclair
Allan Esler Smith
Margaret Smith
Barry and Lynette Spence
James Swan
Dennis Totton
Harry Welshman
Richard Whitford
Norman Whitla
Derek Young

Groups and Organisations:

Ards and North Down Borough Council
Bayburn Historical Society
Belfast and County Down Railway Museum Trust
Downpatrick and County Down Railway
Flame Gasworks Museum
Holywood Over 55s Club
Holywood Women's Institute
Holywood U3A
Holywood Library Archives
Irish Railway Record Society
Libraries NI (Bangor, Central, Downpatrick and Holywood)
Linen Hall Library
National Museums Northern Ireland
North Down Borough Council
North Down Museum
Northern Ireland Environment Agency (Hill Street, Belfast)
Public Record Office Northern Ireland, (the Deputy Keeper of the Records and colleagues)
Railway Preservation Society of Ireland
Queen's University, Belfast
Ulster Scots Agency

Index

(NB Some of the most common place names, eg Bangor, or terms, eg BCDR, are omitted)